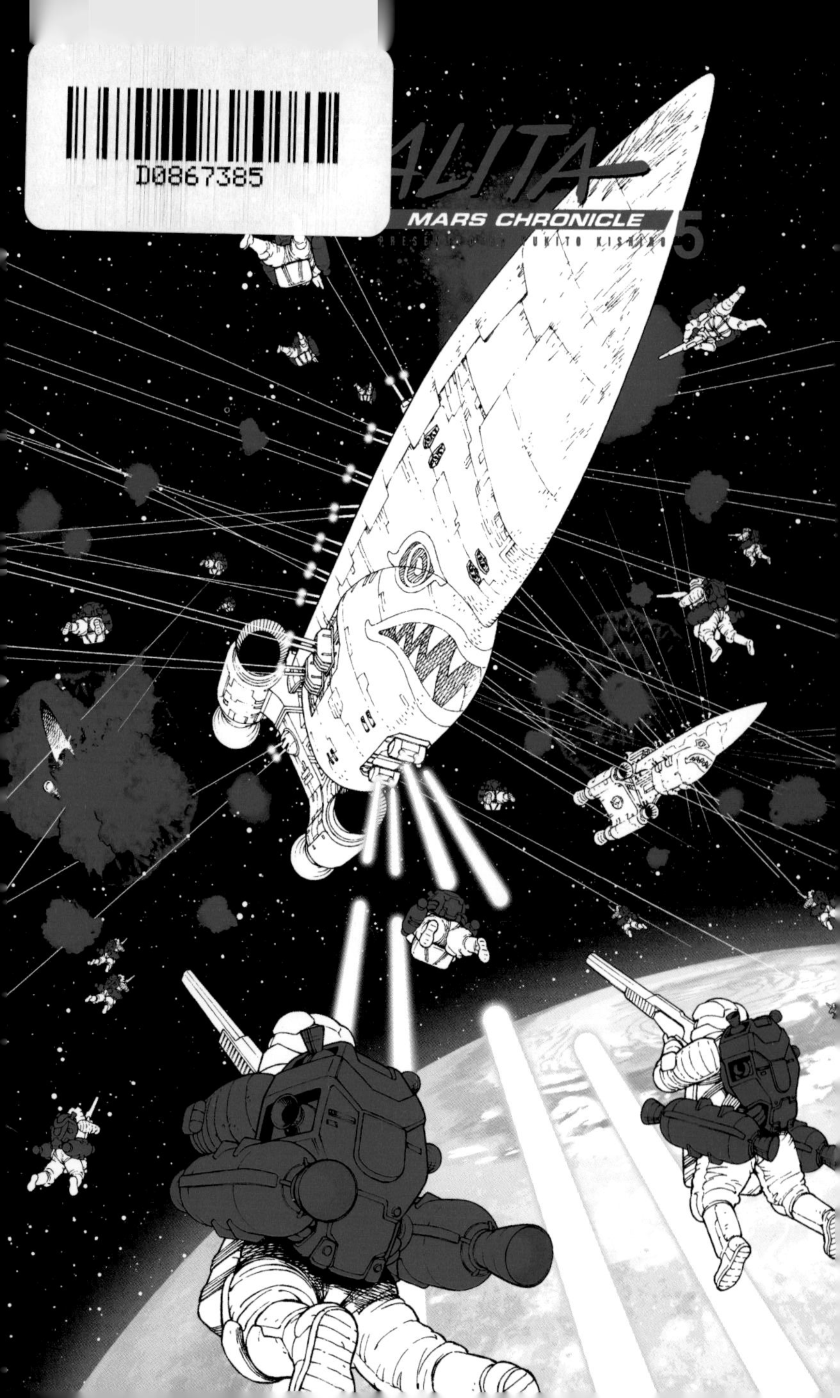
ALITA
MARS CHRONICLE
5

BATTLE ANGEL ALITA MARS CHRONICLE

PRESENTED by YUKITO KISHIRO

C O N T E N T S

LOG:022 P3

CONFESSION OF A MAGGOT

(Evening #10, #12, 2017)

LOG:023 P35

THE DEATH OF YOUNG ITALL

(Evening #13-14, 2017)

LOG:024 P67

NIGHT OF THE HABOOB

(Evening #16-17, 2017)

LOG:025 P99

SOMETHING IMPORTANT

(Evening #19-20, 2017)

LOG:026 P131

SOUL OF THE VAGABOND

(Evening #22-23, 2017)

ADDITIONAL STAFF:
TSUTOMU KISHIRO / EMIYA KINARI

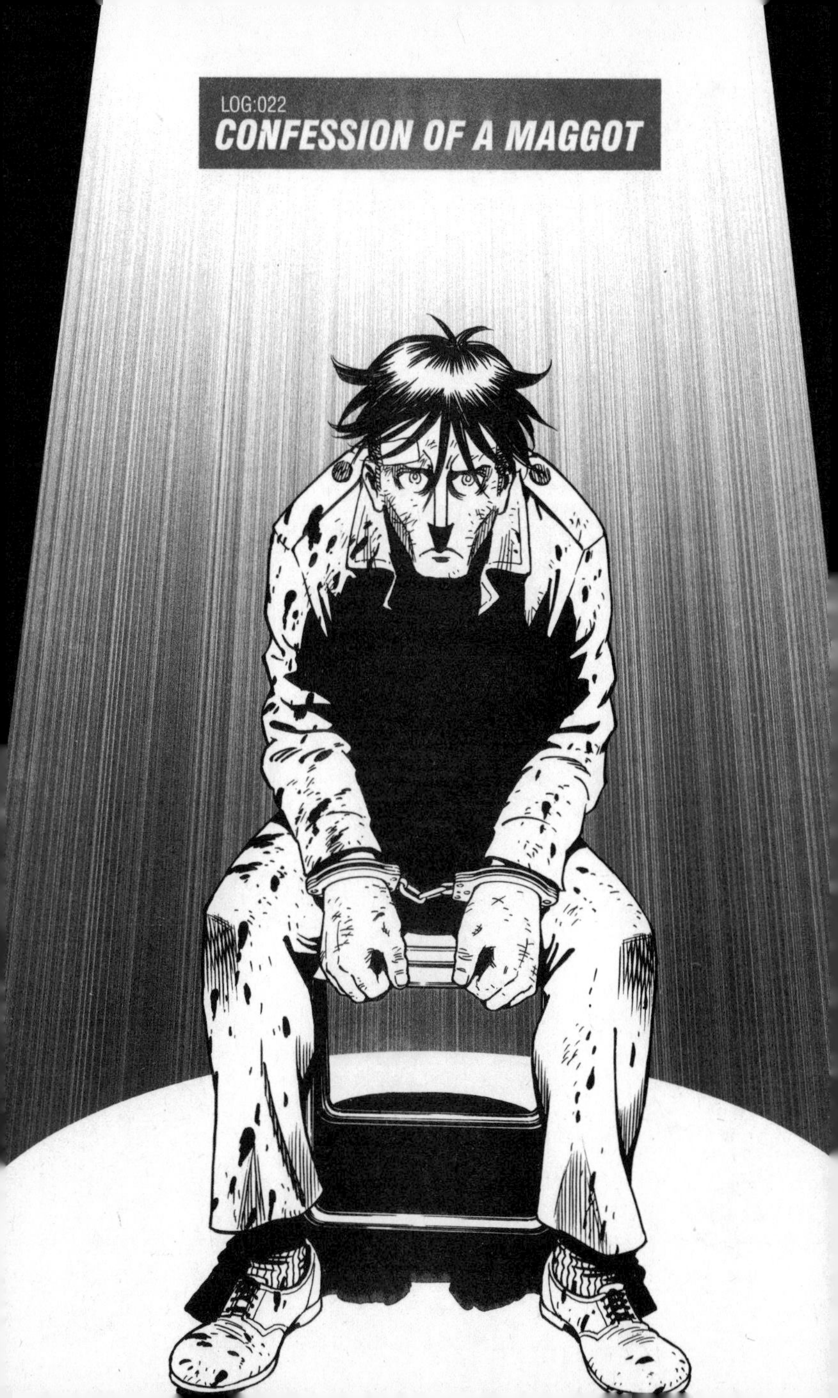
LOG:022
CONFESSION OF A MAGGOT

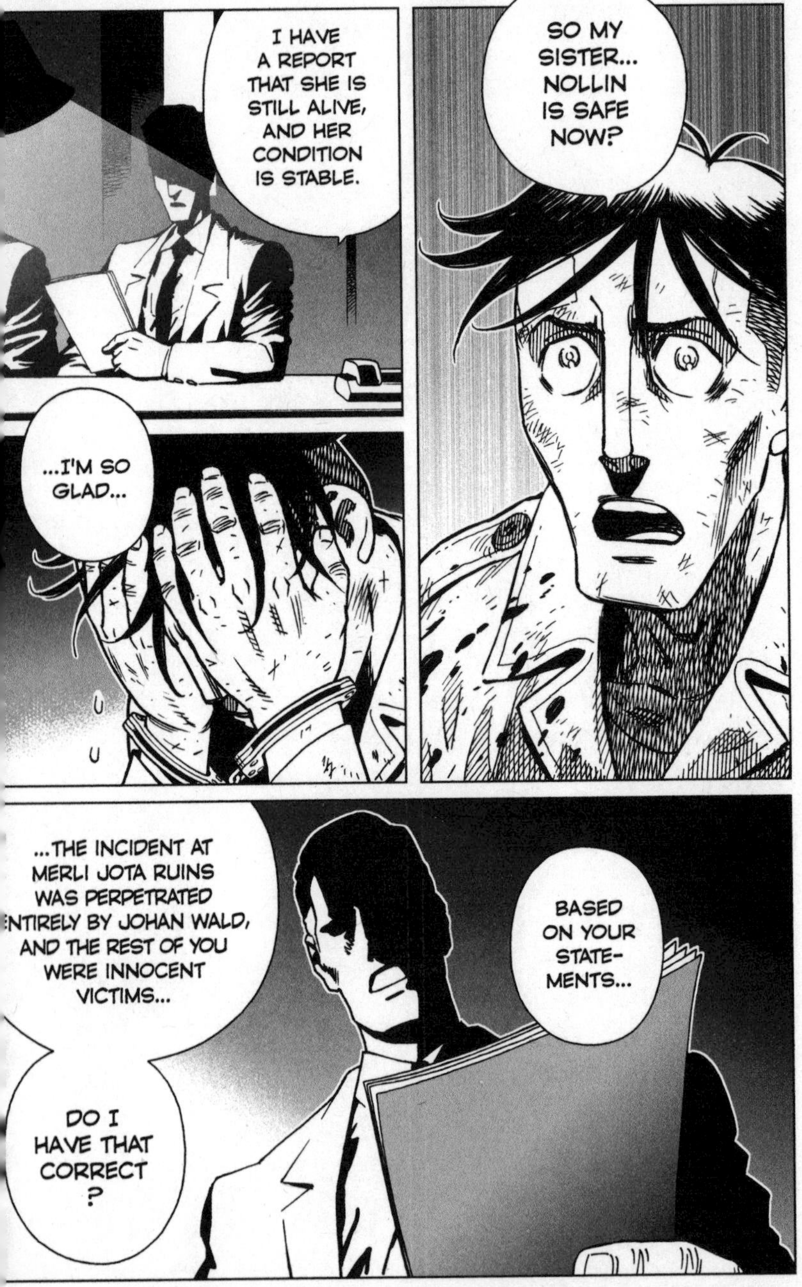
SO MY SISTER... NOLLIN IS SAFE NOW?
I HAVE A REPORT THAT SHE IS STILL ALIVE, AND HER CONDITION IS STABLE.
...I'M SO GLAD...
BASED ON YOUR STATE-MENTS...
...THE INCIDENT AT MERLI JOTA RUINS WAS PERPETRATED ENTIRELY BY JOHAN WALD, AND THE REST OF YOU WERE INNOCENT VICTIMS...
DO I HAVE THAT CORRECT ?

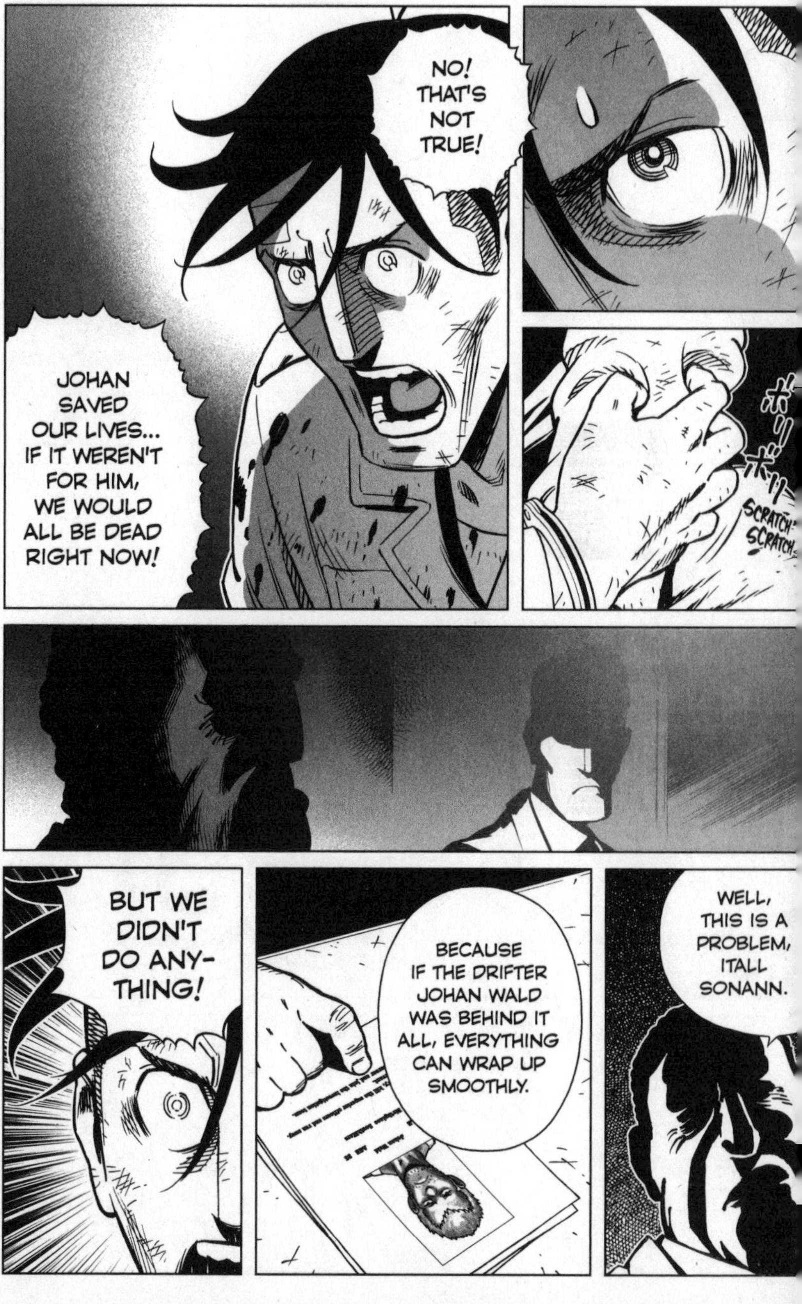
SCRATCH
SCRATCH
NO! THAT'S NOT TRUE!
JOHAN SAVED OUR LIVES... IF IT WEREN'T FOR HIM, WE WOULD ALL BE DEAD RIGHT NOW!
WELL, THIS IS A PROBLEM, ITALL SONANN.
BECAUSE IF THE DRIFTER JOHAN WALD WAS BEHIND IT ALL, EVERYTHING CAN WRAP UP SMOOTHLY.
BUT WE DIDN'T DO ANY-THING!

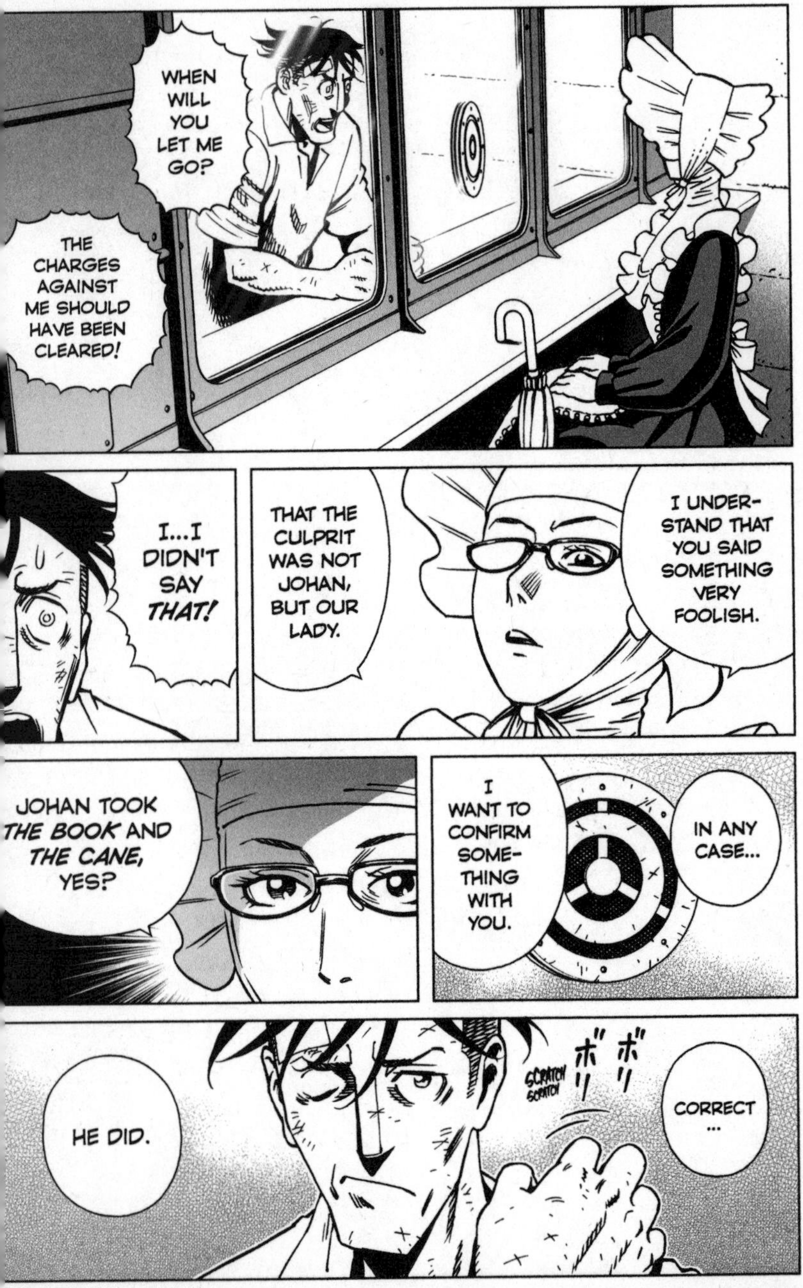
WHEN WILL YOU LET ME GO?
THE CHARGES AGAINST ME SHOULD HAVE BEEN CLEARED!
I UNDER-STAND THAT YOU SAID SOMETHING VERY FOOLISH.
THAT THE CULPRIT WAS NOT JOHAN, BUT OUR LADY.
I...I DIDN'T SAY *THAT!*
IN ANY CASE...
I WANT TO CONFIRM SOME-THING WITH YOU.
JOHAN TOOK *THE BOOK* AND *THE CANE,* YES?
CORRECT ...
ボリボリ
SCRATCH SCRATCH
HE DID.

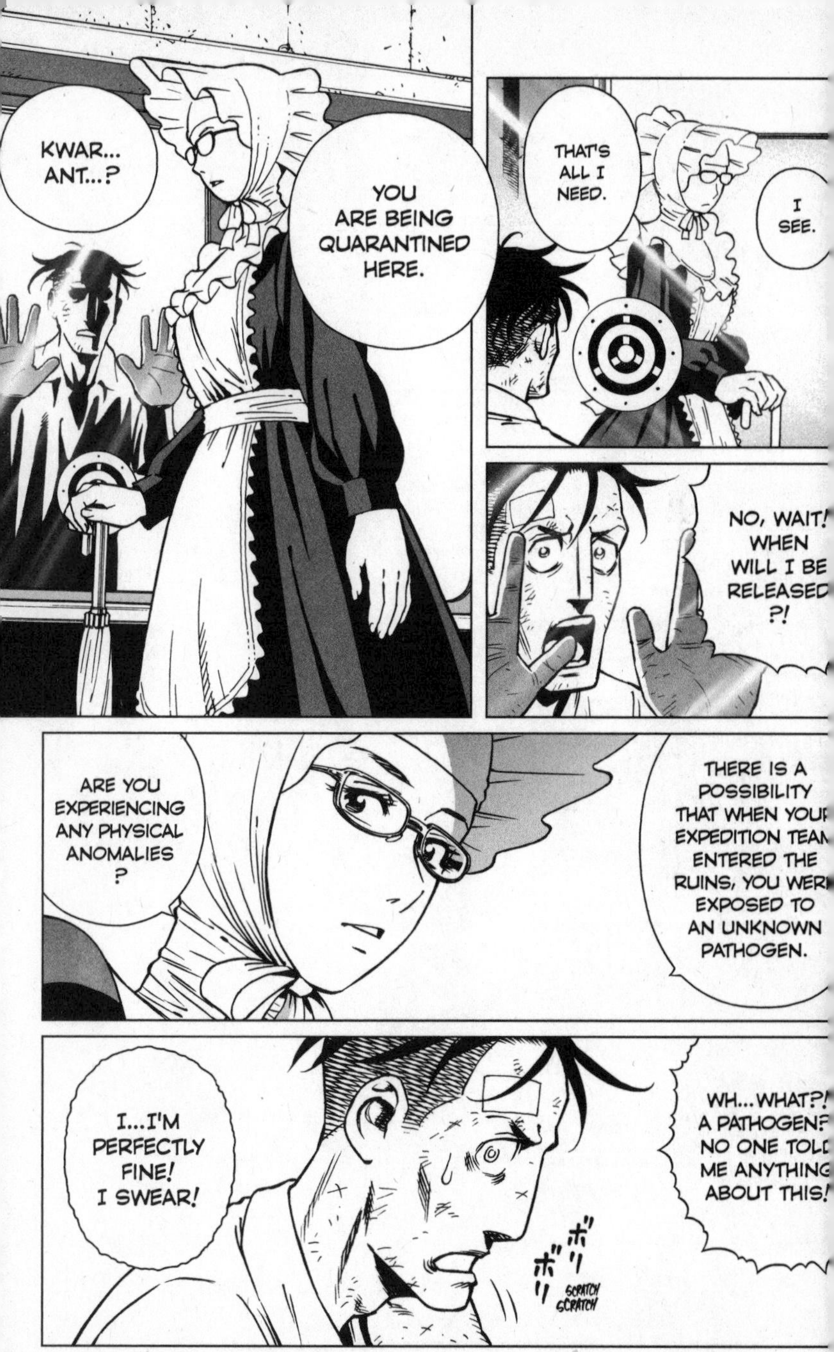
I SEE.
THAT'S ALL I NEED.
NO, WAIT! WHEN WILL I BE RELEASED?!
YOU ARE BEING QUARANTINED HERE.
KWAR... ANT...?
THERE IS A POSSIBILITY THAT WHEN YOUR EXPEDITION TEAM ENTERED THE RUINS, YOU WERE EXPOSED TO AN UNKNOWN PATHOGEN.
ARE YOU EXPERIENCING ANY PHYSICAL ANOMALIES?
WH...WHAT?! A PATHOGEN?! NO ONE TOLD ME ANYTHING ABOUT THIS!
ボリ ボリ
SCRATCH SCRATCH
I...I'M PERFECTLY FINE! I SWEAR!

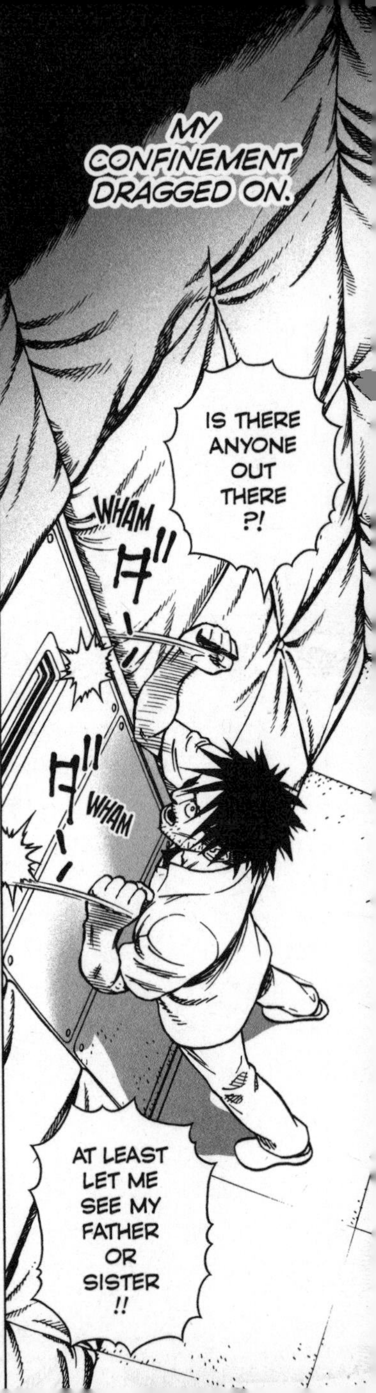
MY CONFINEMENT DRAGGED ON.
IS THERE ANYONE OUT THERE ?!
WHAM
WHAM
AT LEAST LET ME SEE MY FATHER OR SISTER !!

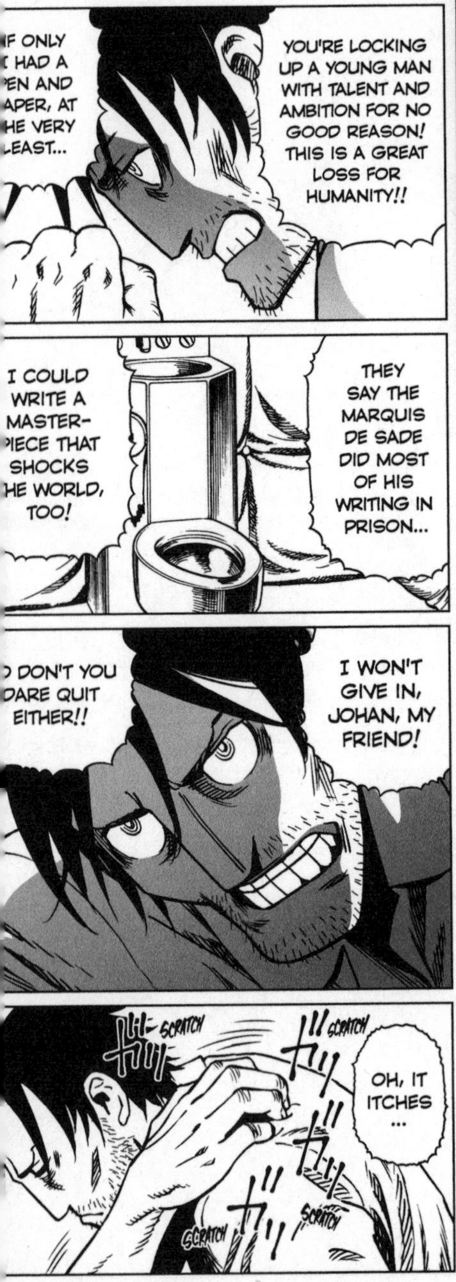
YOU'RE LOCKING UP A YOUNG MAN WITH TALENT AND AMBITION FOR NO GOOD REASON! THIS IS A GREAT LOSS FOR HUMANITY!!
F ONLY HAD A EN AND APER, AT HE VERY EAST...
THEY SAY THE MARQUIS DE SADE DID MOST OF HIS WRITING IN PRISON...
I COULD WRITE A MASTER-IECE THAT SHOCKS HE WORLD, TOO!
I WON'T GIVE IN, JOHAN, MY FRIEND!
DON'T YOU DARE QUIT EITHER!!
SCRATCH
SCRATCH
OH, IT ITCHES ...
SCRATCH
SCRATCH

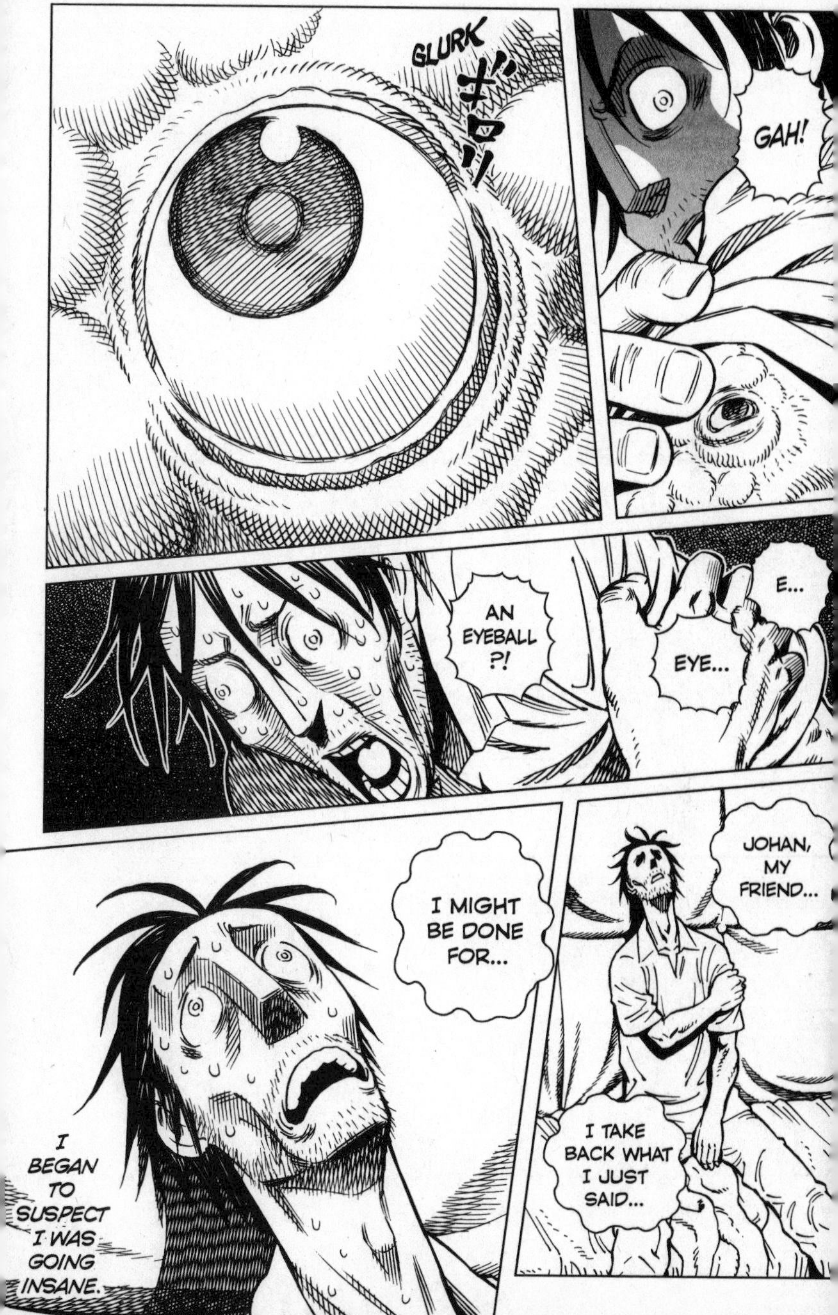
GAH!
GLURK
ギロリ
E...
EYE...
AN EYEBALL ?!
JOHAN, MY FRIEND...
I TAKE BACK WHAT I JUST SAID...
I MIGHT BE DONE FOR...
I BEGAN TO SUSPECT I WAS GOING INSANE.

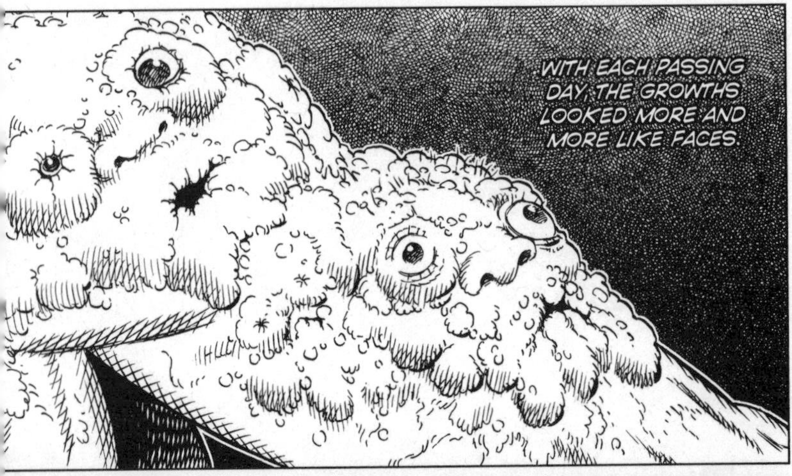
WITH EACH PASSING DAY, THE GROWTHS LOOKED MORE AND MORE LIKE FACES.

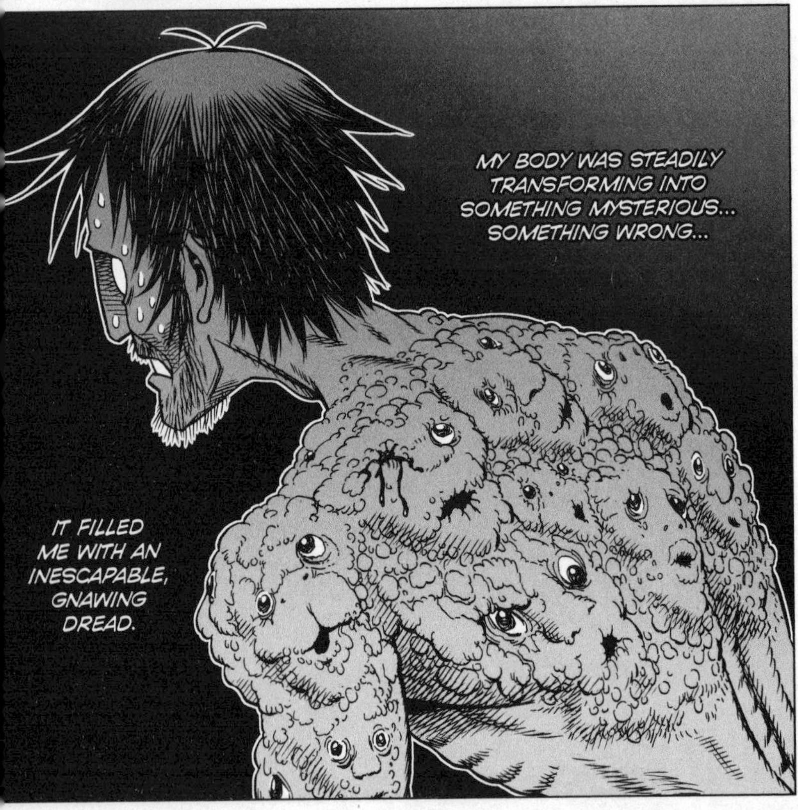
MY BODY WAS STEADILY TRANSFORMING INTO SOMETHING MYSTERIOUS... SOMETHING WRONG...
IT FILLED ME WITH AN INESCAPABLE, GNAWING DREAD.

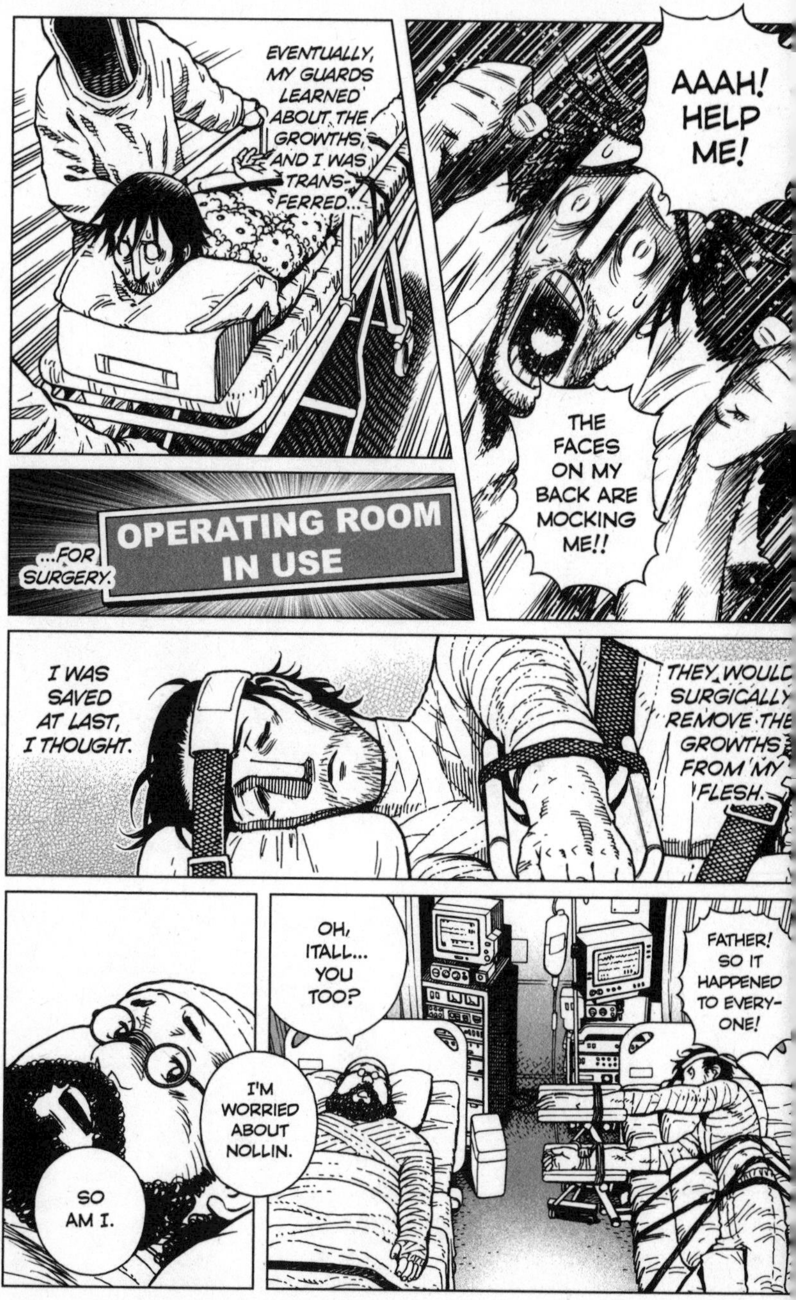

AAAH! HELP ME!
THE FACES ON MY BACK ARE MOCKING ME!!
EVENTUALLY, MY GUARDS LEARNED ABOUT THE GROWTHS, AND I WAS TRANS-FERRED...
OPERATING ROOM IN USE
...FOR SURGERY.
THEY WOULD SURGICALLY REMOVE THE GROWTHS FROM MY FLESH.
I WAS SAVED AT LAST, I THOUGHT.
FATHER! SO IT HAPPENED TO EVERY-ONE!
OH, ITALL... YOU TOO?
I'M WORRIED ABOUT NOLLIN.
SO AM I.

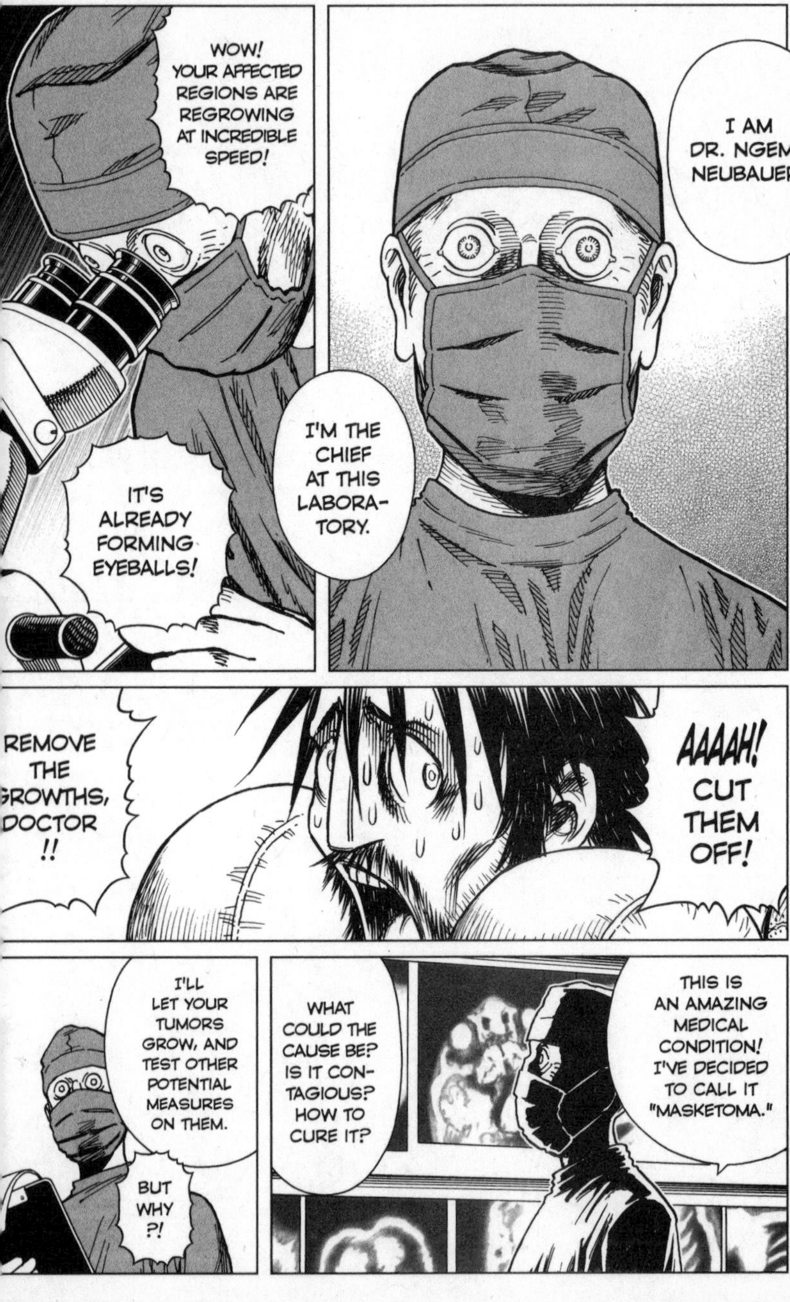
I AM DR. NGEMA NEUBAUER.
I'M THE CHIEF AT THIS LABORA-TORY.
WOW! YOUR AFFECTED REGIONS ARE REGROWING AT INCREDIBLE SPEED!
IT'S ALREADY FORMING EYEBALLS!
AAAAH! CUT THEM OFF!
REMOVE THE GROWTHS, DOCTOR!!
THIS IS AN AMAZING MEDICAL CONDITION! I'VE DECIDED TO CALL IT "MASKETOMA."
WHAT COULD THE CAUSE BE? IS IT CON-TAGIOUS? HOW TO CURE IT?
I'LL LET YOUR TUMORS GROW, AND TEST OTHER POTENTIAL MEASURES ON THEM.
BUT WHY?!

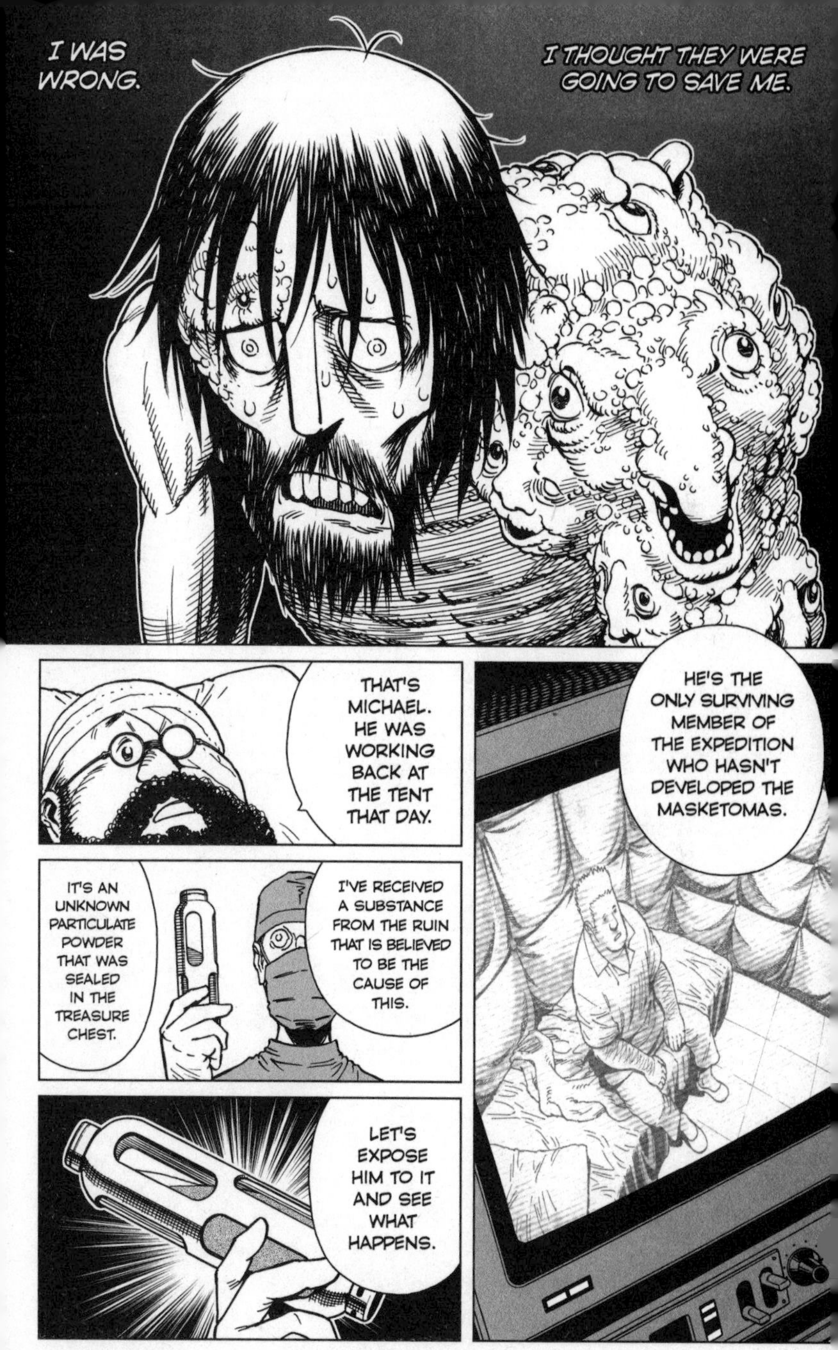

I THOUGHT THEY WERE GOING TO SAVE ME.
I WAS WRONG.
HE'S THE ONLY SURVIVING MEMBER OF THE EXPEDITION WHO HASN'T DEVELOPED THE MASKETOMAS.
THAT'S MICHAEL. HE WAS WORKING BACK AT THE TENT THAT DAY.
I'VE RECEIVED A SUBSTANCE FROM THE RUIN THAT IS BELIEVED TO BE THE CAUSE OF THIS.
IT'S AN UNKNOWN PARTICULATE POWDER THAT WAS SEALED IN THE TREASURE CHEST.
LET'S EXPOSE HIM TO IT AND SEE WHAT HAPPENS.

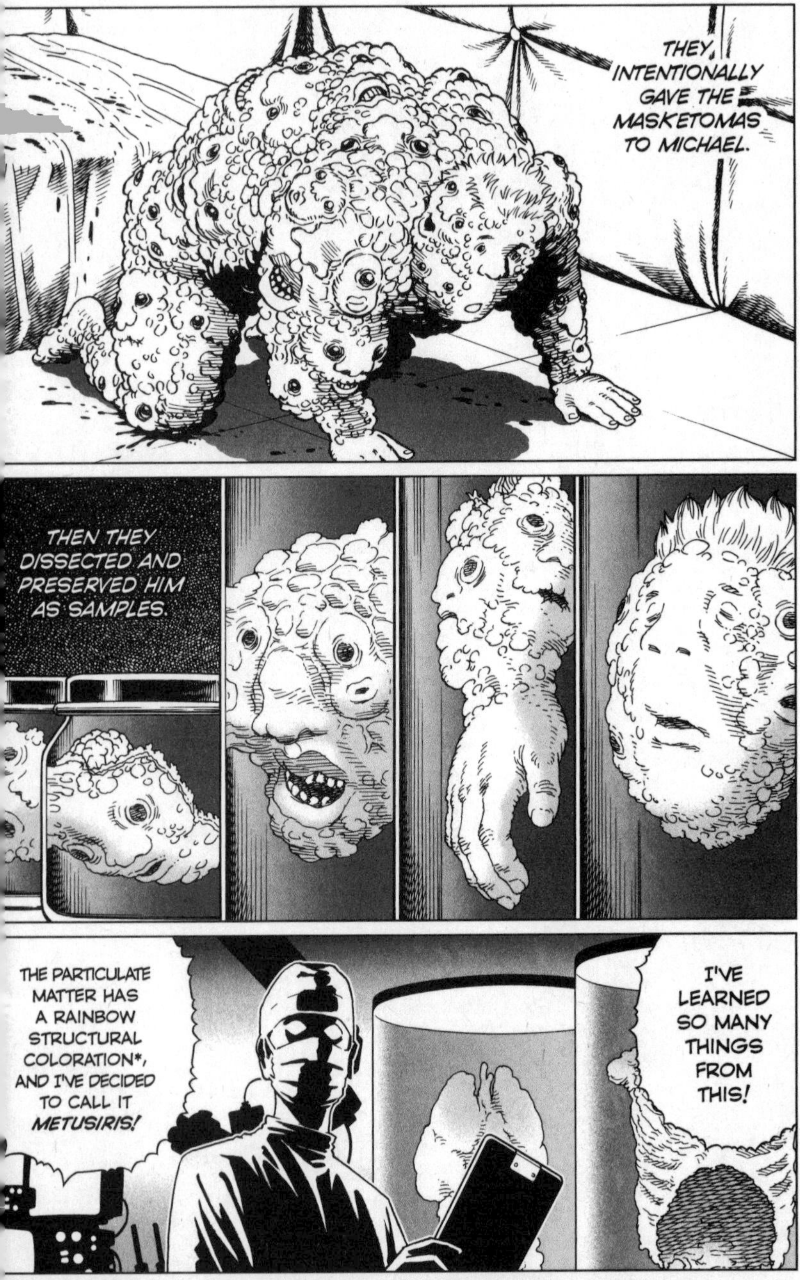
THEY INTENTIONALLY GAVE THE MASKETOMAS TO MICHAEL.
THEN THEY DISSECTED AND PRESERVED HIM AS SAMPLES.
I'VE LEARNED SO MANY THINGS FROM THIS!
THE PARTICULATE MATTER HAS A RAINBOW STRUCTURAL COLORATION*, AND I'VE DECIDED TO CALL IT *METUSIRIS!*

TRUCTURAL COLORATION: A phenomenon in which a material's microscopic structure interferes with light, producing olor it does not actually possess. Some familiar examples would be compact discs, soap bubbles, or pearls.

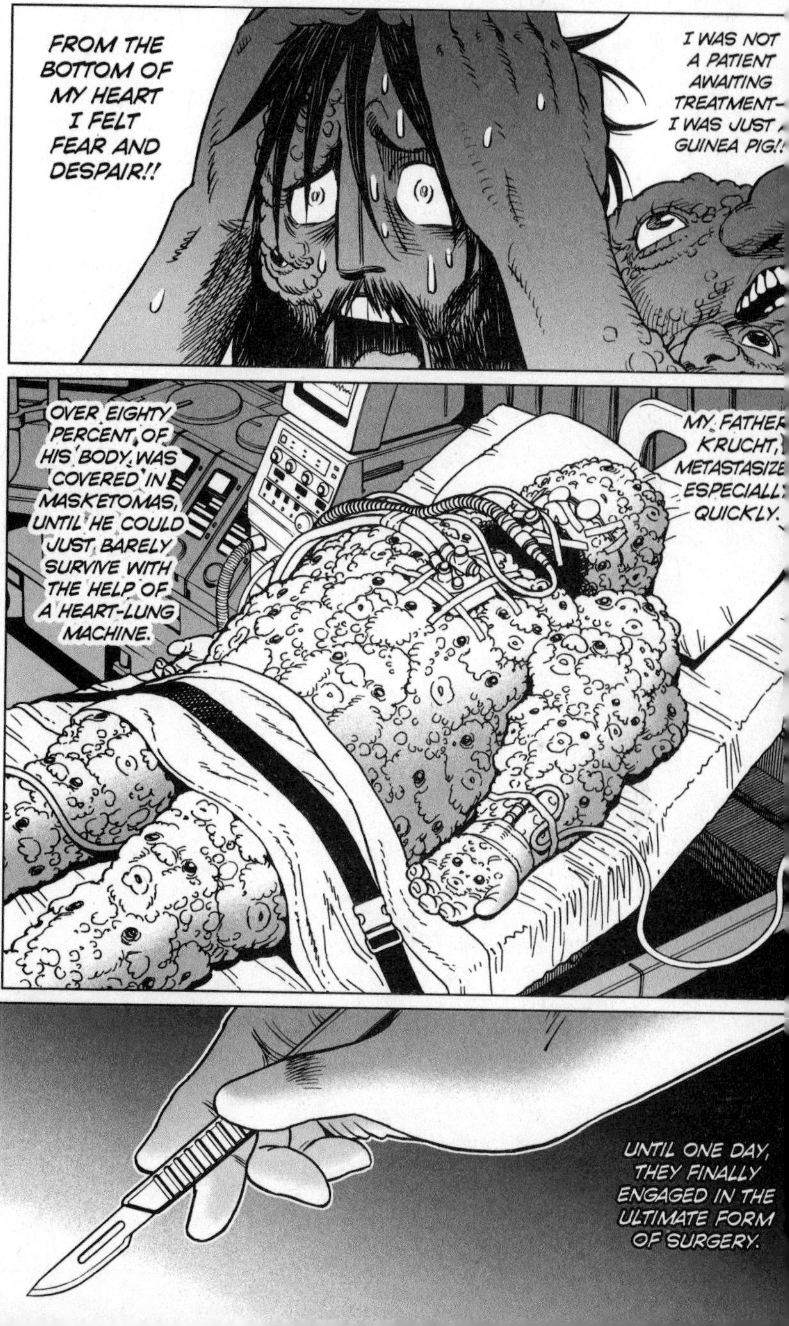
I WAS NOT A PATIENT AWAITING TREATMENT- I WAS JUST A GUINEA PIG!!
FROM THE BOTTOM OF MY HEART I FELT FEAR AND DESPAIR!!
MY FATHER KRUCHT, METASTASIZE ESPECIALL QUICKLY.
OVER EIGHTY PERCENT OF HIS BODY WAS COVERED IN MASKETOMAS, UNTIL HE COULD JUST BARELY SURVIVE WITH THE HELP OF A HEART-LUNG MACHINE.
UNTIL ONE DAY, THEY FINALLY ENGAGED IN THE ULTIMATE FORM OF SURGERY.

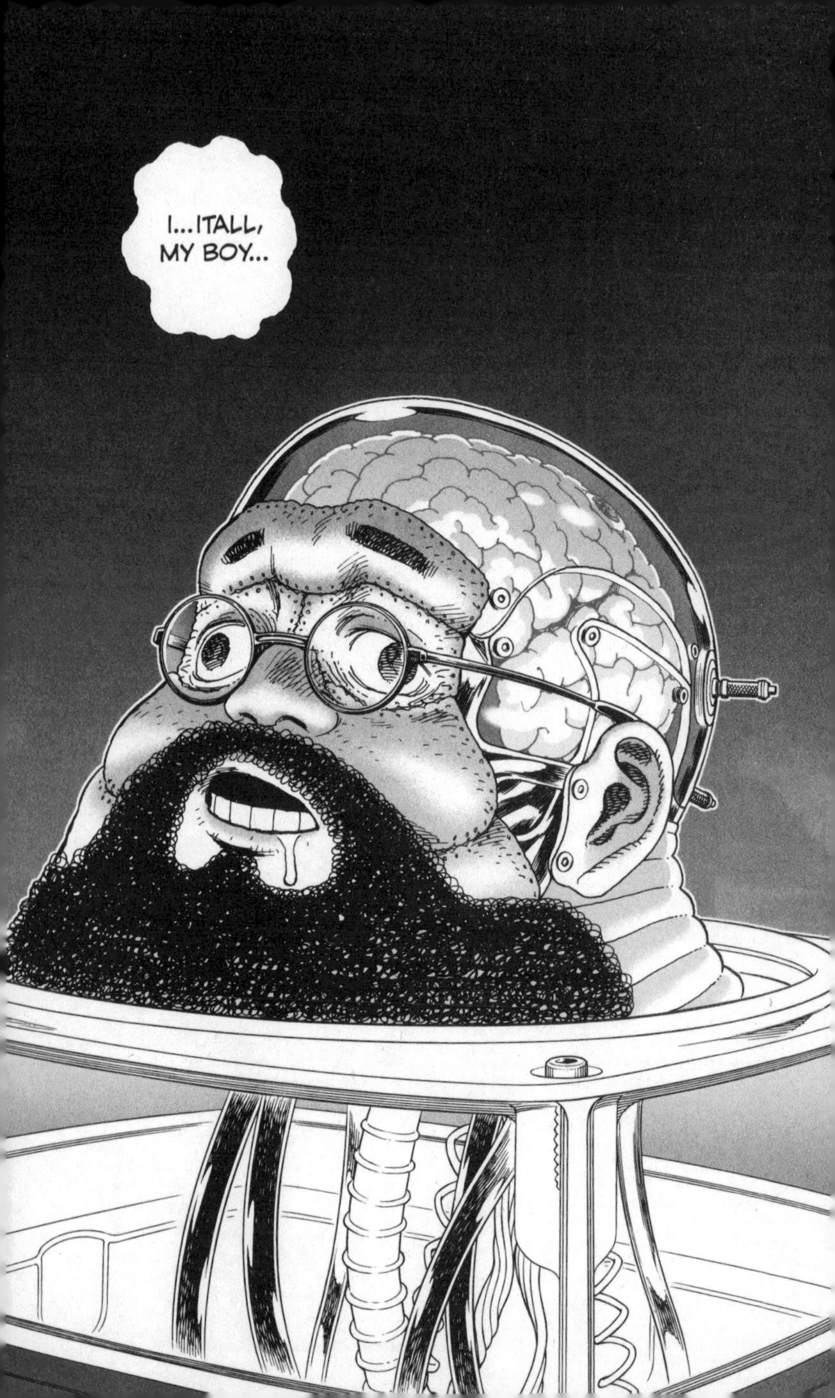
I...ITALL, MY BOY...

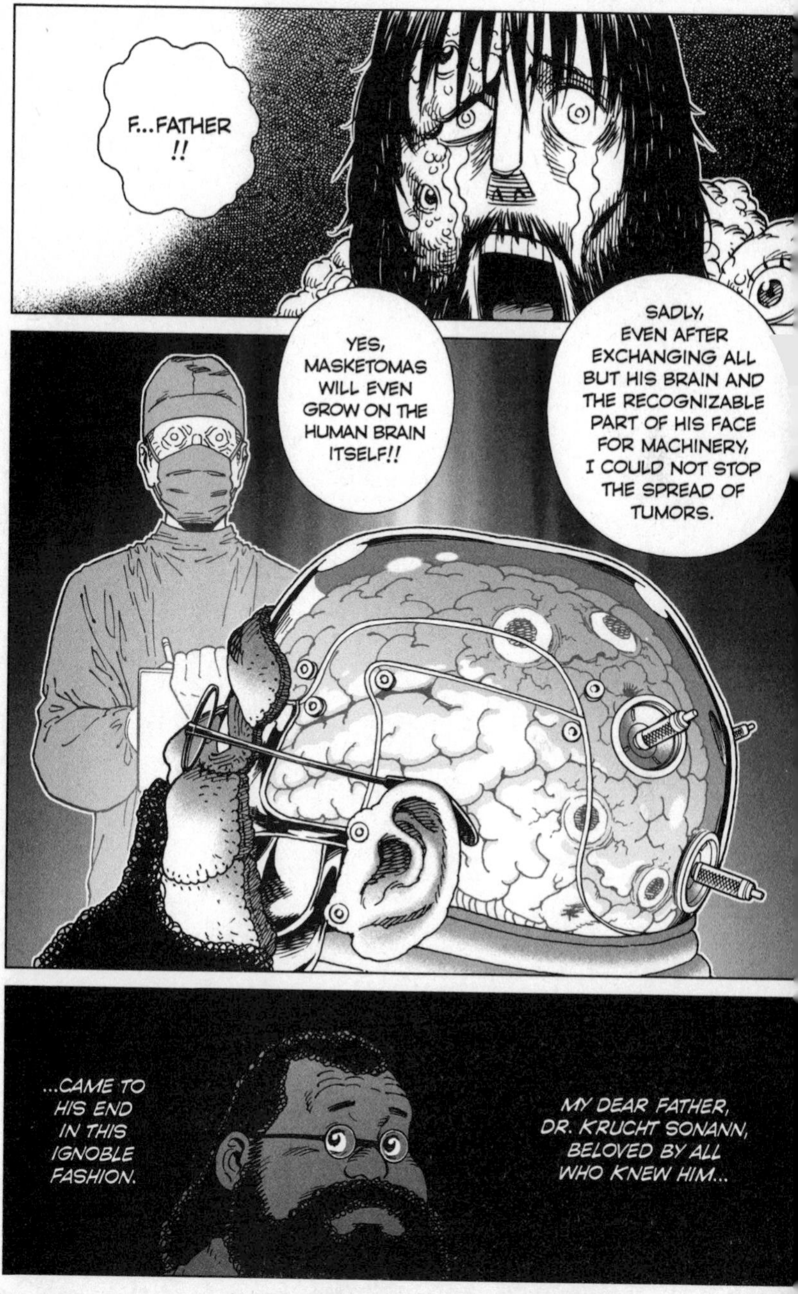
F...FATHER !!
SADLY, EVEN AFTER EXCHANGING ALL BUT HIS BRAIN AND THE RECOGNIZABLE PART OF HIS FACE FOR MACHINERY, I COULD NOT STOP THE SPREAD OF TUMORS.
YES, MASKETOMAS WILL EVEN GROW ON THE HUMAN BRAIN ITSELF!!
MY DEAR FATHER, DR. KRUCHT SONANN, BELOVED BY ALL WHO KNEW HIM...
...CAME TO HIS END IN THIS IGNOBLE FASHION.

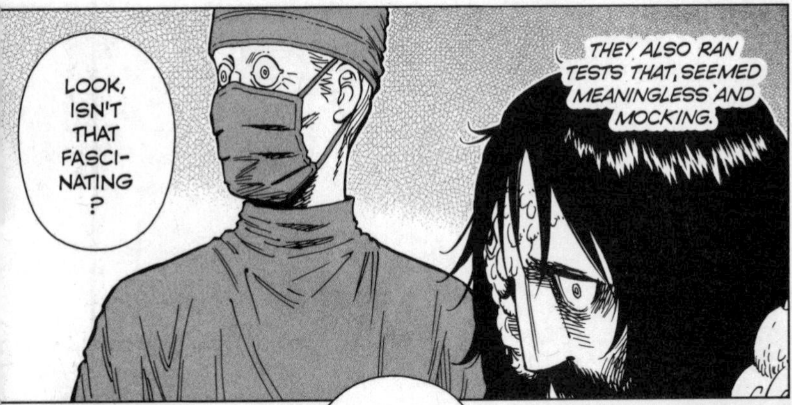
THEY ALSO RAN TESTS THAT SEEMED MEANINGLESS AND MOCKING.
LOOK, ISN'T THAT FASCINATING?
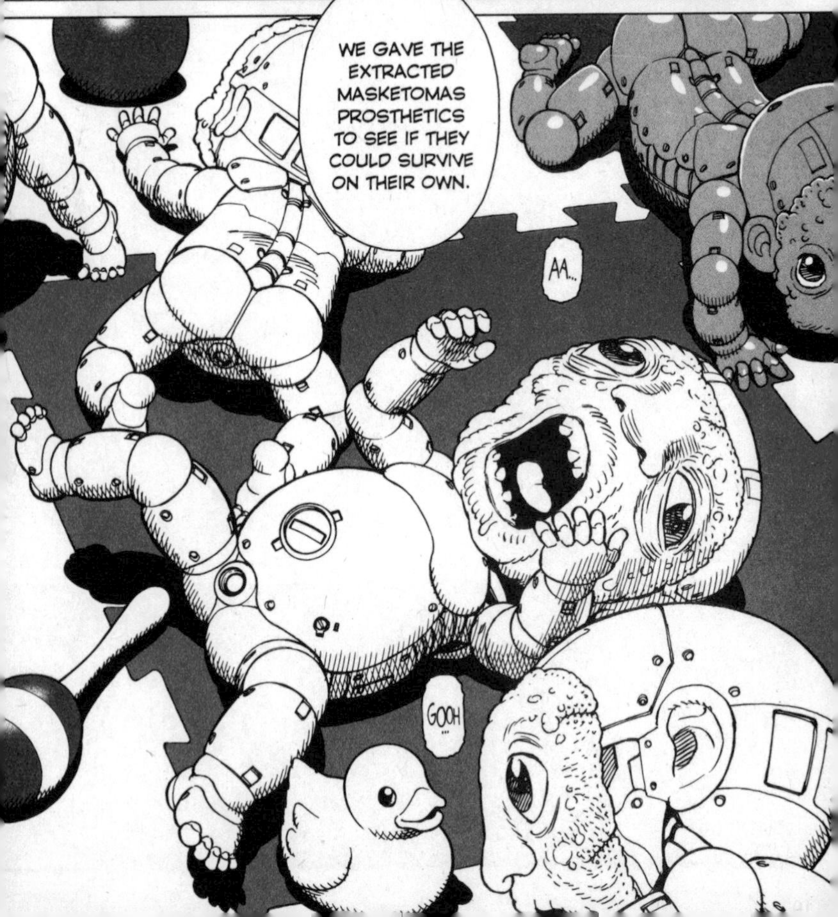
WE GAVE THE EXTRACTED MASKETOMAS PROSTHETICS TO SEE IF THEY COULD SURVIVE ON THEIR OWN.
AA...
GOOH...

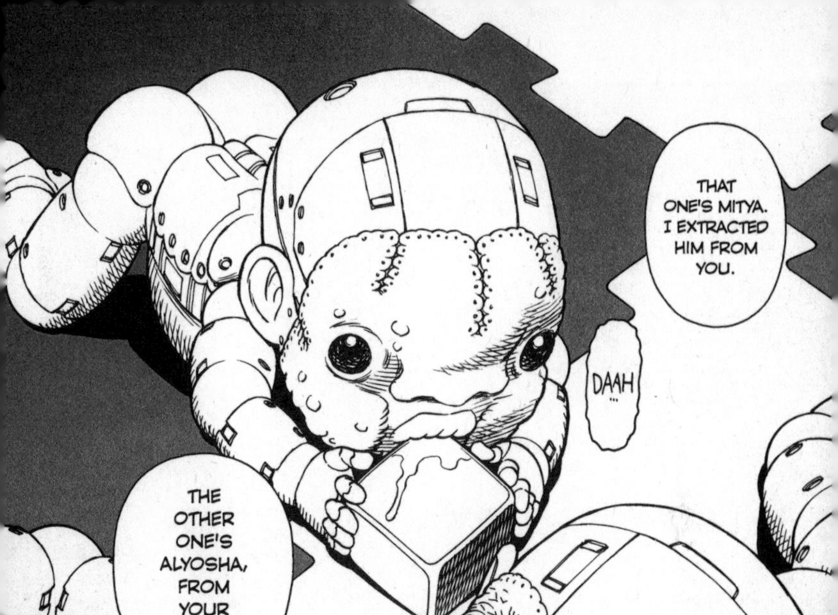
THAT ONE'S MITYA. I EXTRACTED HIM FROM YOU.
DAAH...
THE OTHER ONE'S ALYOSHA, FROM YOUR FATHER.

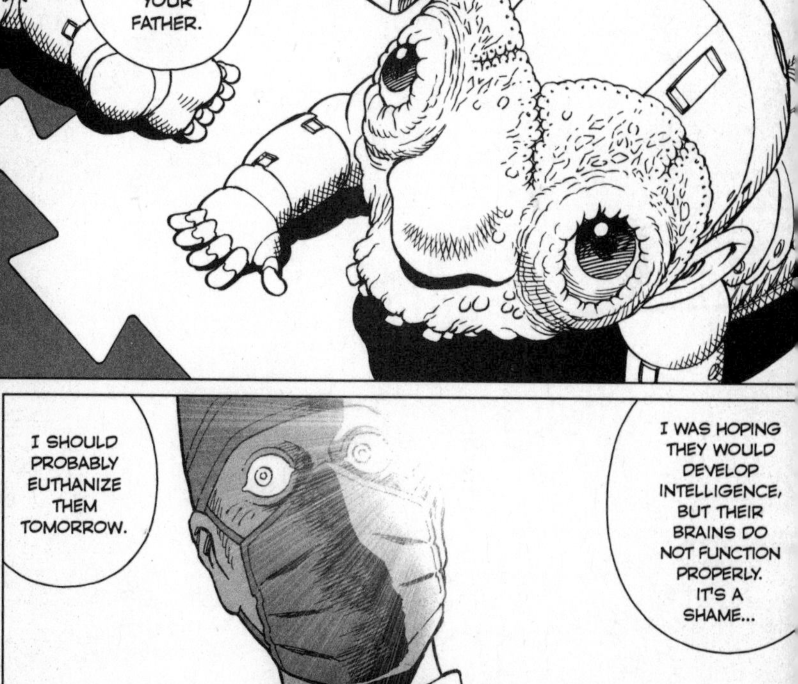
I WAS HOPING THEY WOULD DEVELOP INTELLIGENCE, BUT THEIR BRAINS DO NOT FUNCTION PROPERLY. IT'S A SHAME...
I SHOULD PROBABLY EUTHANIZE THEM TOMORROW.

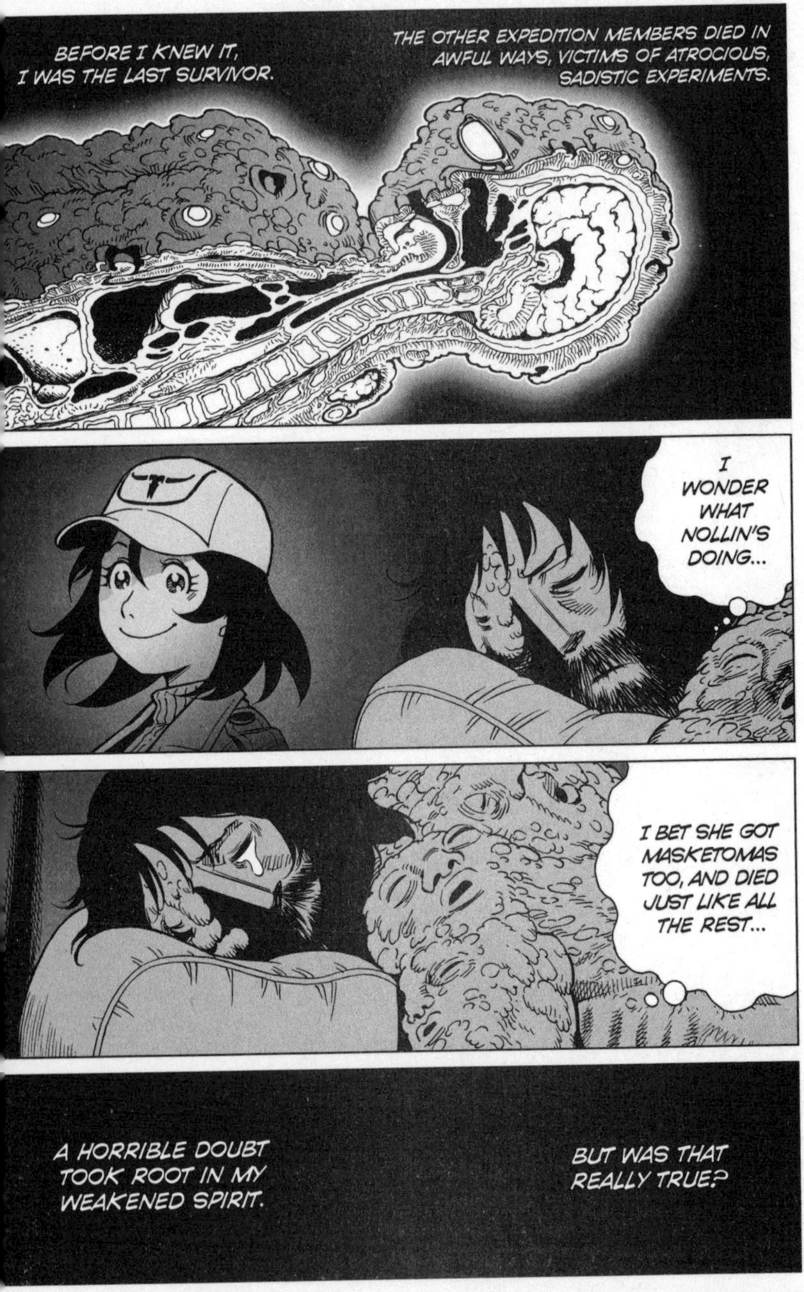
THE OTHER EXPEDITION MEMBERS DIED IN AWFUL WAYS, VICTIMS OF ATROCIOUS, SADISTIC EXPERIMENTS.
BEFORE I KNEW IT, I WAS THE LAST SURVIVOR.
I WONDER WHAT NOLLIN'S DOING...
I BET SHE GOT MASKETOMAS TOO, AND DIED JUST LIKE ALL THE REST...
BUT WAS THAT REALLY TRUE?
A HORRIBLE DOUBT TOOK ROOT IN MY WEAKENED SPIRIT.

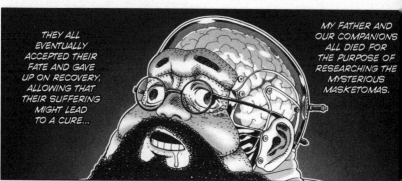

MY FATHER AND OUR COMPANIONS ALL DIED FOR THE PURPOSE OF RESEARCHING THE MYSTERIOUS MASKETOMAS.
THEY ALL EVENTUALLY ACCEPTED THEIR FATE AND GAVE UP ON RECOVERY, ALLOWING THAT THEIR SUFFERING MIGHT LEAD TO A CURE...
BUT WHAT IF THE MASKETOMAS WERE NOTHING BUT A VICIOUS LIE?!
WHAT IF WE'D MERELY BEEN LED TO BELIEVE IN THEM THROUGH A COMBINATION OF DRUGS AND PROSTHETIC SPECIAL EFFECTS?!
THEN MY FATHER! AND MY SISTER! AND OUR PARTNERS! WERE ALL KILLED FOR NOTHING!!
I BURNED WITH A RIGHTEOUS FURY!!

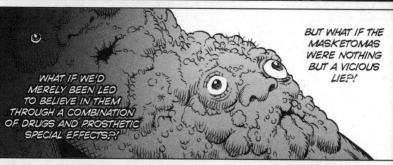

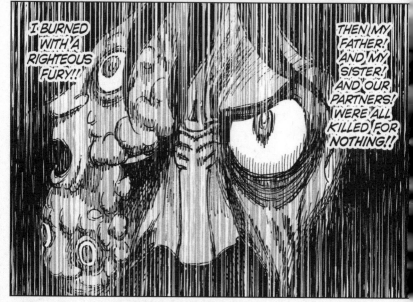

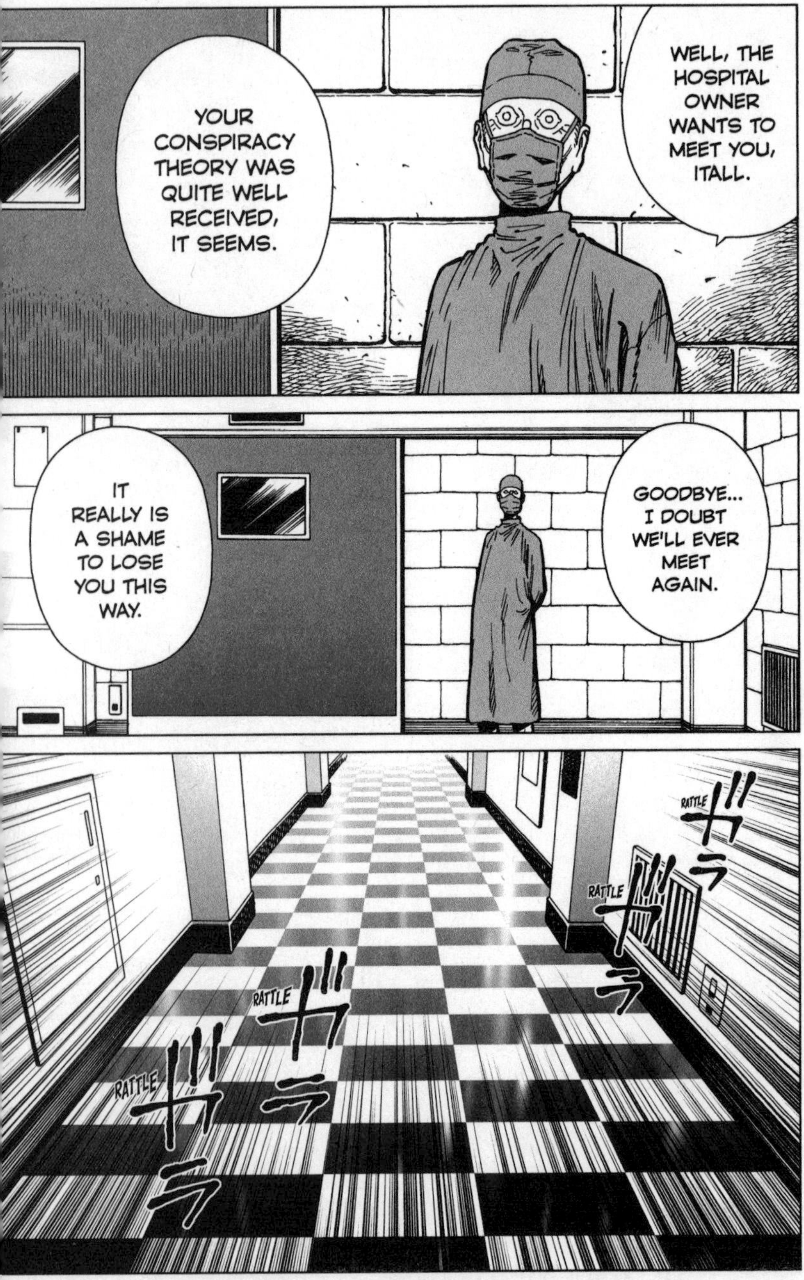

WELL, THE HOSPITAL OWNER WANTS TO MEET YOU, ITALL.
YOUR CONSPIRACY THEORY WAS QUITE WELL RECEIVED, IT SEEMS.
GOODBYE... I DOUBT WE'LL EVER MEET AGAIN.
IT REALLY IS A SHAME TO LOSE YOU THIS WAY.
RATTLE ガラ
RATTLE ガラ
RATTLE ガラ
RATTLE ガラ

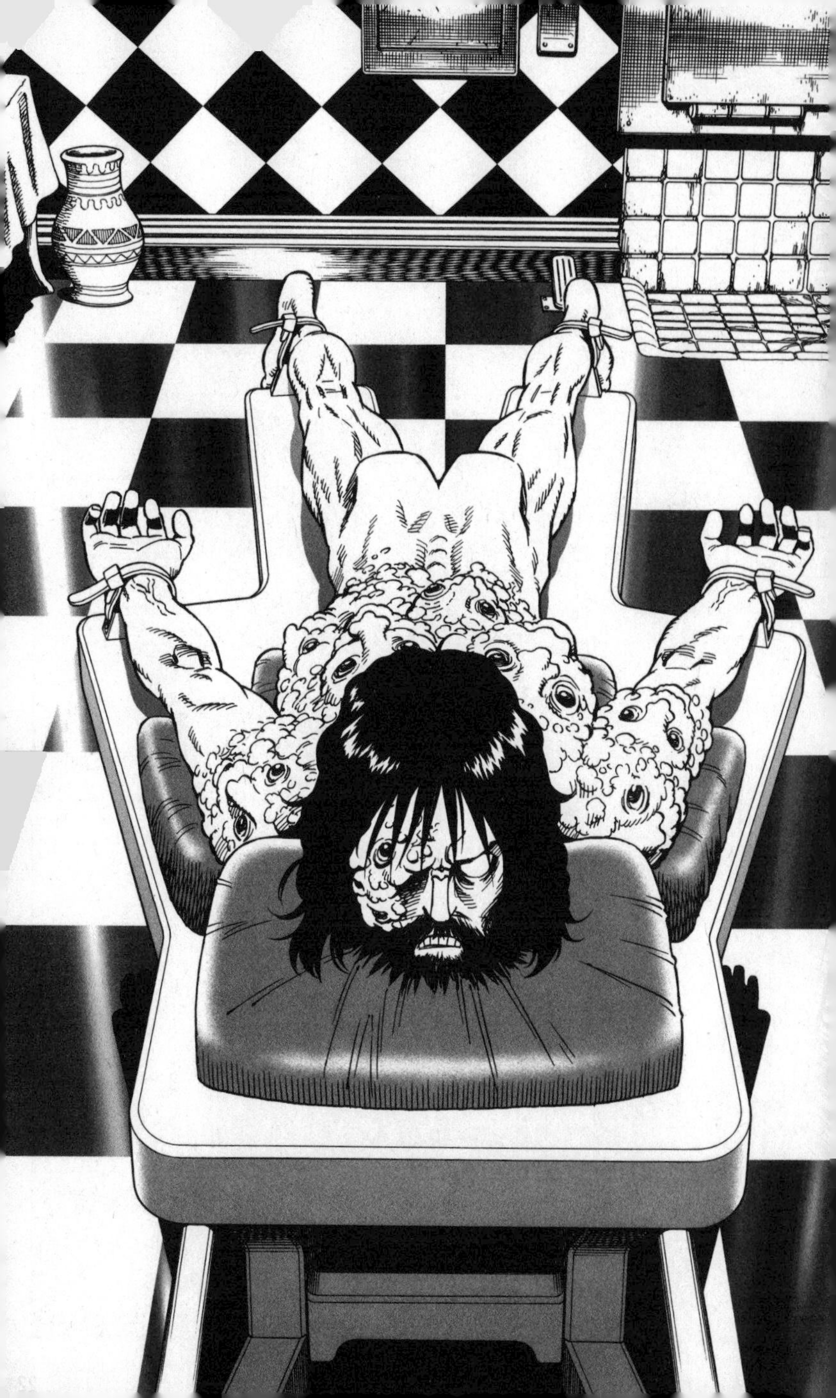

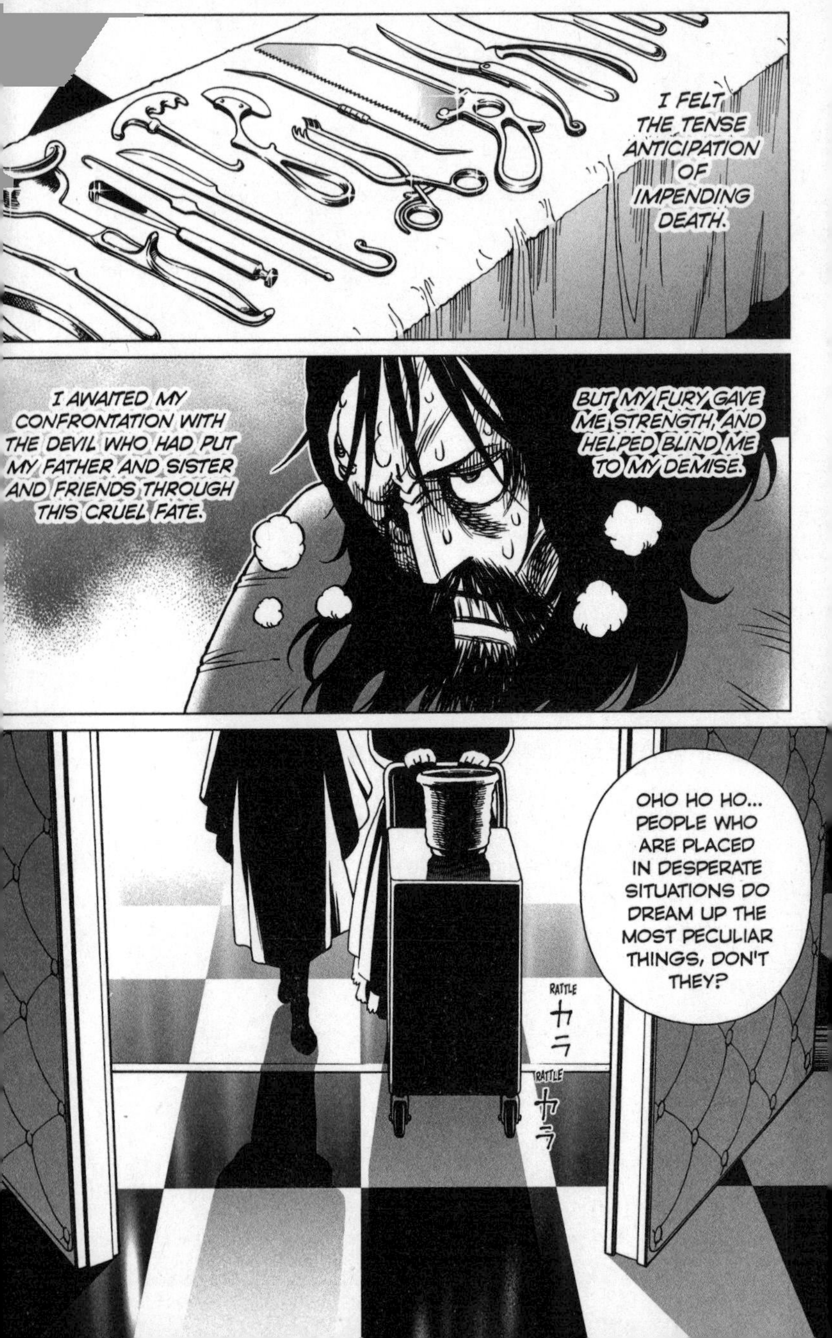
I FELT THE TENSE ANTICIPATION OF IMPENDING DEATH.
BUT MY FURY GAVE ME STRENGTH, AND HELPED BLIND ME TO MY DEMISE.
I AWAITED MY CONFRONTATION WITH THE DEVIL WHO HAD PUT MY FATHER AND SISTER AND FRIENDS THROUGH THIS CRUEL FATE.
OHO HO HO... PEOPLE WHO ARE PLACED IN DESPERATE SITUATIONS DO DREAM UP THE MOST PECULIAR THINGS, DON'T THEY?
RATTLE
カラ
RATTLE
カラ

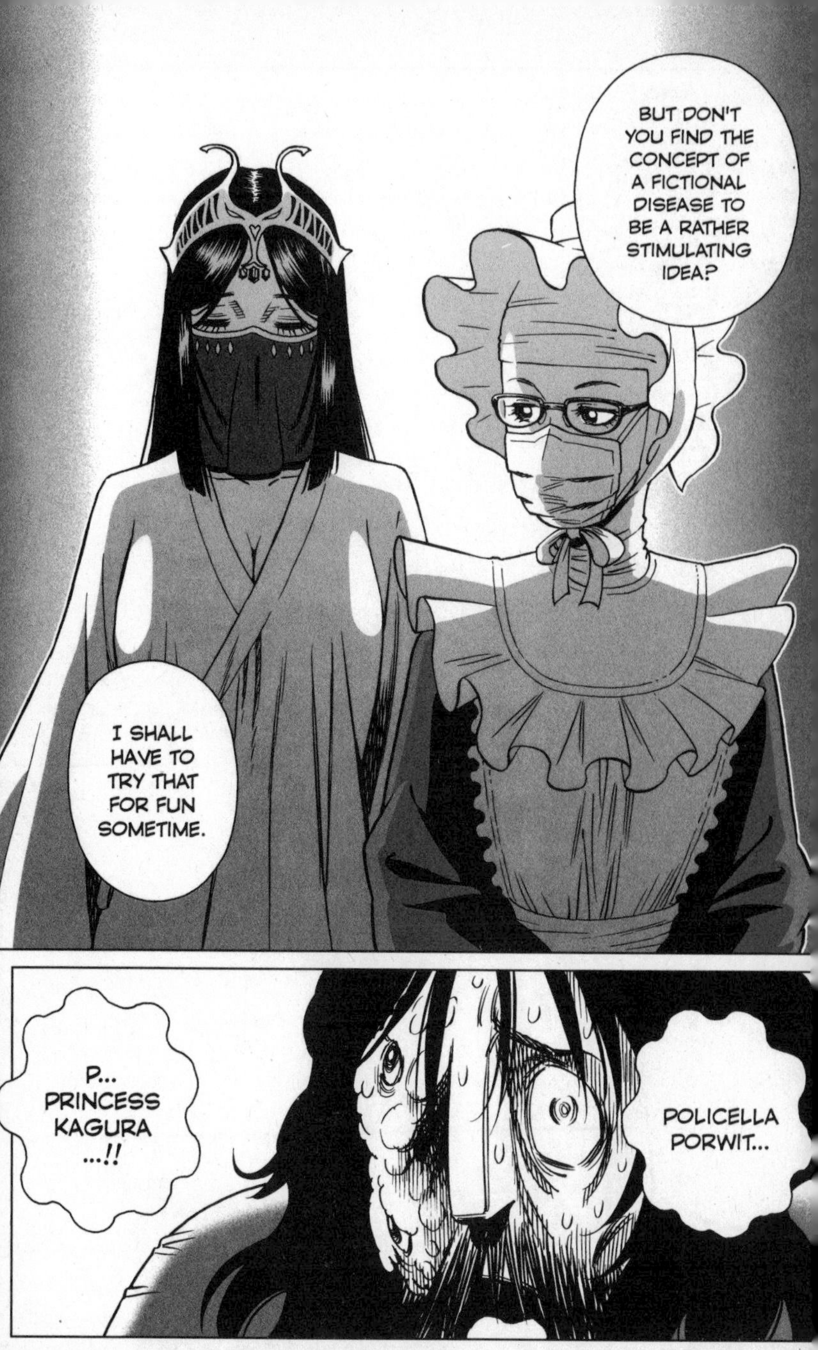
BUT DON'T YOU FIND THE CONCEPT OF A FICTIONAL DISEASE TO BE A RATHER STIMULATING IDEA?
I SHALL HAVE TO TRY THAT FOR FUN SOMETIME.
POLICELLA PORWIT...
P... PRINCESS KAGURA ...!!

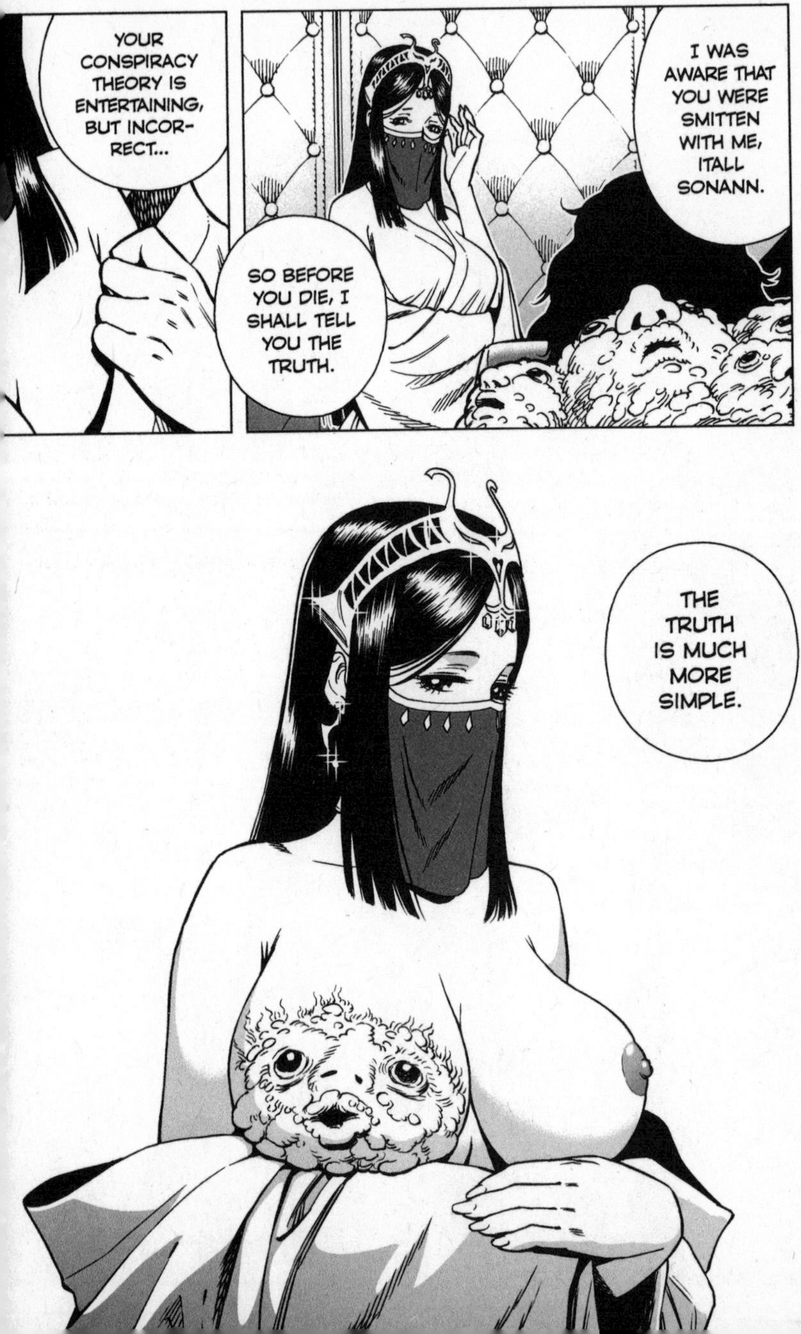
I WAS AWARE THAT YOU WERE SMITTEN WITH ME, ITALL SONANN.
SO BEFORE YOU DIE, I SHALL TELL YOU THE TRUTH.
YOUR CONSPIRACY THEORY IS ENTERTAINING, BUT INCORRECT...
THE TRUTH IS MUCH MORE SIMPLE.

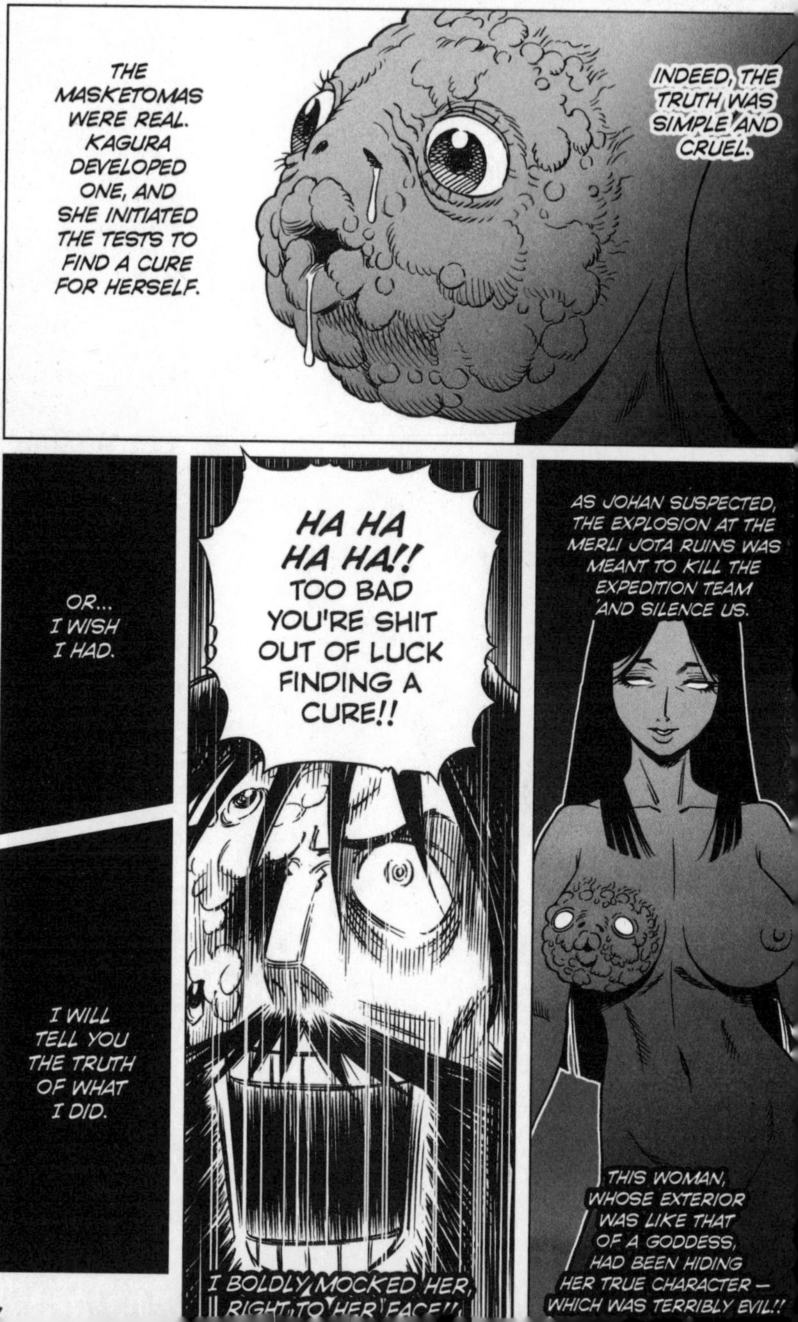
INDEED, THE TRUTH WAS SIMPLE AND CRUEL.
THE MASKETOMAS WERE REAL. KAGURA DEVELOPED ONE, AND SHE INITIATED THE TESTS TO FIND A CURE FOR HERSELF.
AS JOHAN SUSPECTED, THE EXPLOSION AT THE MERLI JOTA RUINS WAS MEANT TO KILL THE EXPEDITION TEAM AND SILENCE US.
THIS WOMAN, WHOSE EXTERIOR WAS LIKE THAT OF A GODDESS, HAD BEEN HIDING HER TRUE CHARACTER — WHICH WAS TERRIBLY EVIL!!
HA HA HA HA!! TOO BAD YOU'RE SHIT OUT OF LUCK FINDING A CURE!!
I BOLDLY MOCKED HER, RIGHT TO HER FACE!!
OR... I WISH I HAD.
I WILL TELL YOU THE TRUTH OF WHAT I DID.

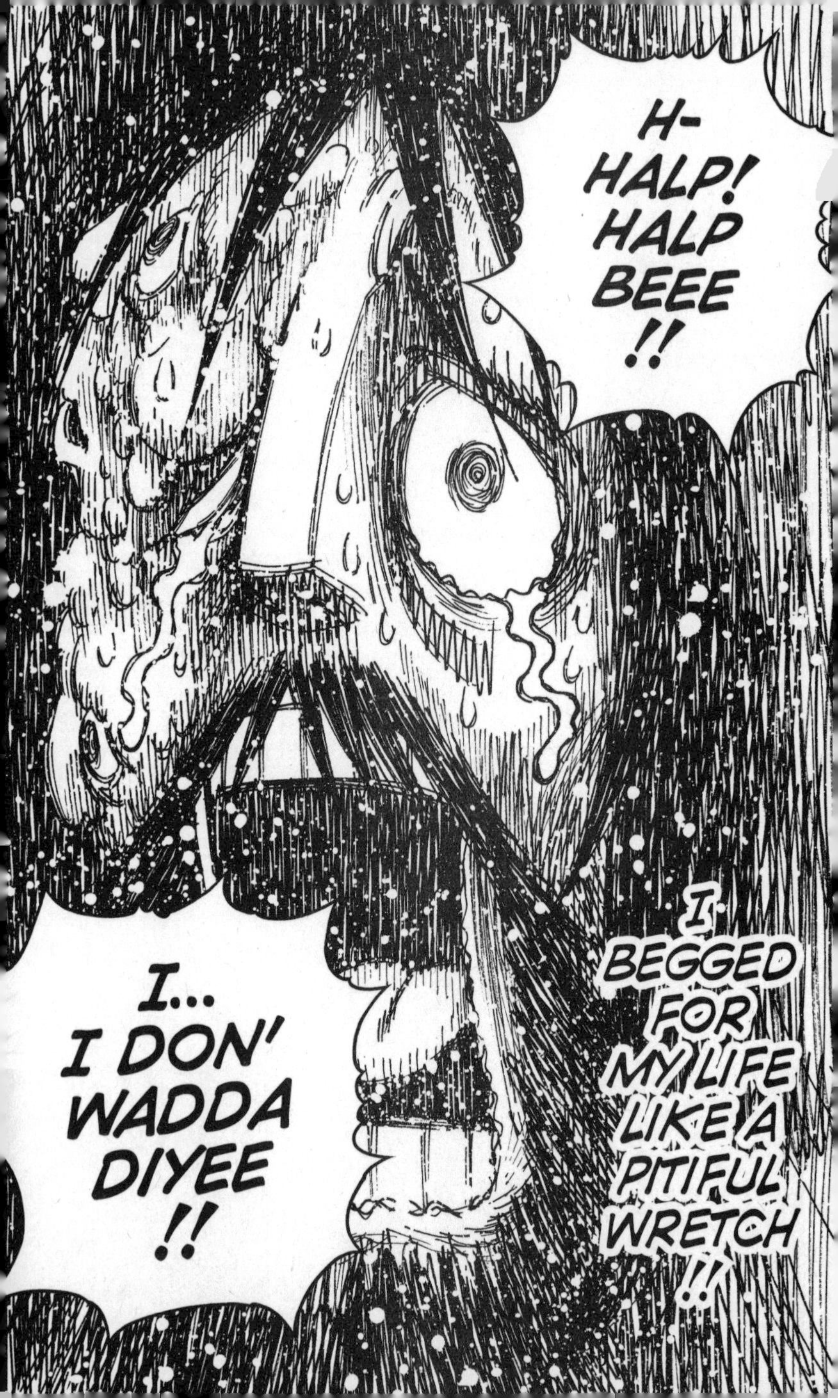
H-HALP! HALP BEEE !!
I BEGGED FOR MY LIFE LIKE A PITIFUL WRETCH !!
I... I DON' WADDA DIYEE !!

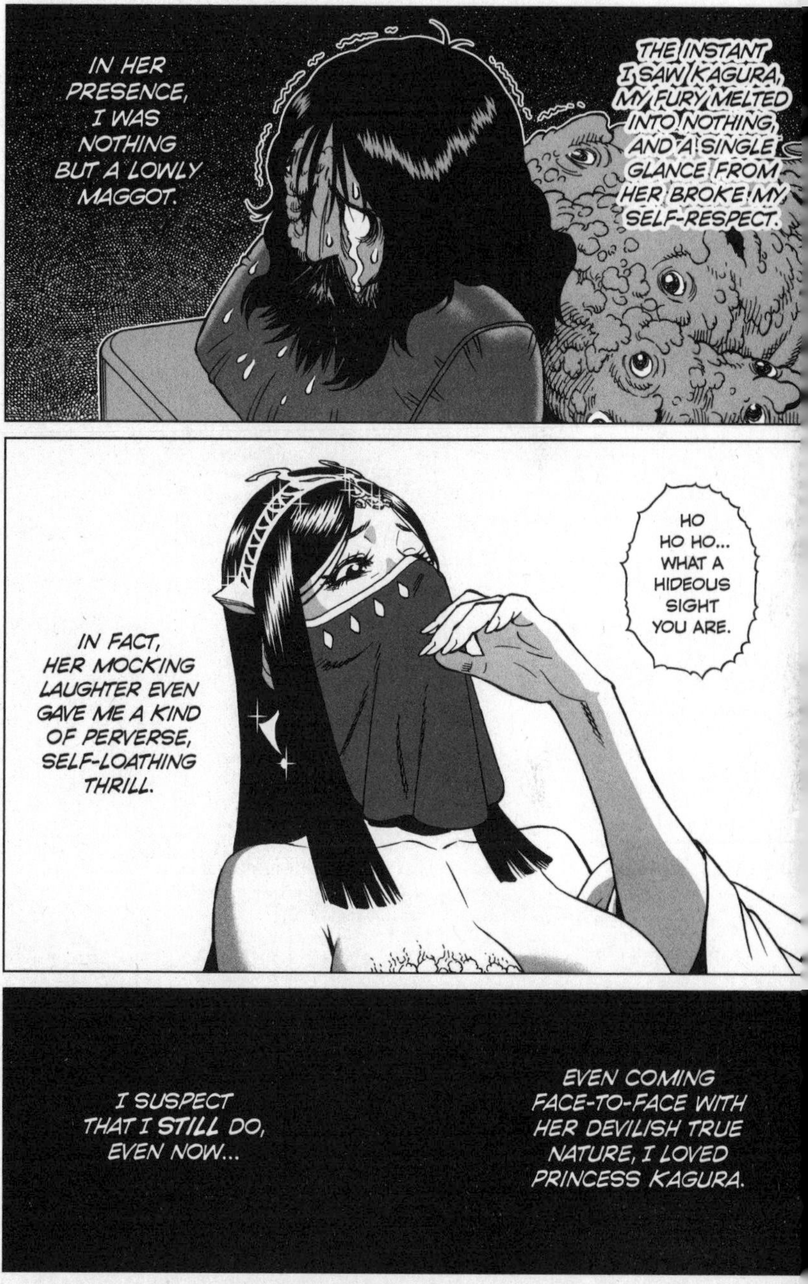
THE INSTANT I SAW KAGURA, MY FURY MELTED INTO NOTHING, AND A SINGLE GLANCE FROM HER BROKE MY SELF-RESPECT.
IN HER PRESENCE, I WAS NOTHING BUT A LOWLY MAGGOT.
HO HO HO... WHAT A HIDEOUS SIGHT YOU ARE.
IN FACT, HER MOCKING LAUGHTER EVEN GAVE ME A KIND OF PERVERSE, SELF-LOATHING THRILL.
EVEN COMING FACE-TO-FACE WITH HER DEVILISH TRUE NATURE, I LOVED PRINCESS KAGURA.
I SUSPECT THAT I **STILL** DO, EVEN NOW...

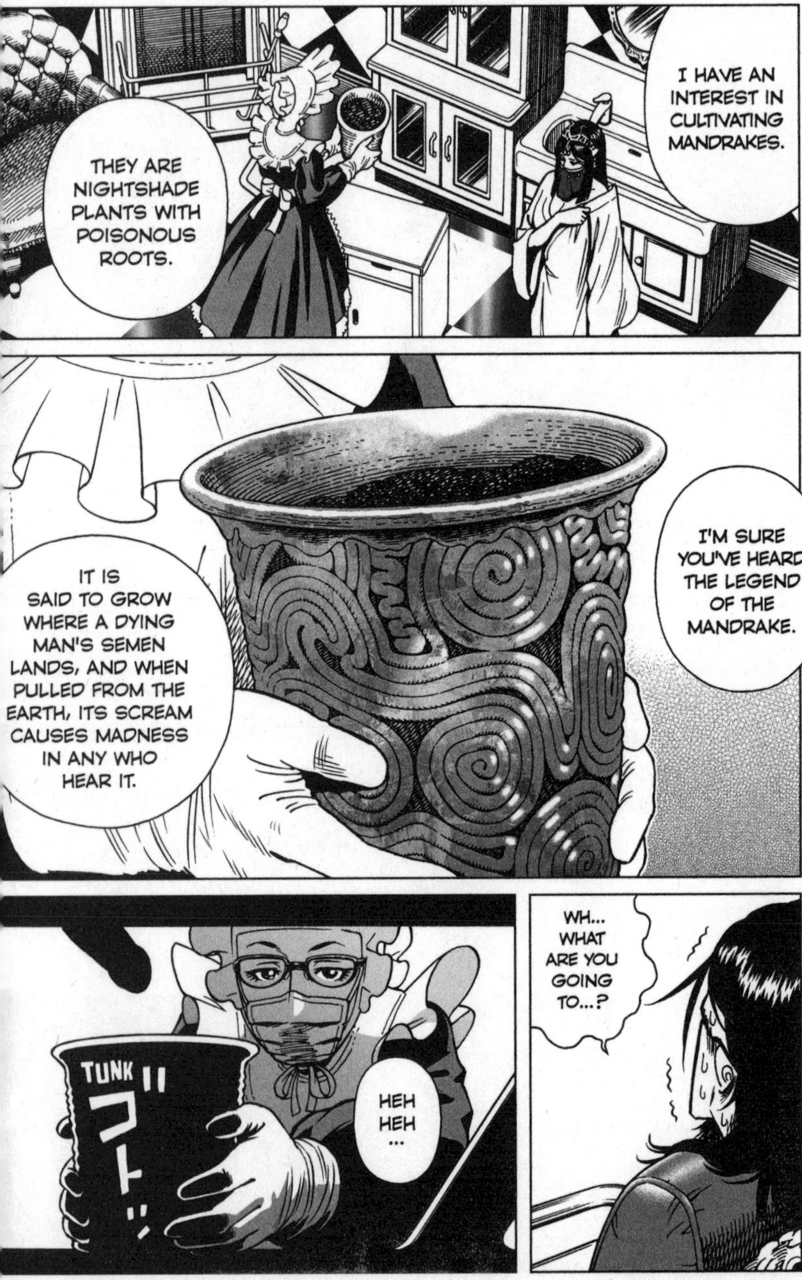
I HAVE AN INTEREST IN CULTIVATING MANDRAKES.
THEY ARE NIGHTSHADE PLANTS WITH POISONOUS ROOTS.
I'M SURE YOU'VE HEARD THE LEGEND OF THE MANDRAKE.
IT IS SAID TO GROW WHERE A DYING MAN'S SEMEN LANDS, AND WHEN PULLED FROM THE EARTH, ITS SCREAM CAUSES MADNESS IN ANY WHO HEAR IT.
WH... WHAT ARE YOU GOING TO...?
HEH HEH ...
TUNK
コトッ

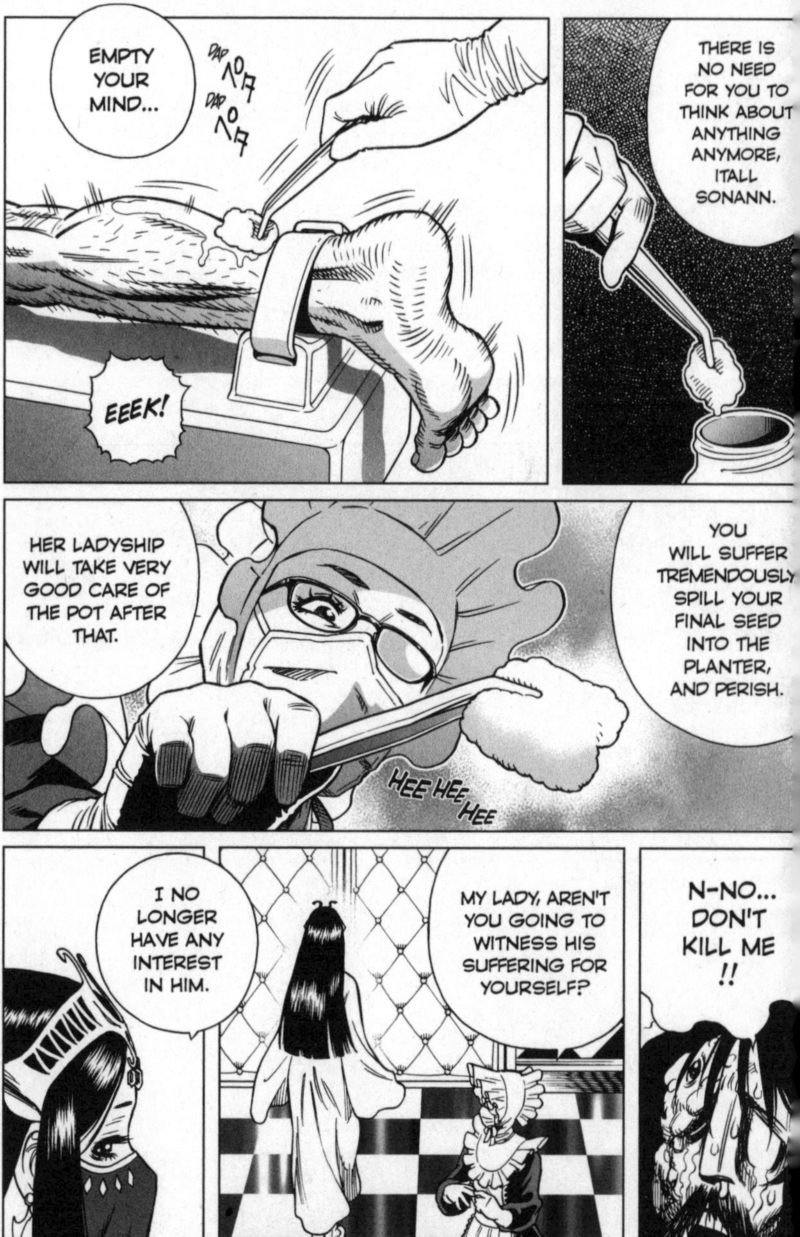
THERE IS NO NEED FOR YOU TO THINK ABOUT ANYTHING ANYMORE, ITALL SONANN.
EMPTY YOUR MIND...
DAP
DAP
EEEK!
YOU WILL SUFFER TREMENDOUSLY, SPILL YOUR FINAL SEED INTO THE PLANTER, AND PERISH.
HER LADYSHIP WILL TAKE VERY GOOD CARE OF THE POT AFTER THAT.
HEE HEE HEE
N-NO... DON'T KILL ME !!
MY LADY, AREN'T YOU GOING TO WITNESS HIS SUFFERING FOR YOURSELF?
I NO LONGER HAVE ANY INTEREST IN HIM.

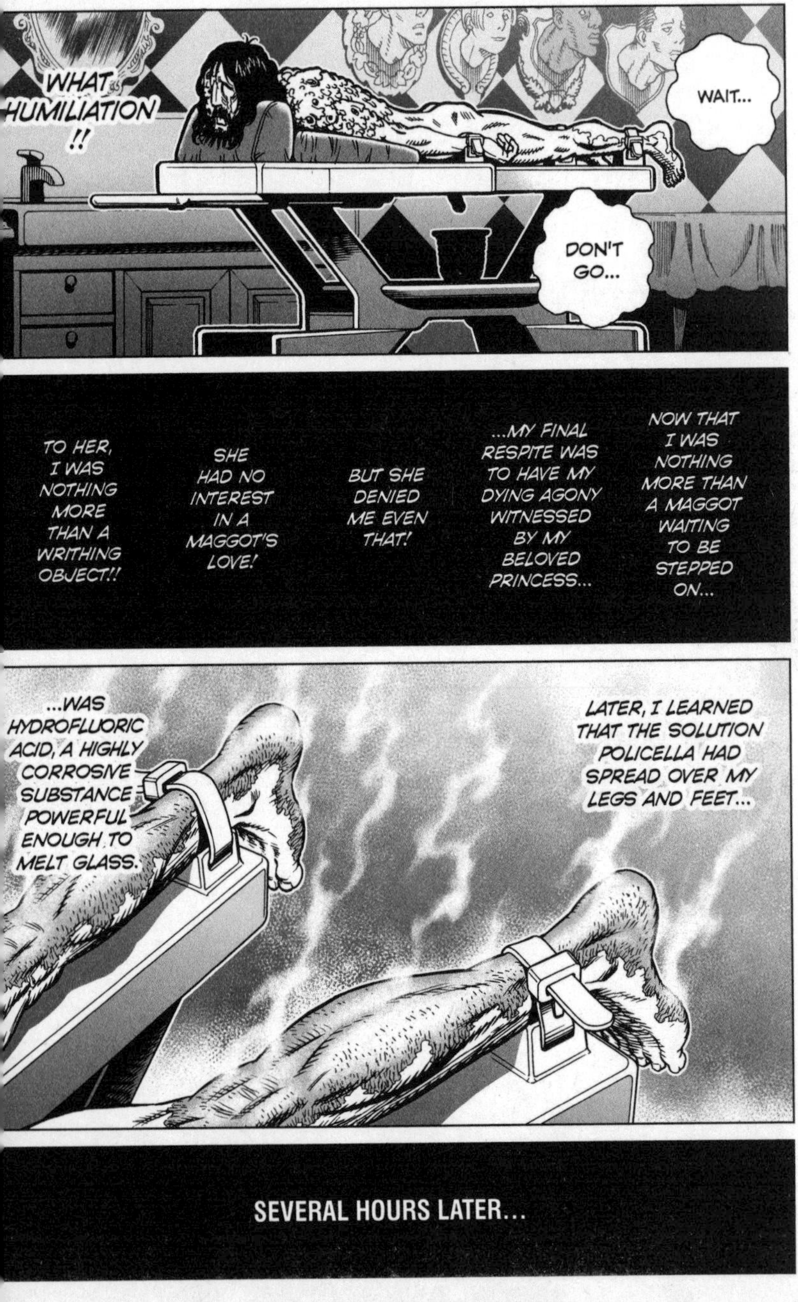
WAIT...
DON'T GO...
WHAT HUMILIATION!!
NOW THAT I WAS NOTHING MORE THAN A MAGGOT WAITING TO BE STEPPED ON...
...MY FINAL RESPITE WAS TO HAVE MY DYING AGONY WITNESSED BY MY BELOVED PRINCESS...
BUT SHE DENIED ME EVEN THAT!
SHE HAD NO INTEREST IN A MAGGOT'S LOVE!
TO HER, I WAS NOTHING MORE THAN A WRITHING OBJECT!!
LATER, I LEARNED THAT THE SOLUTION POLICELLA HAD SPREAD OVER MY LEGS AND FEET...
...WAS HYDROFLUORIC ACID, A HIGHLY CORROSIVE SUBSTANCE POWERFUL ENOUGH TO MELT GLASS.
SEVERAL HOURS LATER...

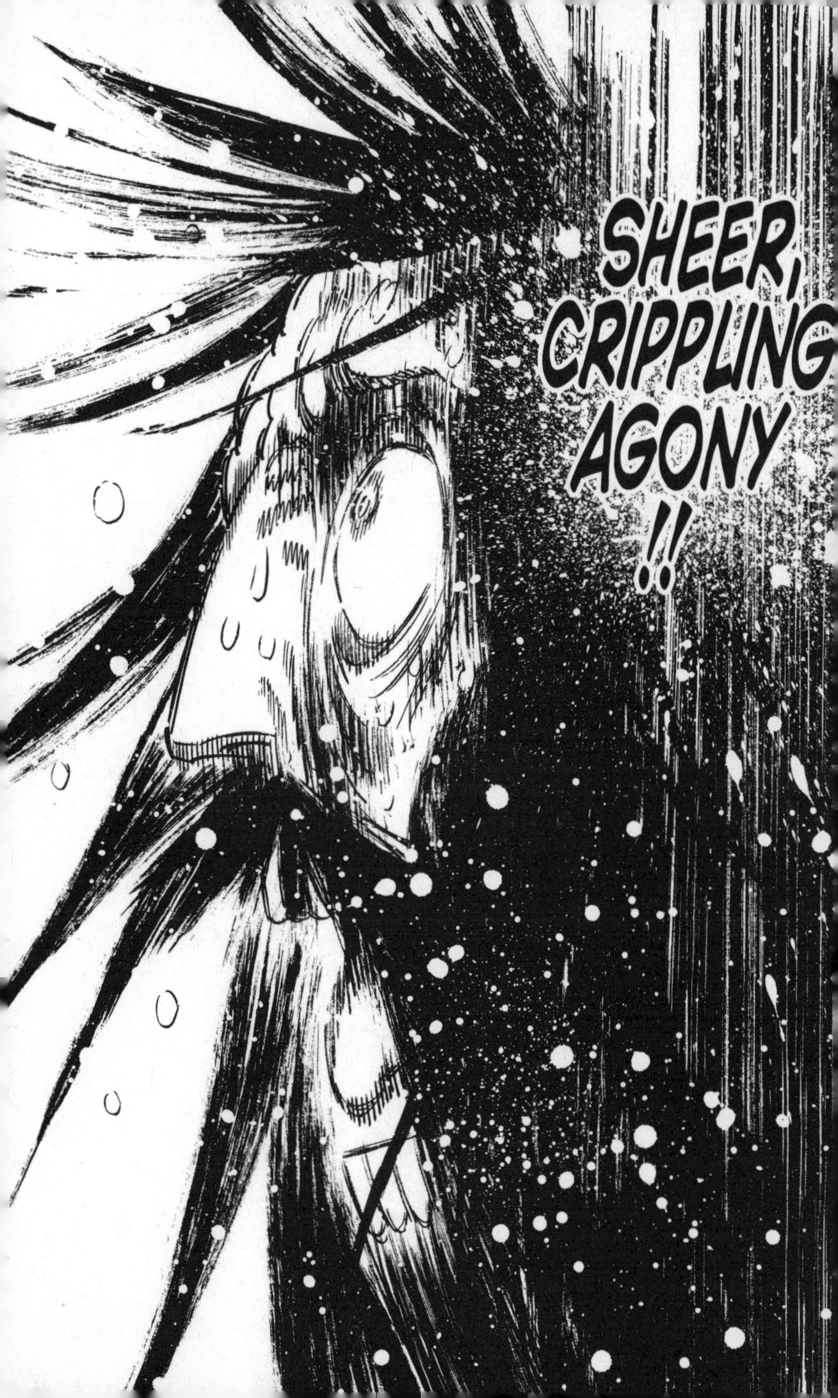
SHEER, CRIPPLING AGONY !!

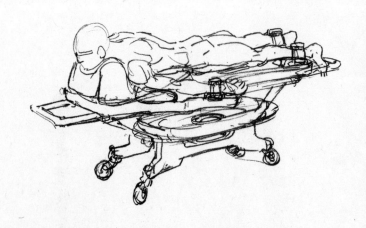

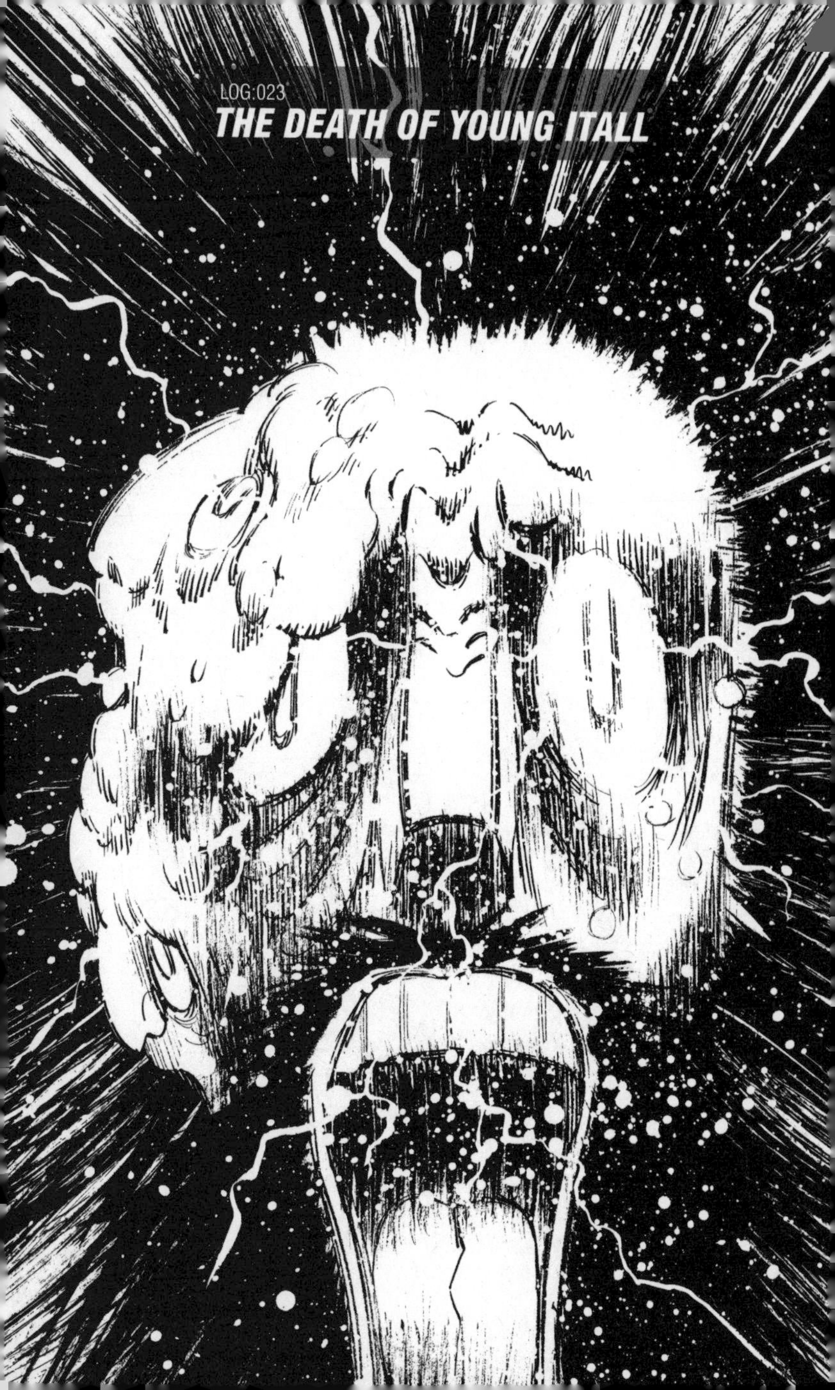
LOG:023
THE DEATH OF YOUNG ITALL

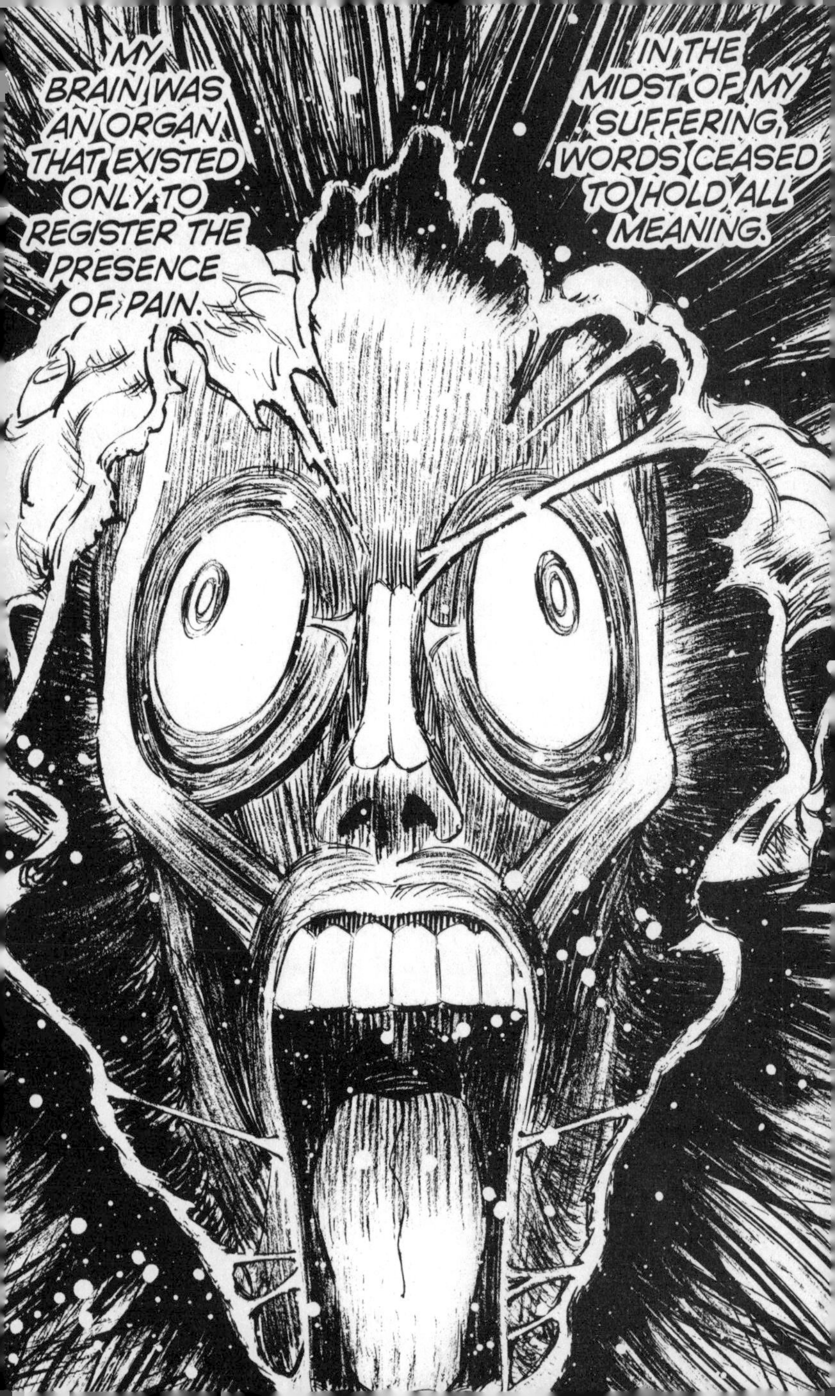
IN THE MIDST OF MY SUFFERING, WORDS CEASED TO HOLD ALL MEANING.
MY BRAIN WAS AN ORGAN THAT EXISTED ONLY TO REGISTER THE PRESENCE OF PAIN.

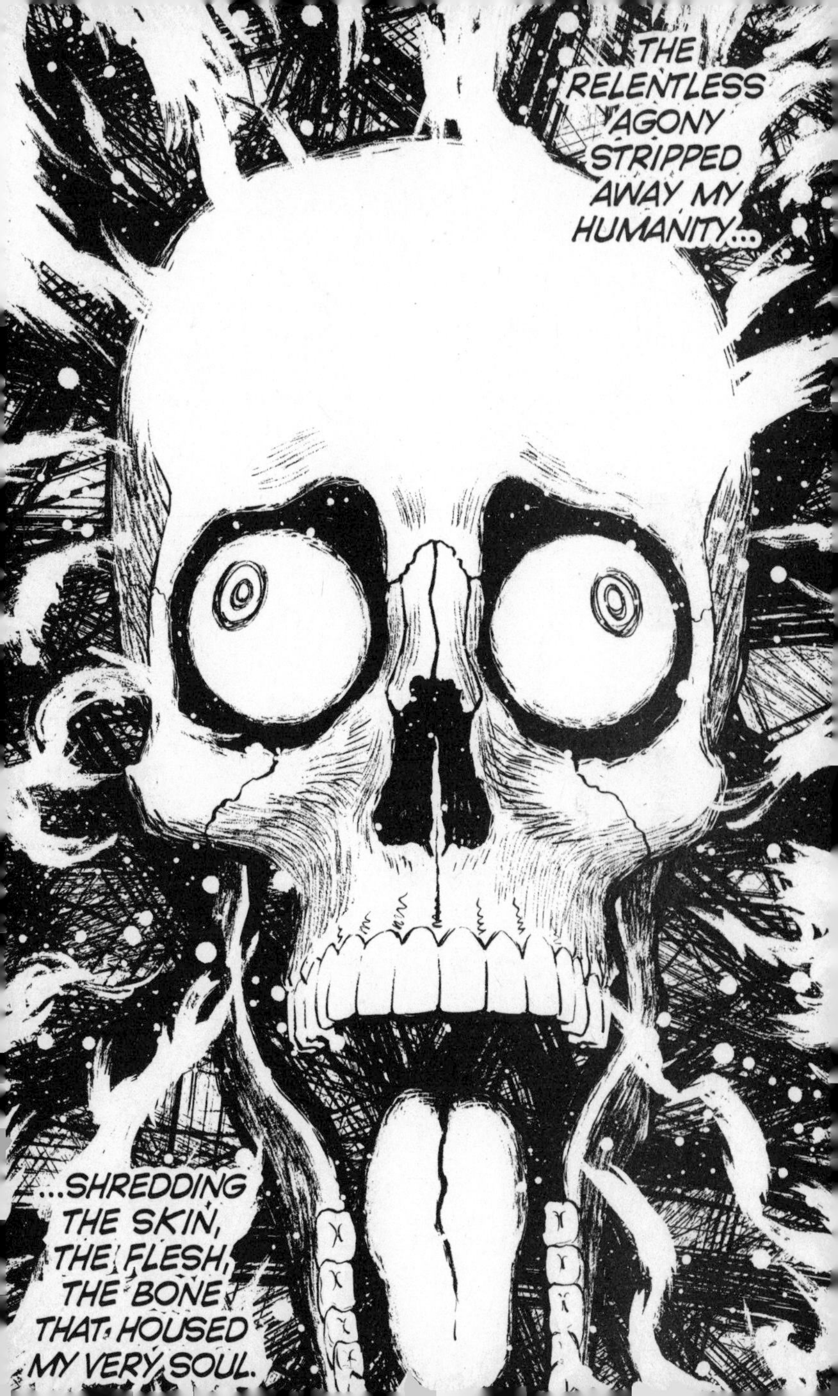
THE RELENTLESS AGONY STRIPPED AWAY MY HUMANITY...
...SHREDDING THE SKIN, THE FLESH, THE BONE THAT HOUSED MY VERY SOUL.

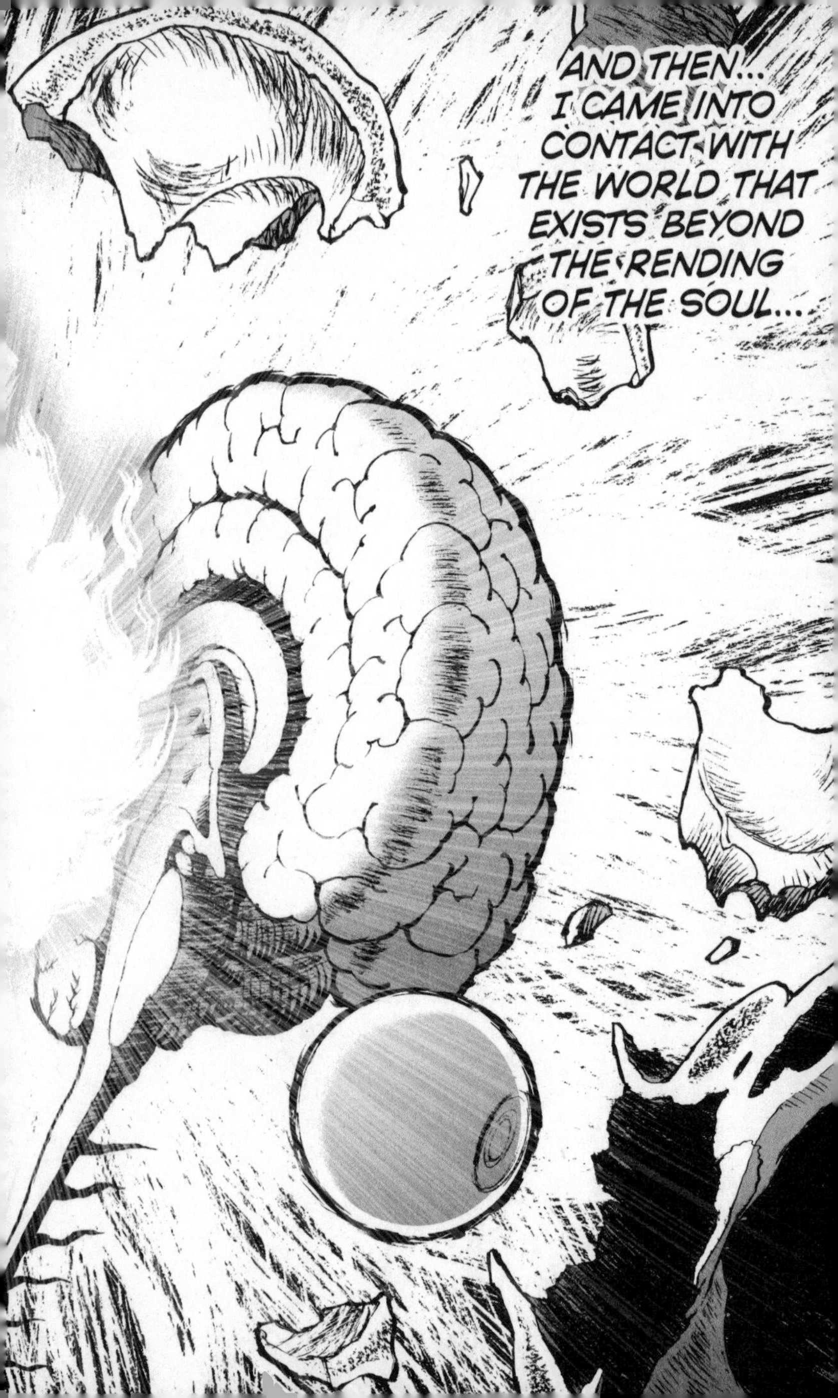
AND THEN... I CAME INTO CONTACT WITH THE WORLD THAT EXISTS BEYOND THE RENDING OF THE SOUL...

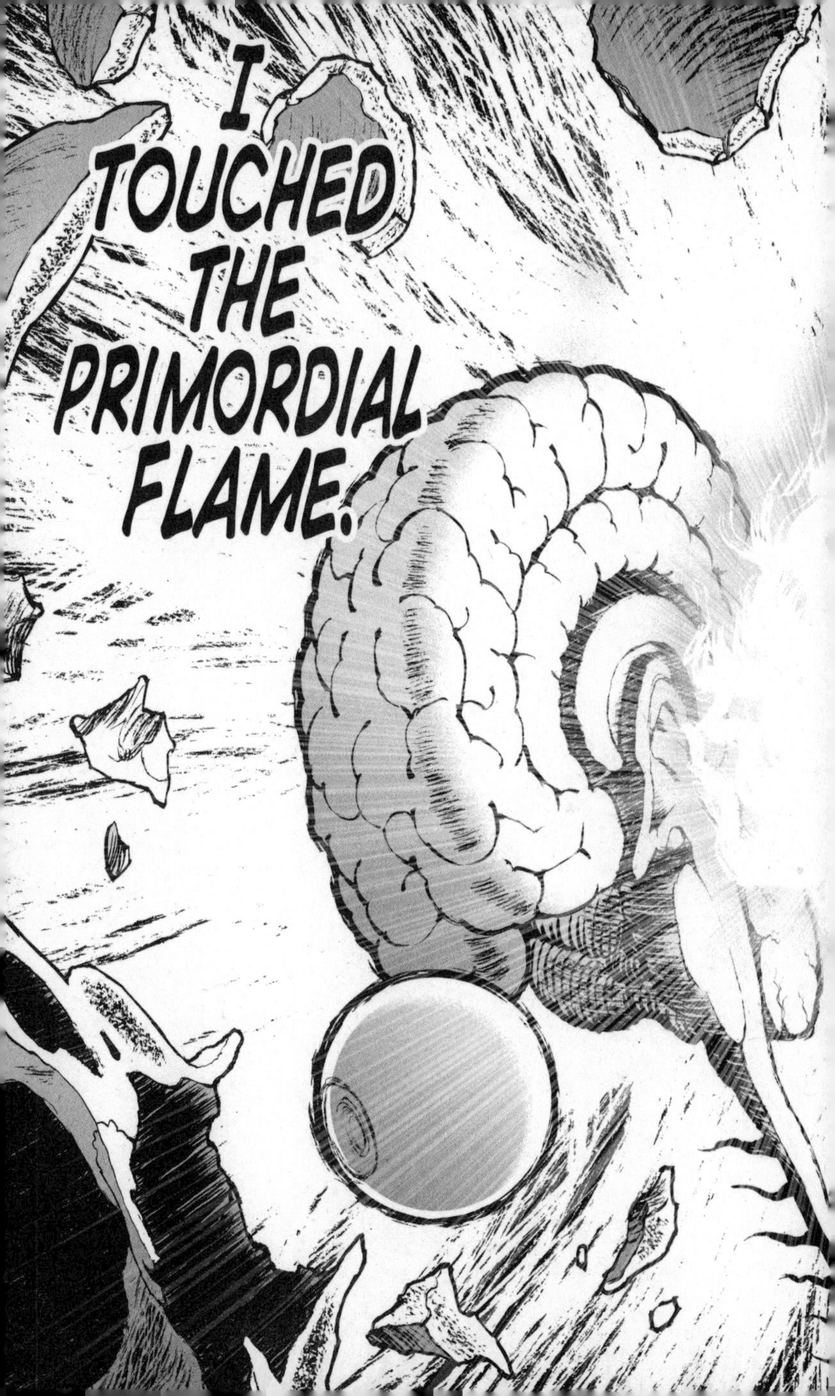
I TOUCHED THE PRIMORDIAL FLAME.

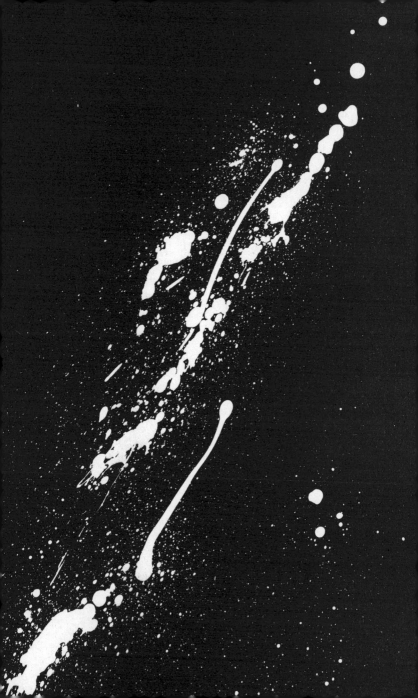

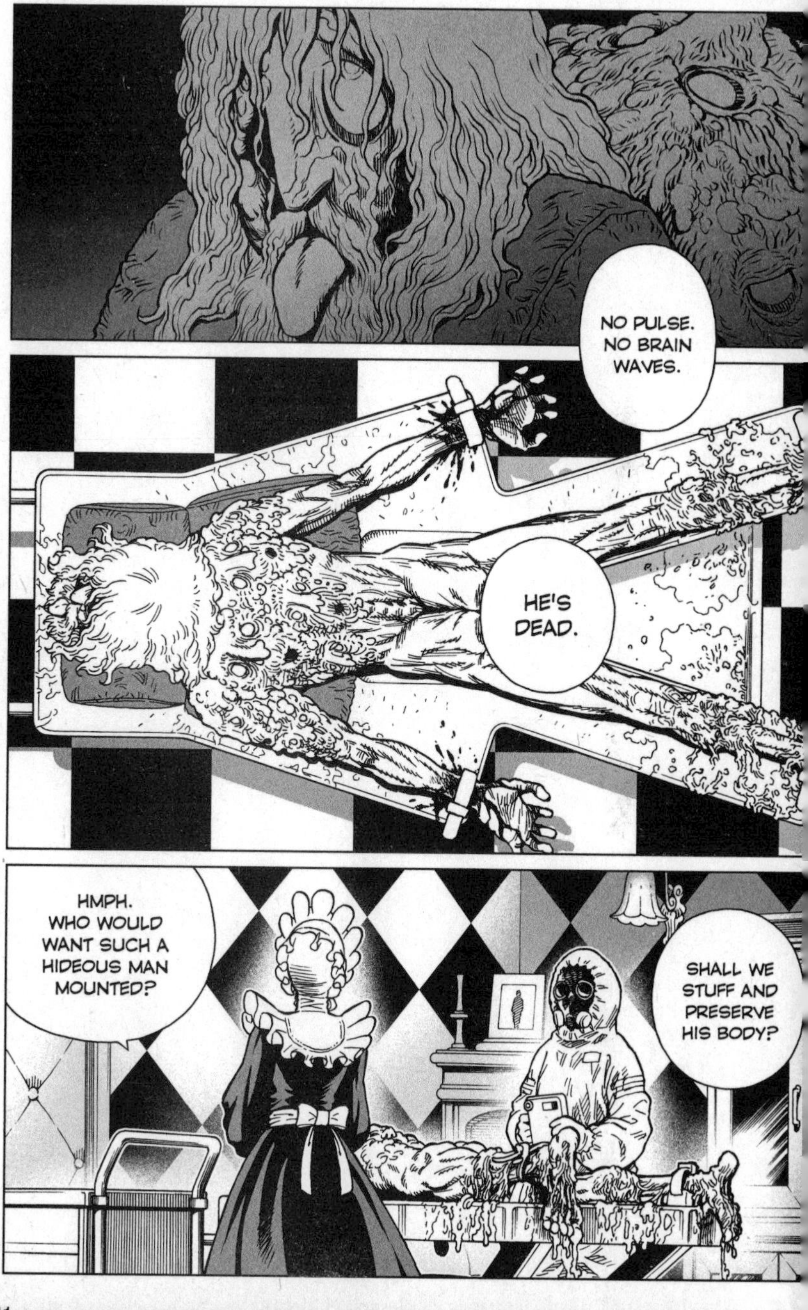
NO PULSE. NO BRAIN WAVES.
HE'S DEAD.
SHALL WE STUFF AND PRESERVE HIS BODY?
HMPH. WHO WOULD WANT SUCH A HIDEOUS MAN MOUNTED?

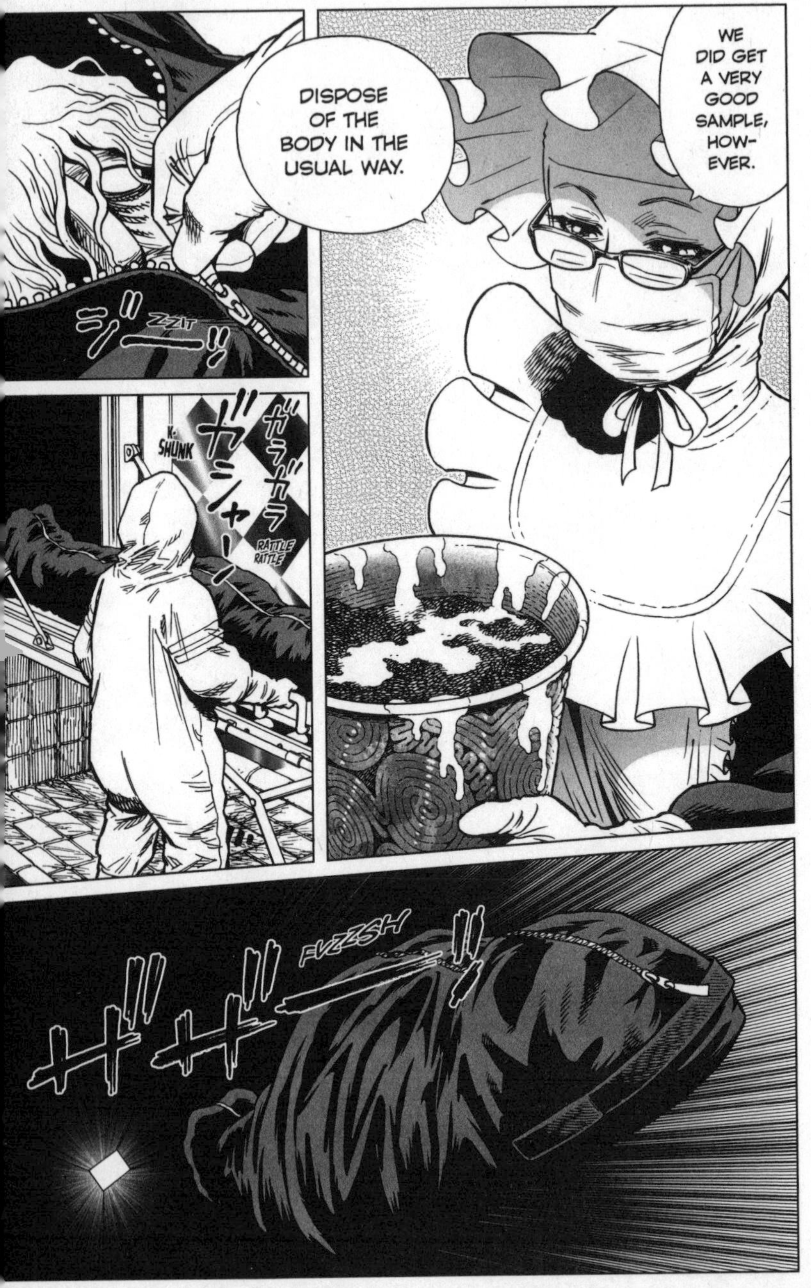
WE DID GET A VERY GOOD SAMPLE, HOW-EVER.
DISPOSE OF THE BODY IN THE USUAL WAY.
ジー!!
ZZZIT
ガラガラ
RATTLE RATTLE
ガシャーン
K-SHUNK
FVZZSH

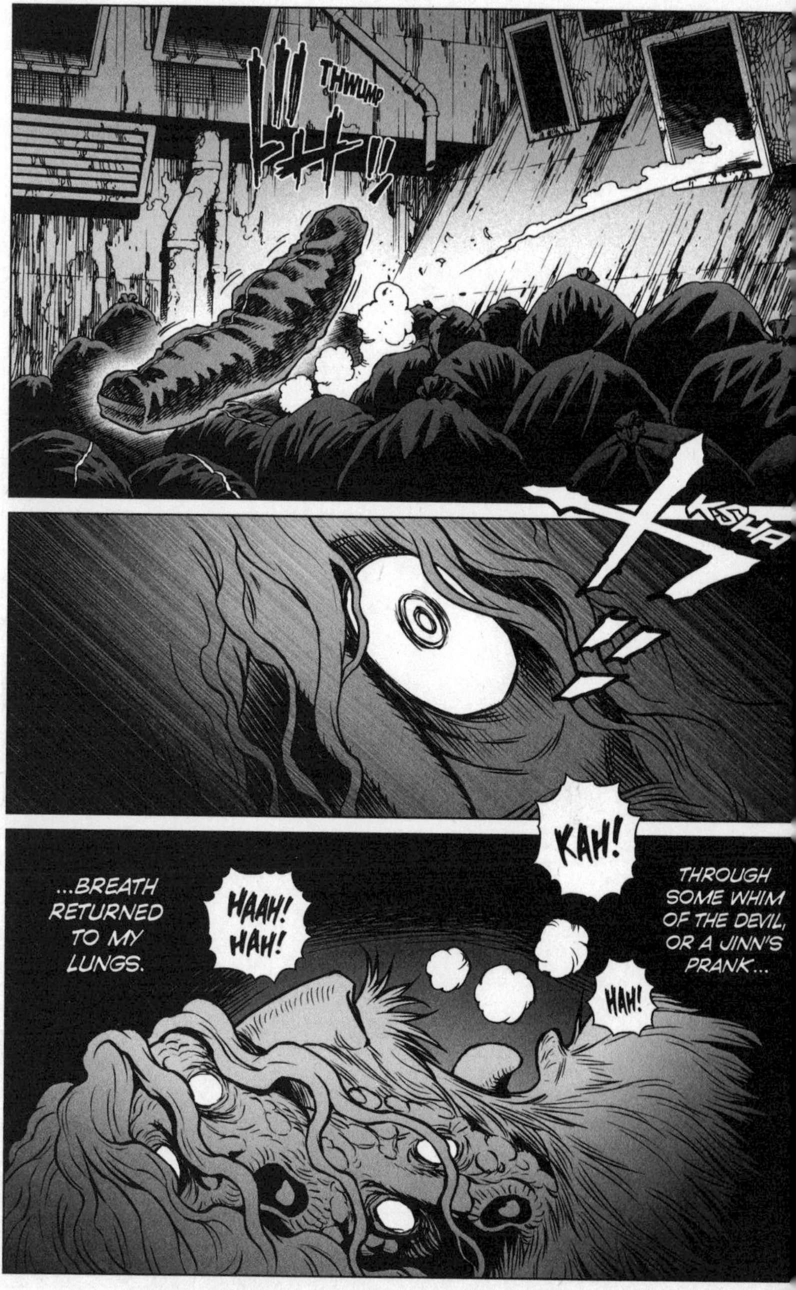
THWUMP
KSHA
KAH!
THROUGH SOME WHIM OF THE DEVIL, OR A JINN'S PRANK...
HAH!
HAAH! HAH!
...BREATH RETURNED TO MY LUNGS.

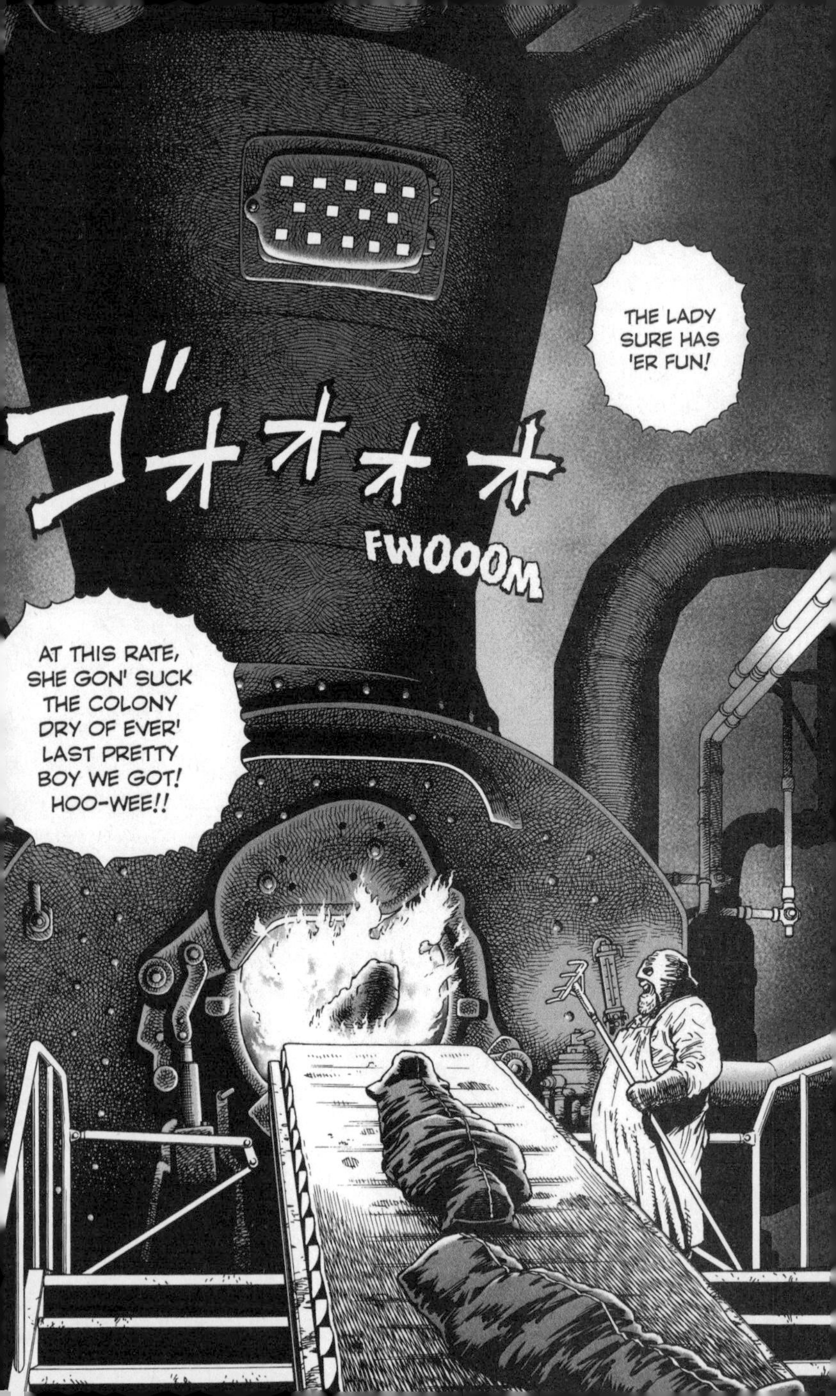
THE LADY SURE HAS 'ER FUN!
ゴォオォオ
FWOOOM
AT THIS RATE, SHE GON' SUCK THE COLONY DRY OF EVER' LAST PRETTY BOY WE GOT! HOO-WEE!!

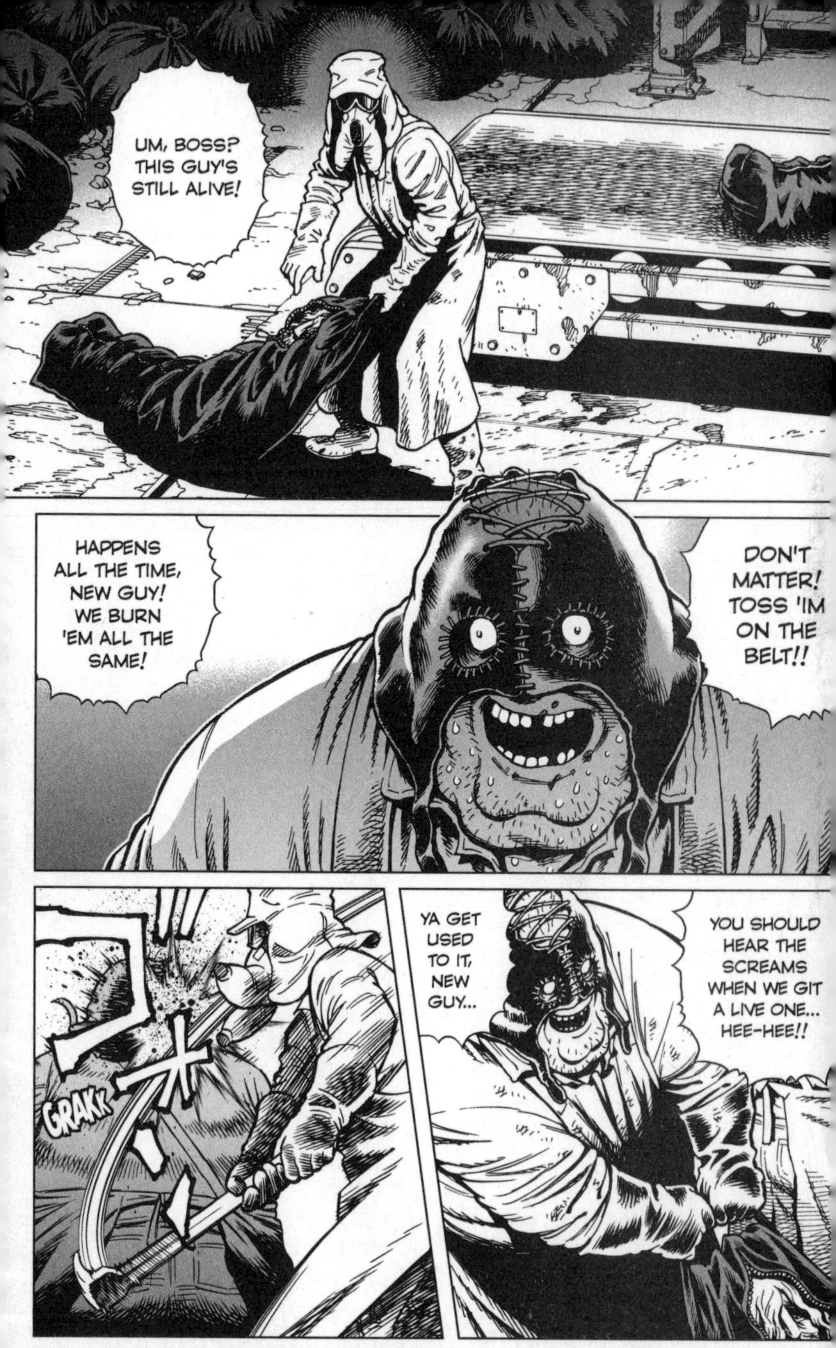
UM, BOSS? THIS GUY'S STILL ALIVE!
DON'T MATTER! TOSS 'IM ON THE BELT!!
HAPPENS ALL THE TIME, NEW GUY! WE BURN 'EM ALL THE SAME!
YOU SHOULD HEAR THE SCREAMS WHEN WE GIT A LIVE ONE... HEE-HEE!!
YA GET USED TO IT, NEW GUY...
GRAKK

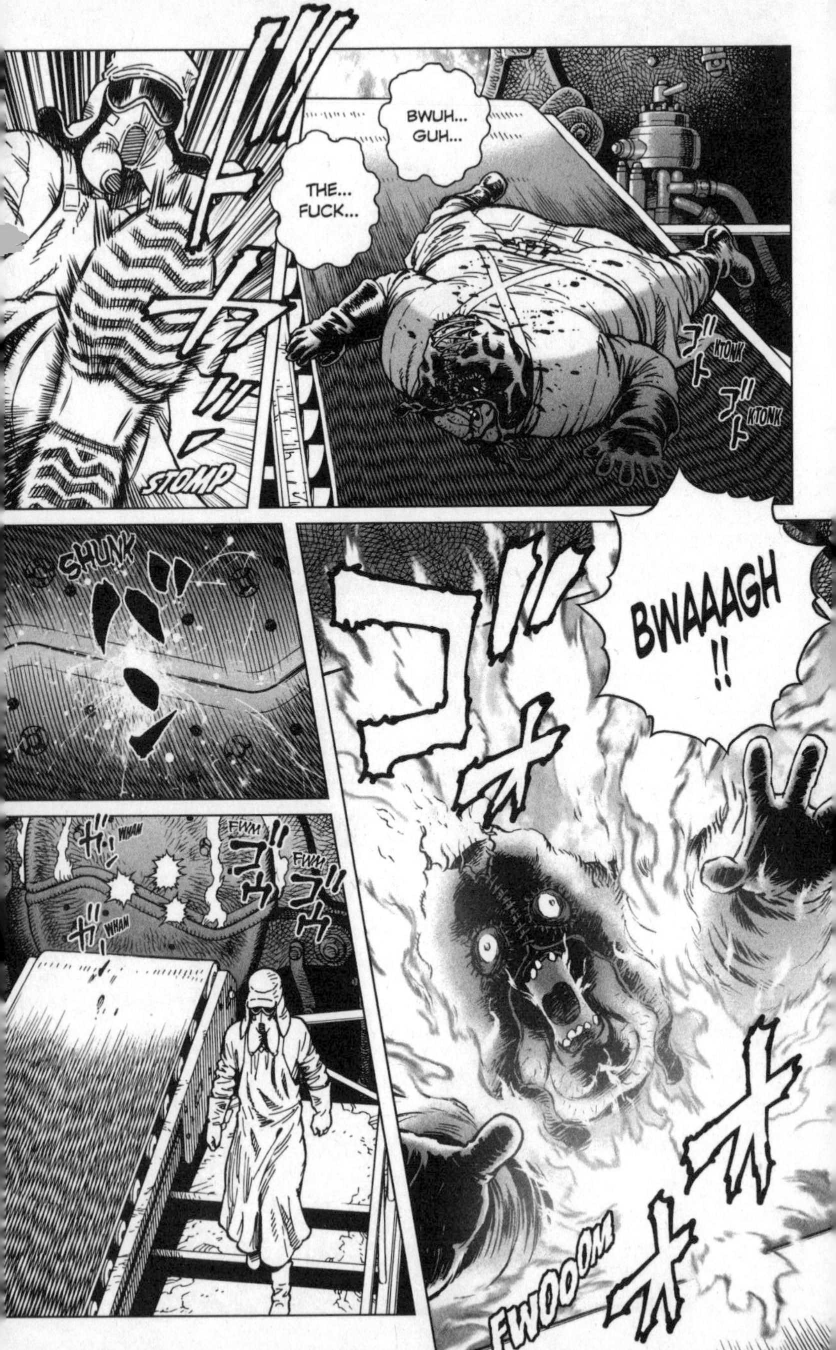

BWUH... GUH...
THE... FUCK...
KTONK
KTONK
STOMP
BWAAAGH!!
FWOOOM
SHUNK
FWM
FWM
WHAM
WHAM

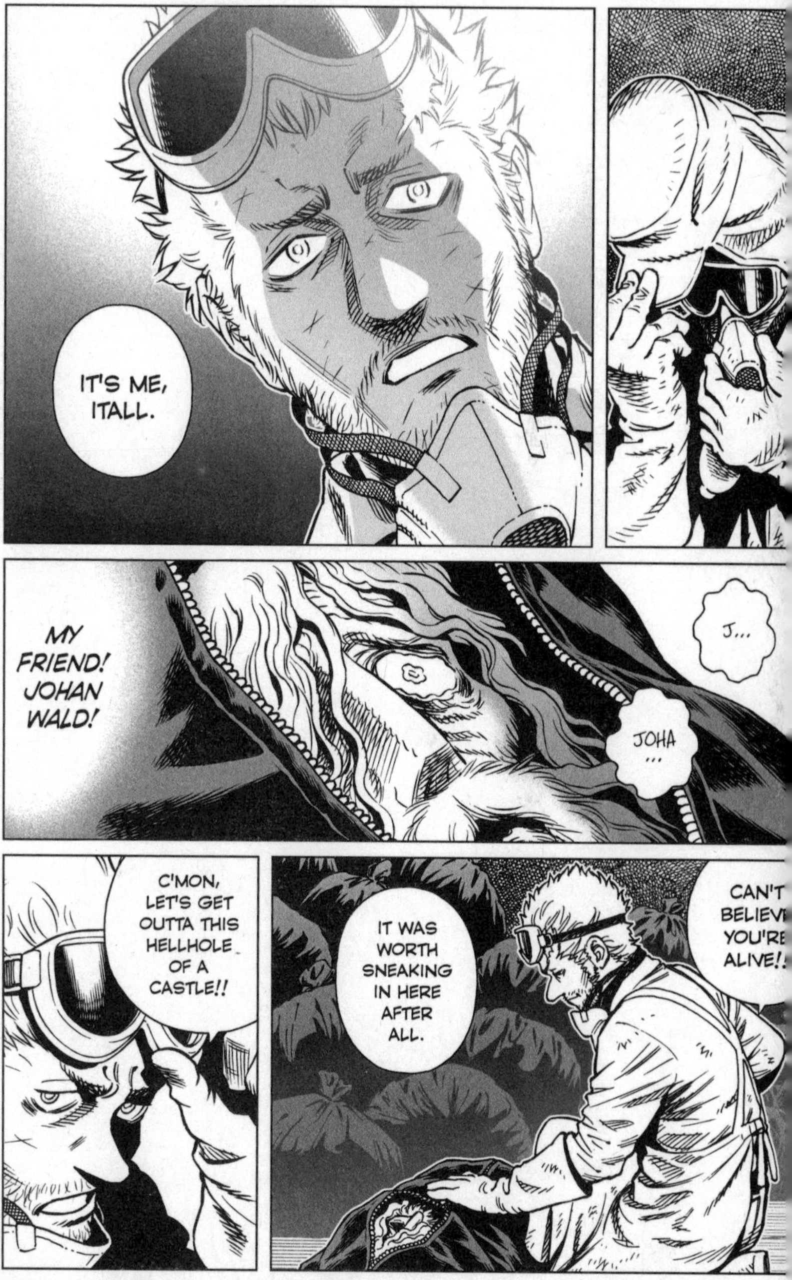
IT'S ME, ITALL.
J...
JOHA ...
MY FRIEND! JOHAN WALD!
CAN'T BELIEV YOU'RE ALIVE!
IT WAS WORTH SNEAKING IN HERE AFTER ALL.
C'MON, LET'S GET OUTTA THIS HELLHOLE OF A CASTLE!!

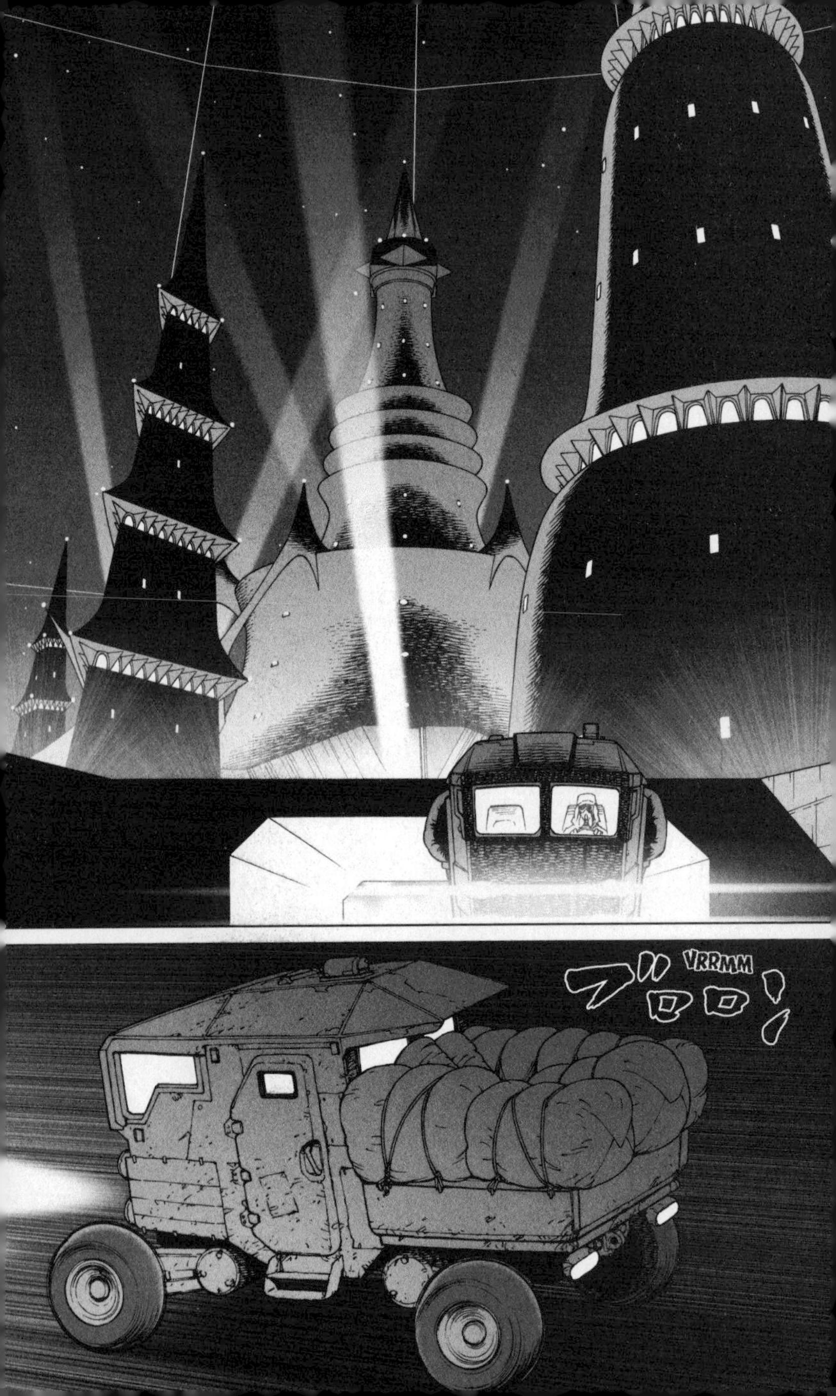

ブロロ!
VRRMM

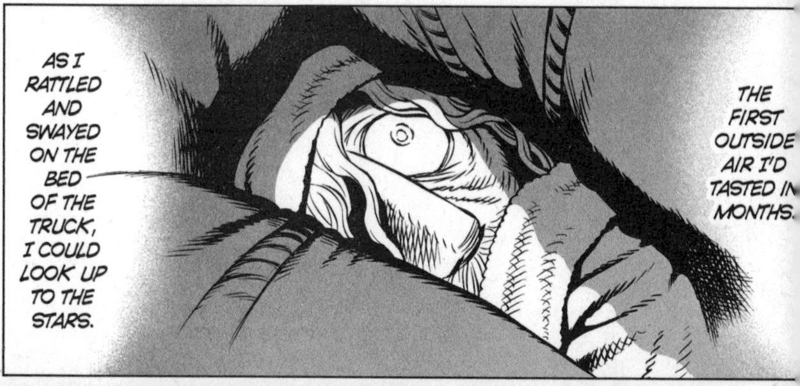
THE FIRST OUTSIDE AIR I'D TASTED IN MONTHS.
AS I RATTLED AND SWAYED ON THE BED OF THE TRUCK, I COULD LOOK UP TO THE STARS.

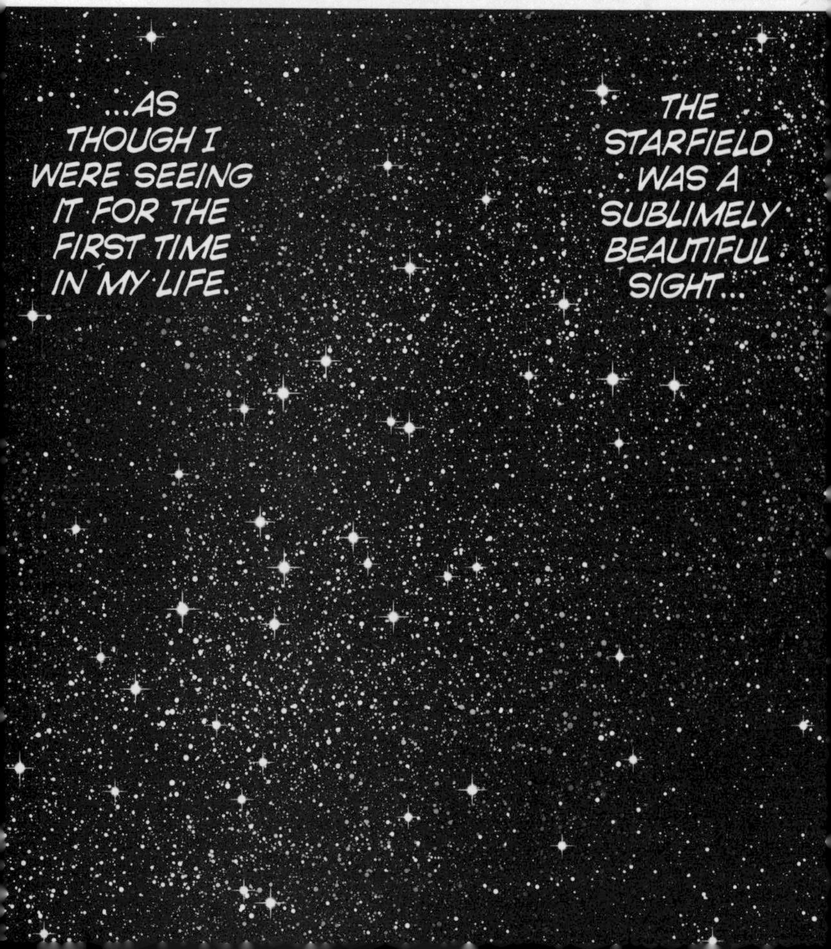
THE STARFIELD WAS A SUBLIMELY BEAUTIFUL SIGHT...
...AS THOUGH I WERE SEEING IT FOR THE FIRST TIME IN MY LIFE.

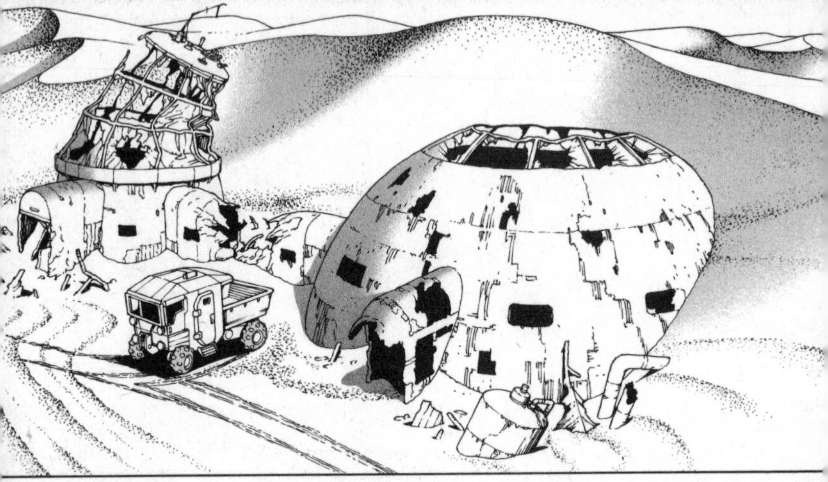

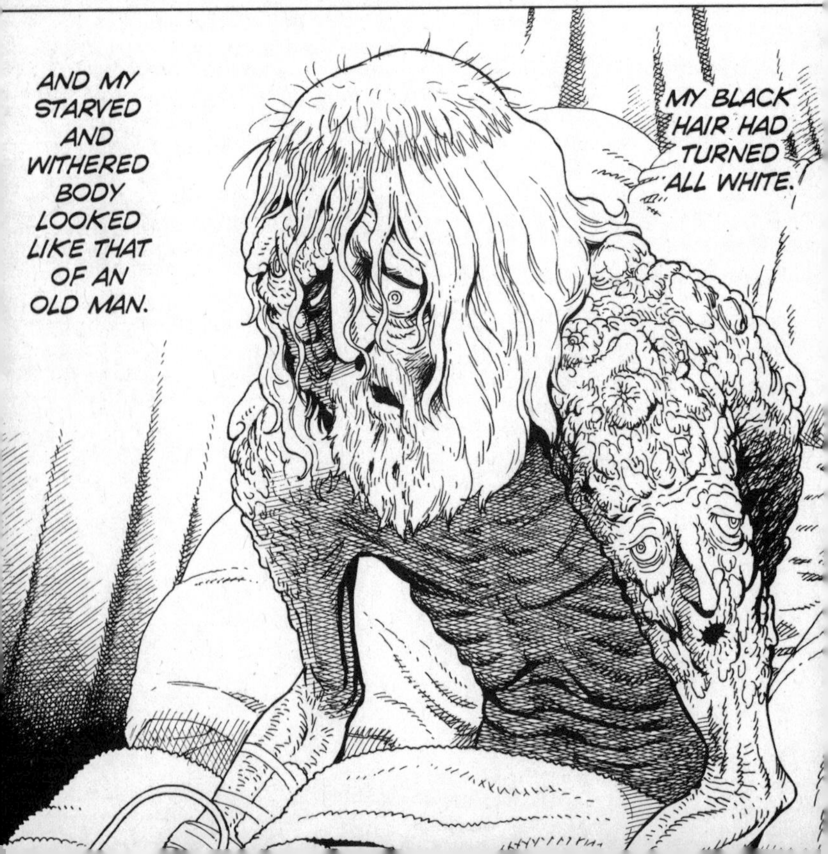
MY BLACK HAIR HAD TURNED ALL WHITE.
AND MY STARVED AND WITHERED BODY LOOKED LIKE THAT OF AN OLD MAN.

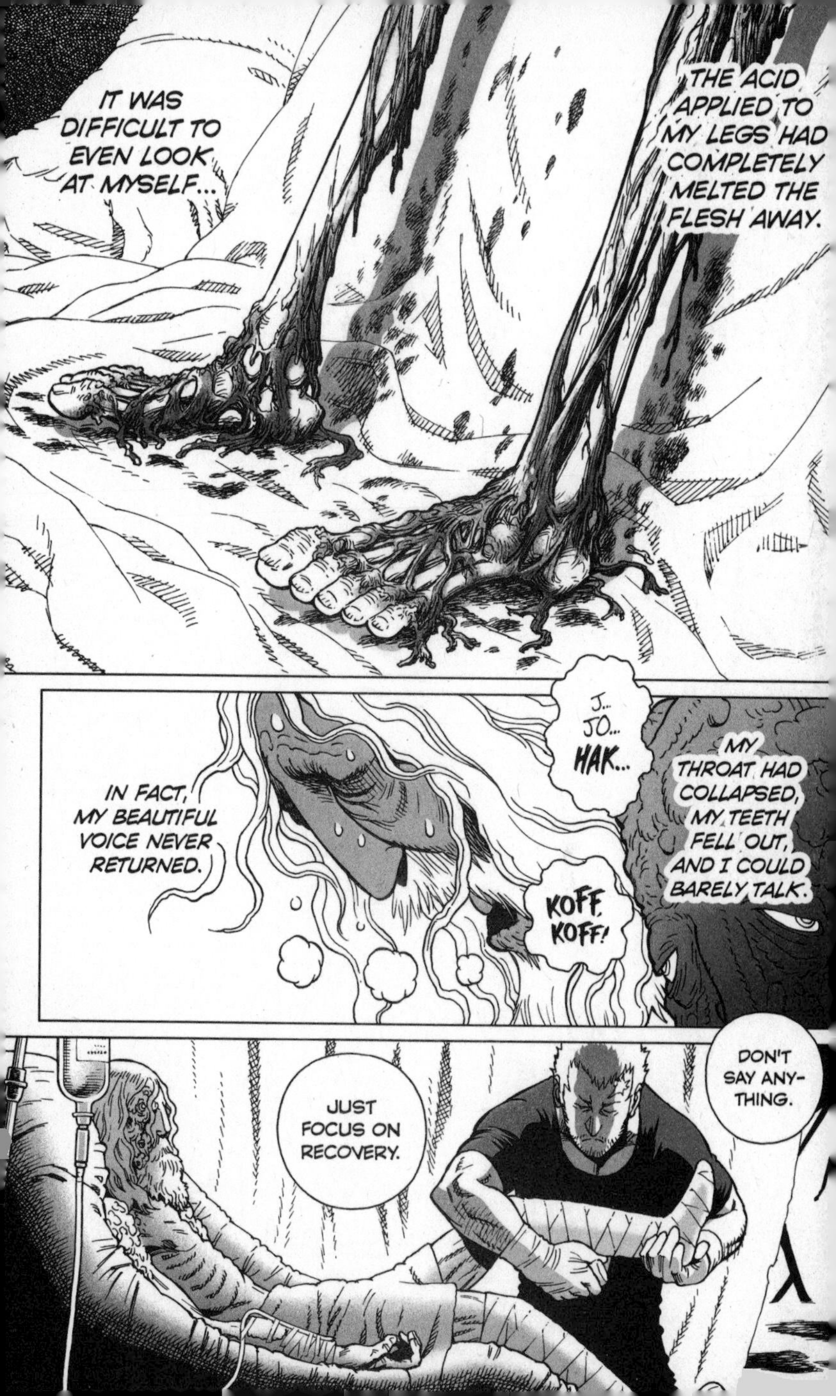
THE ACID APPLIED TO MY LEGS HAD COMPLETELY MELTED THE FLESH AWAY.
IT WAS DIFFICULT TO EVEN LOOK AT MYSELF...
MY THROAT HAD COLLAPSED, MY TEETH FELL OUT, AND I COULD BARELY TALK.
J... JO... HAK...
KOFF, KOFF!
IN FACT, MY BEAUTIFUL VOICE NEVER RETURNED.
DON'T SAY ANY-THING.
JUST FOCUS ON RECOVERY.

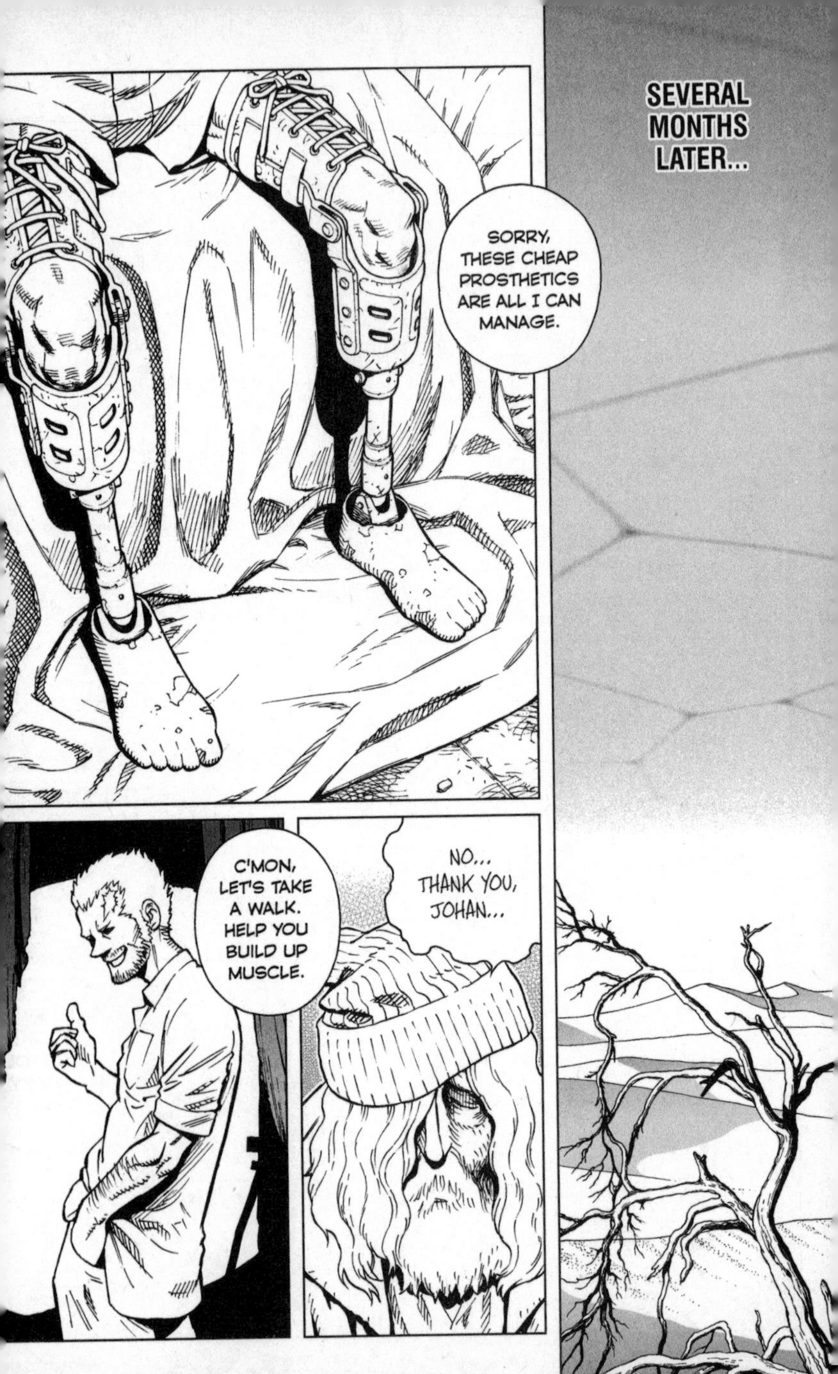
SEVERAL MONTHS LATER...
SORRY, THESE CHEAP PROSTHETICS ARE ALL I CAN MANAGE.
NO... THANK YOU, JOHAN...
C'MON, LET'S TAKE A WALK. HELP YOU BUILD UP MUSCLE.

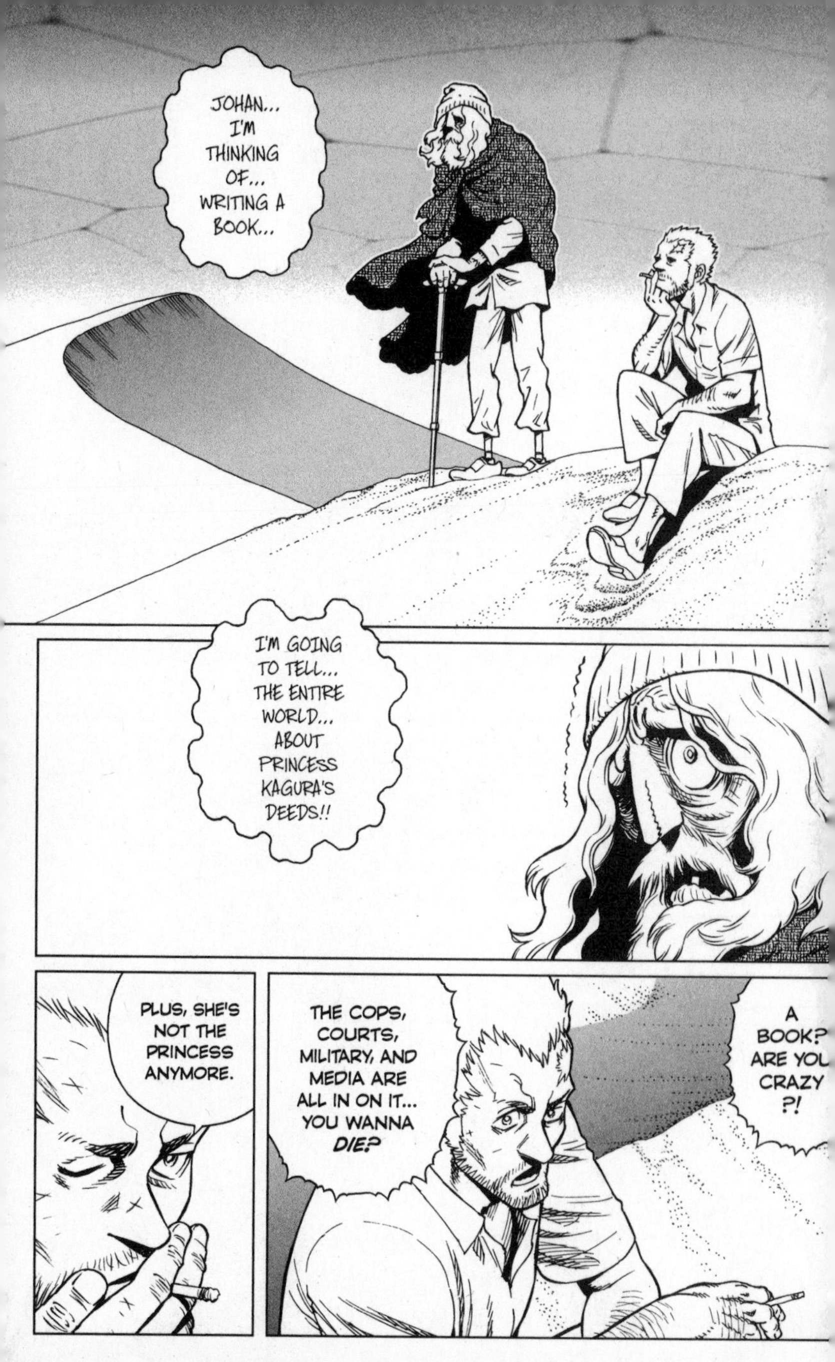
JOHAN... I'M THINKING OF... WRITING A BOOK...
I'M GOING TO TELL... THE ENTIRE WORLD... ABOUT PRINCESS KAGURA'S DEEDS!!
A BOOK? ARE YOU CRAZY?!
THE COPS, COURTS, MILITARY, AND MEDIA ARE ALL IN ON IT... YOU WANNA *DIE?*
PLUS, SHE'S NOT THE PRINCESS ANYMORE.

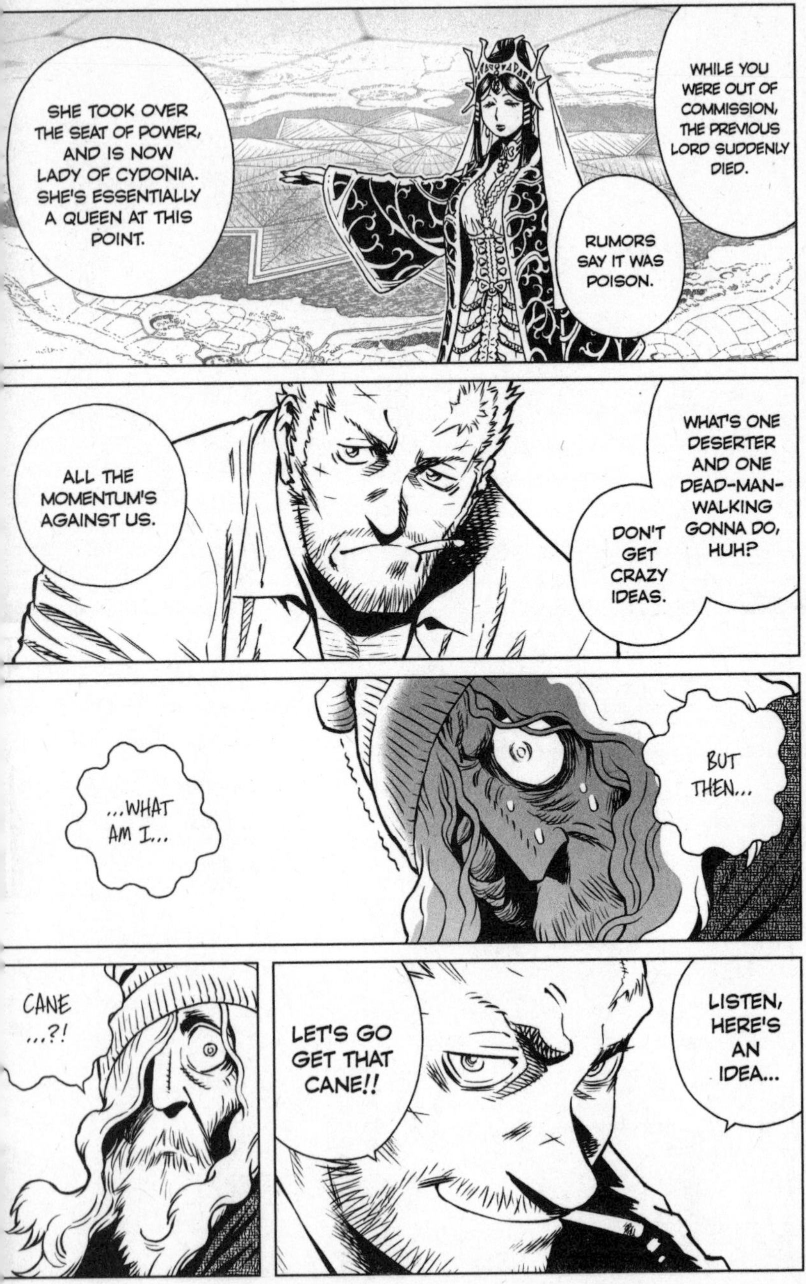

WHILE YOU WERE OUT OF COMMISSION, THE PREVIOUS LORD SUDDENLY DIED.
RUMORS SAY IT WAS POISON.
SHE TOOK OVER THE SEAT OF POWER, AND IS NOW LADY OF CYDONIA. SHE'S ESSENTIALLY A QUEEN AT THIS POINT.
WHAT'S ONE DESERTER AND ONE DEAD-MAN-WALKING GONNA DO, HUH?
DON'T GET CRAZY IDEAS.
ALL THE MOMENTUM'S AGAINST US.
BUT THEN...
...WHAT AM I...
LISTEN, HERE'S AN IDEA...
LET'S GO GET THAT CANE!!
CANE ...?!

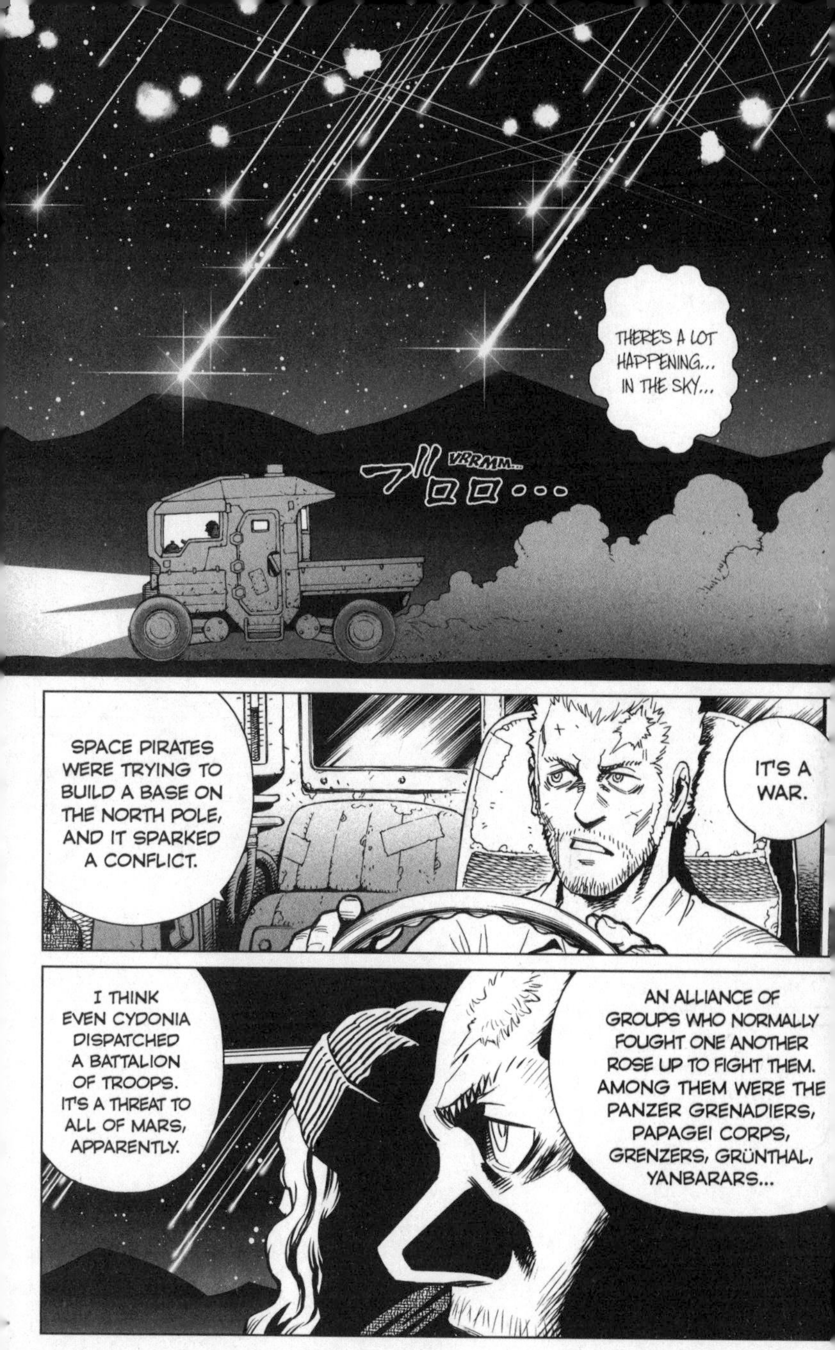
THERE'S A LOT HAPPENING... IN THE SKY...
VRRMM...
IT'S A WAR.
SPACE PIRATES WERE TRYING TO BUILD A BASE ON THE NORTH POLE, AND IT SPARKED A CONFLICT.
AN ALLIANCE OF GROUPS WHO NORMALLY FOUGHT ONE ANOTHER ROSE UP TO FIGHT THEM. AMONG THEM WERE THE PANZER GRENADIERS, PAPAGEI CORPS, GRENZERS, GRÜNTHAL, YANBARARS...
I THINK EVEN CYDONIA DISPATCHED A BATTALION OF TROOPS. IT'S A THREAT TO ALL OF MARS, APPARENTLY.

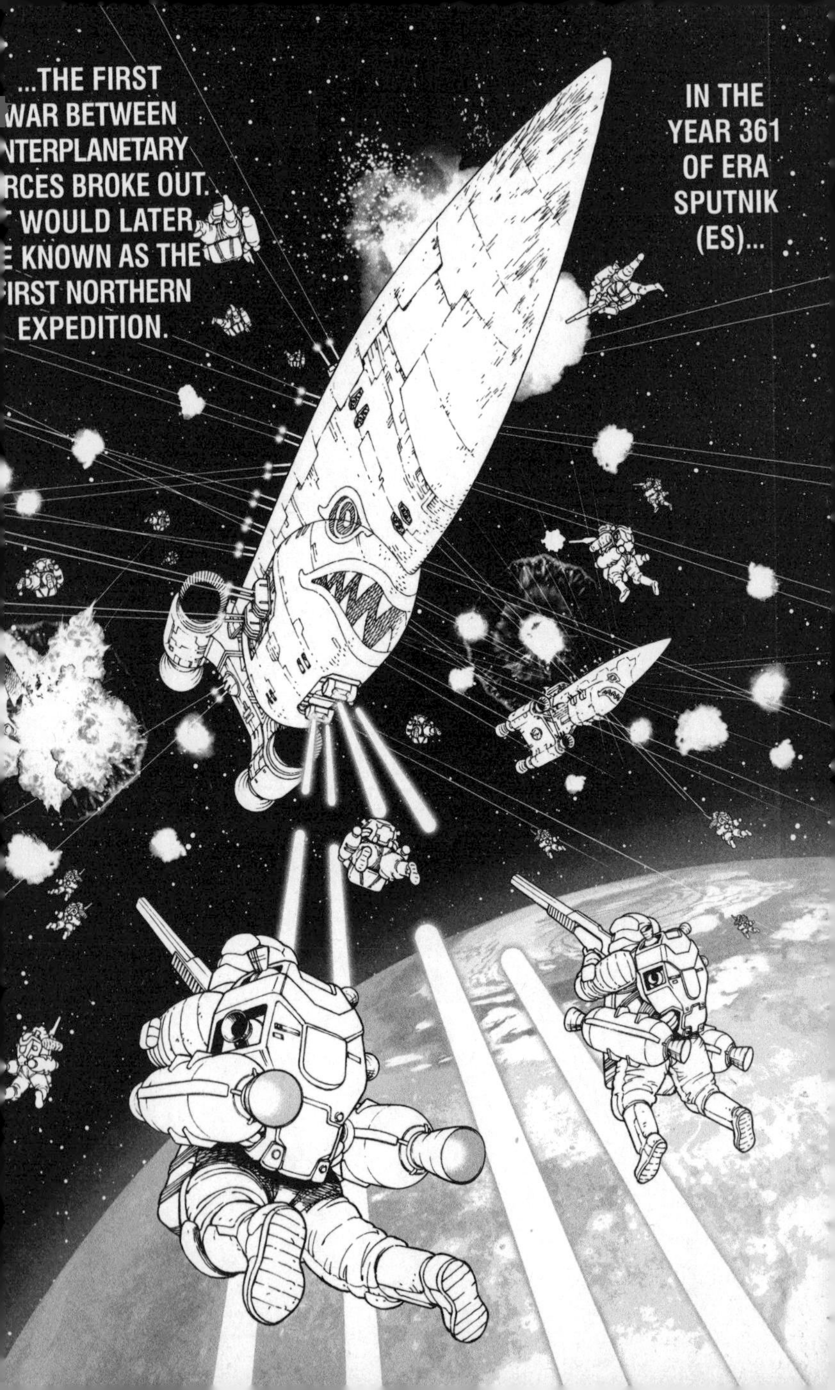
IN THE YEAR 361 OF ERA SPUTNIK (ES)...
...THE FIRST WAR BETWEEN NTERPLANETARY RCES BROKE OUT. WOULD LATER E KNOWN AS THE IRST NORTHERN EXPEDITION.

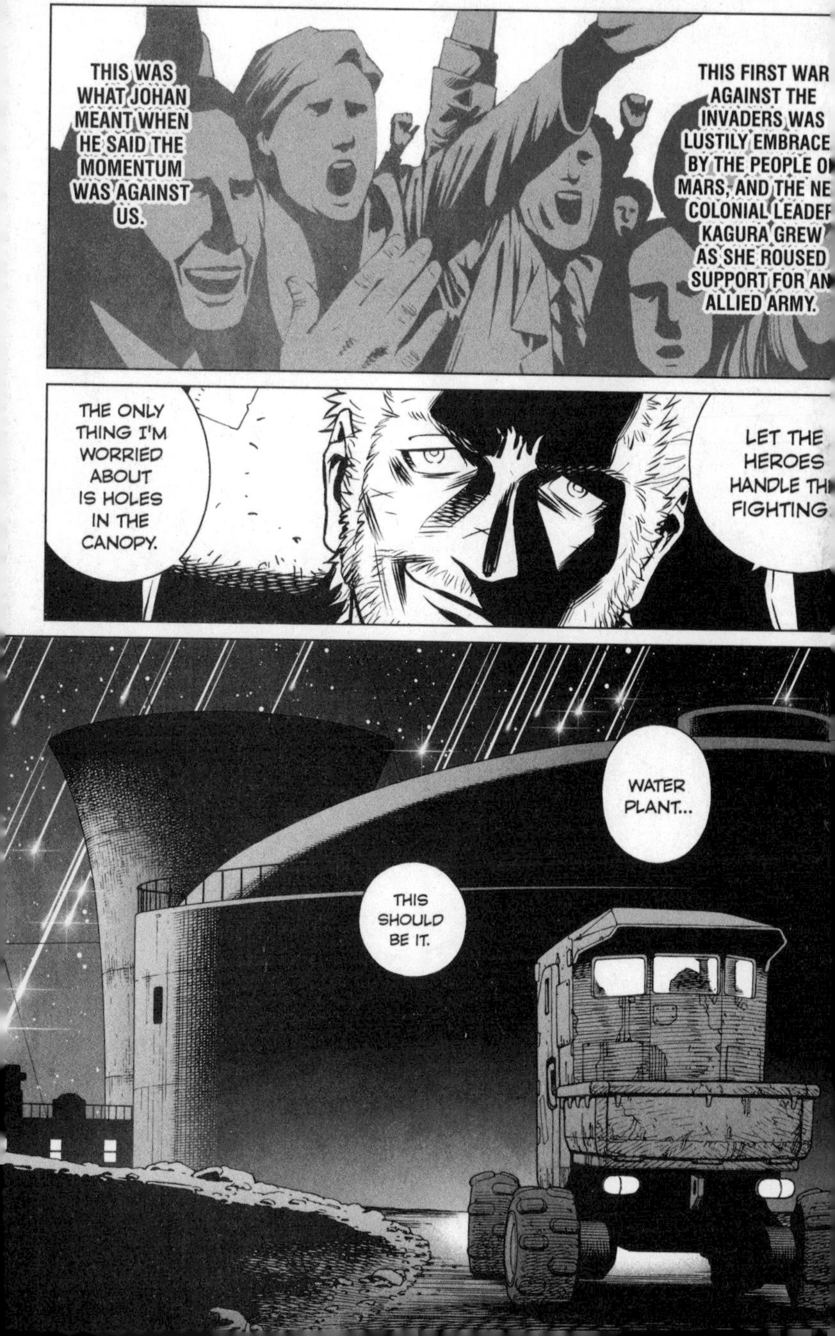
THIS FIRST WAR AGAINST THE INVADERS WAS LUSTILY EMBRACE BY THE PEOPLE O MARS, AND THE NE COLONIAL LEADE KAGURA GREW AS SHE ROUSED SUPPORT FOR AN ALLIED ARMY.
THIS WAS WHAT JOHAN MEANT WHEN HE SAID THE MOMENTUM WAS AGAINST US.
LET THE HEROES HANDLE TH FIGHTING
THE ONLY THING I'M WORRIED ABOUT IS HOLES IN THE CANOPY.
WATER PLANT...
THIS SHOULD BE IT.

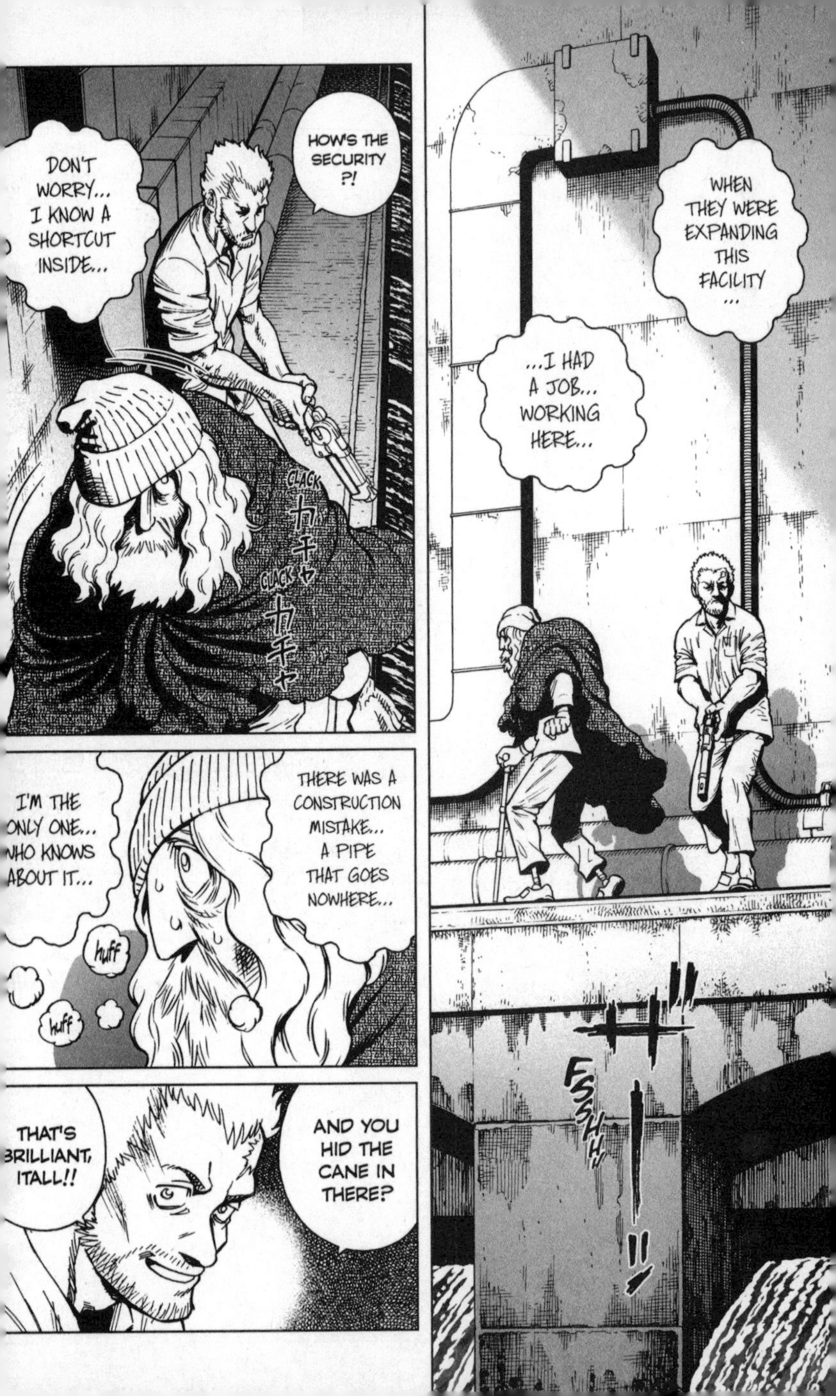

WHEN THEY WERE EXPANDING THIS FACILITY...
...I HAD A JOB... WORKING HERE...
FSSH!!
HOW'S THE SECURITY?!
DON'T WORRY... I KNOW A SHORTCUT INSIDE...
CLACK
カチャ
CLACK
カチャ
THERE WAS A CONSTRUCTION MISTAKE... A PIPE THAT GOES NOWHERE...
I'M THE ONLY ONE... WHO KNOWS ABOUT IT...
huff
huff
AND YOU HID THE CANE IN THERE?
THAT'S BRILLIANT, ITALL!!

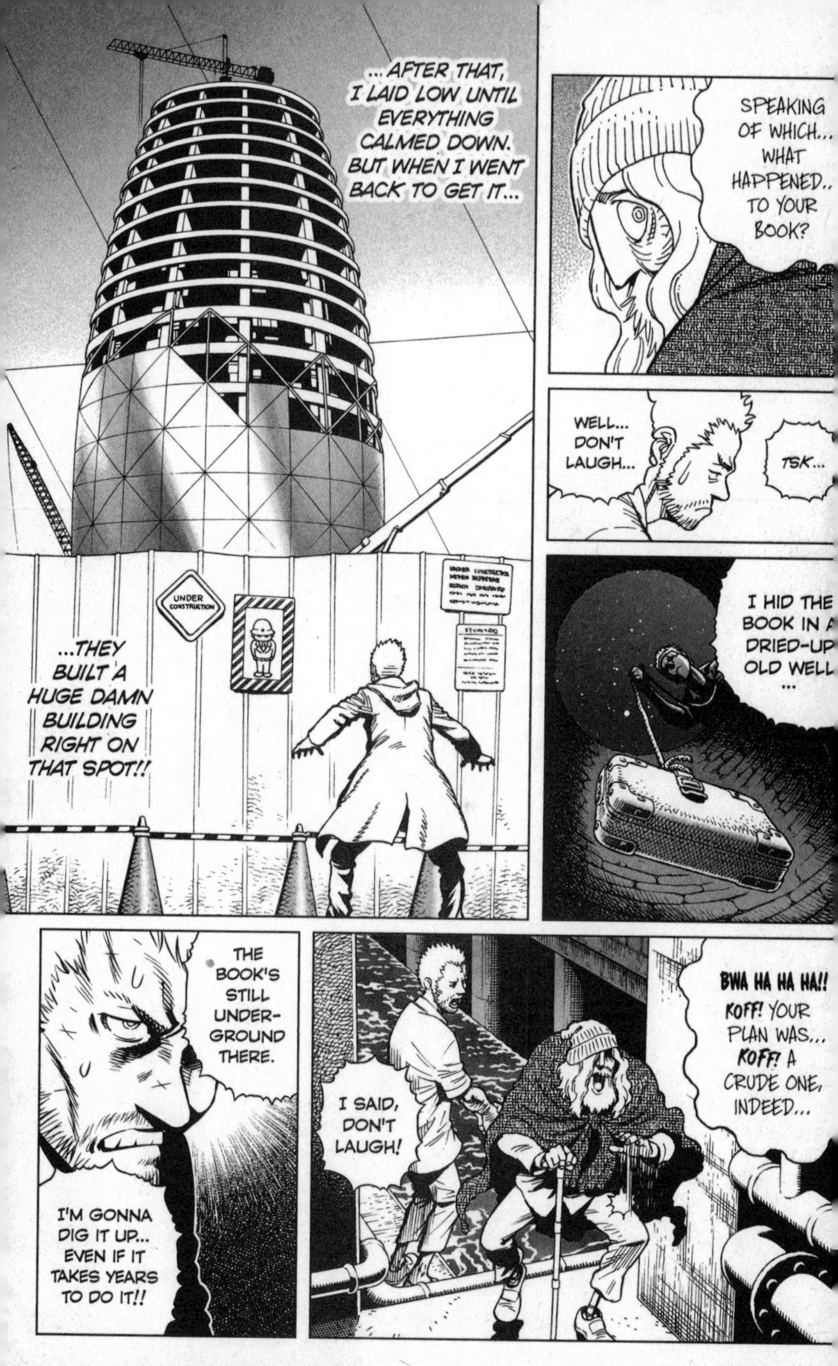
SPEAKING OF WHICH... WHAT HAPPENED.. TO YOUR BOOK?
TSK...
WELL... DON'T LAUGH...
I HID THE BOOK IN A DRIED-UP OLD WELL ...
...AFTER THAT, I LAID LOW UNTIL EVERYTHING CALMED DOWN. BUT WHEN I WENT BACK TO GET IT...
UNDER CONSTRUCTION
...THEY BUILT A HUGE DAMN BUILDING RIGHT ON THAT SPOT!!
BWA HA HA HA!!
KOFF! YOUR PLAN WAS... KOFF! A CRUDE ONE, INDEED...
I SAID, DON'T LAUGH!
THE BOOK'S STILL UNDER-GROUND THERE.
I'M GONNA DIG IT UP... EVEN IF IT TAKES YEARS TO DO IT!!

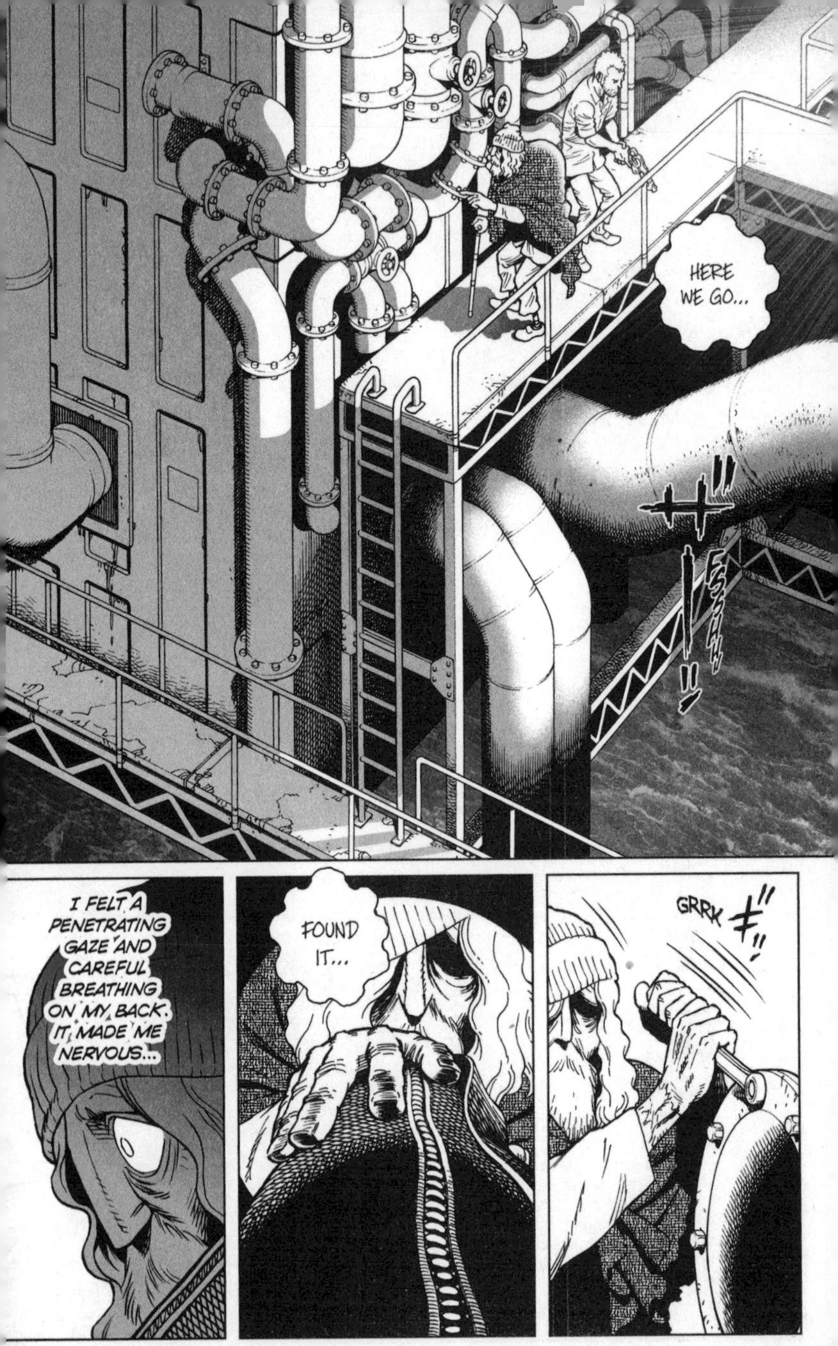
HERE WE GO...
GRRK
FOUND IT...
I FELT A PENETRATING GAZE AND CAREFUL BREATHING ON MY BACK. IT MADE ME NERVOUS...

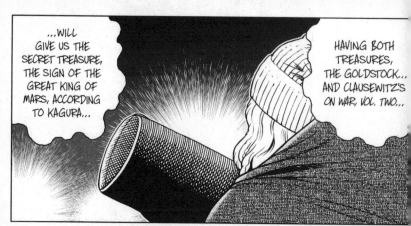

HAVING BOTH TREASURES, THE GOLDSTOCK... AND CLAUSEWITZ'S ON WAR, VOL. TWO...
...WILL GIVE US THE SECRET TREASURE, THE SIGN OF THE GREAT KING OF MARS, ACCORDING TO KAGURA...
S-SO LET'S GO AND FIND THIS GREAT MARTIAN TREASURE TOGETHER... THE TWO OF US!!
WE CAN PROVE TO THE WORLD THAT WE'RE NOT JUST A PAIR OF DOWNTRODDEN LOSERS...

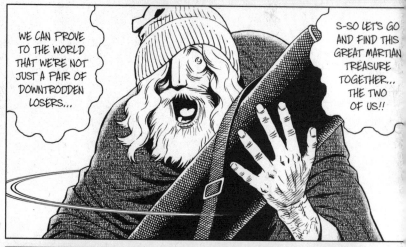

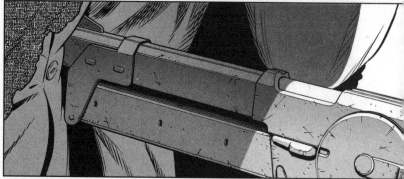

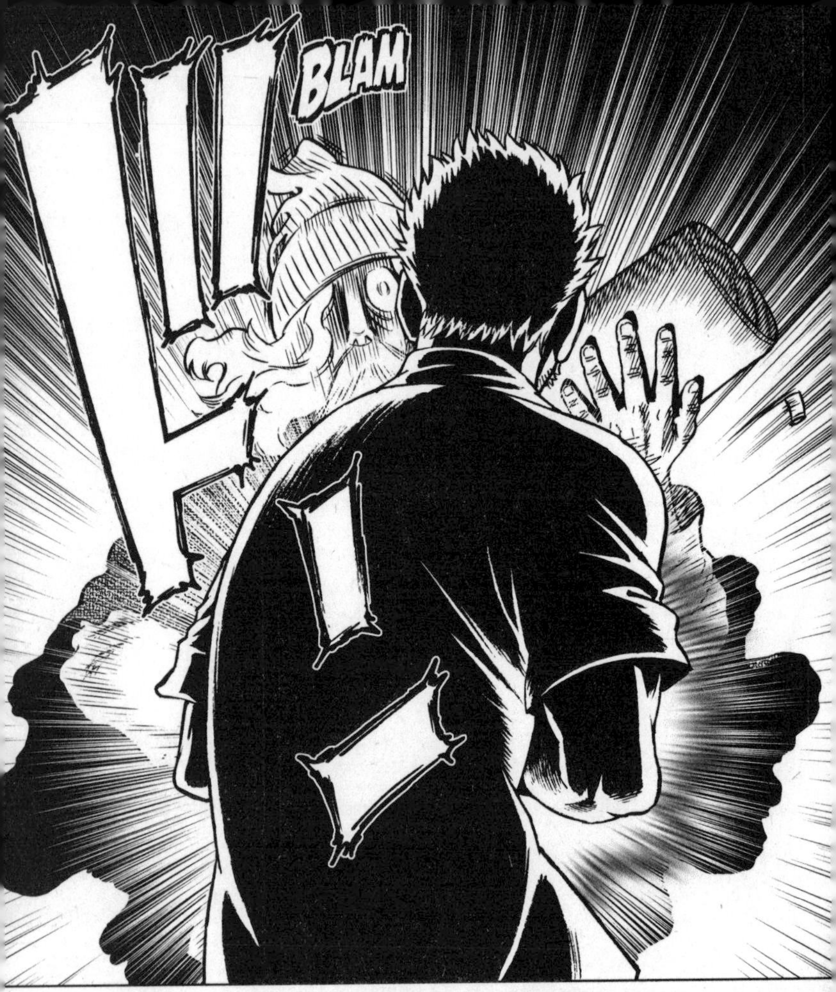
BLAM

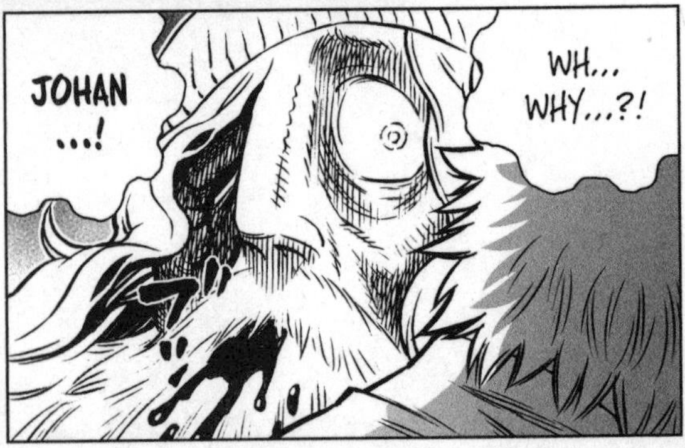
WH... WHY...?!
JOHAN ...!

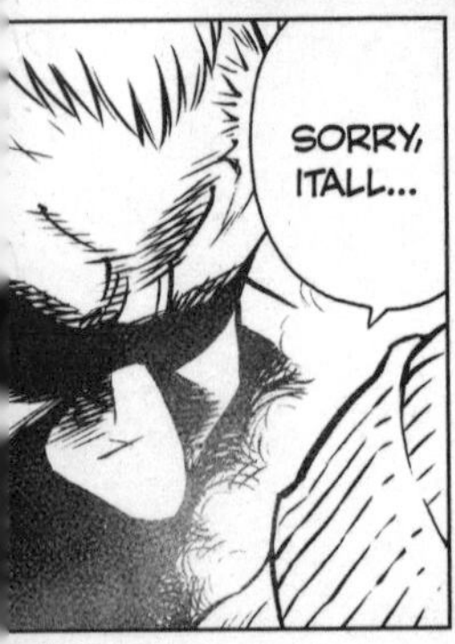
SORRY, ITALL...

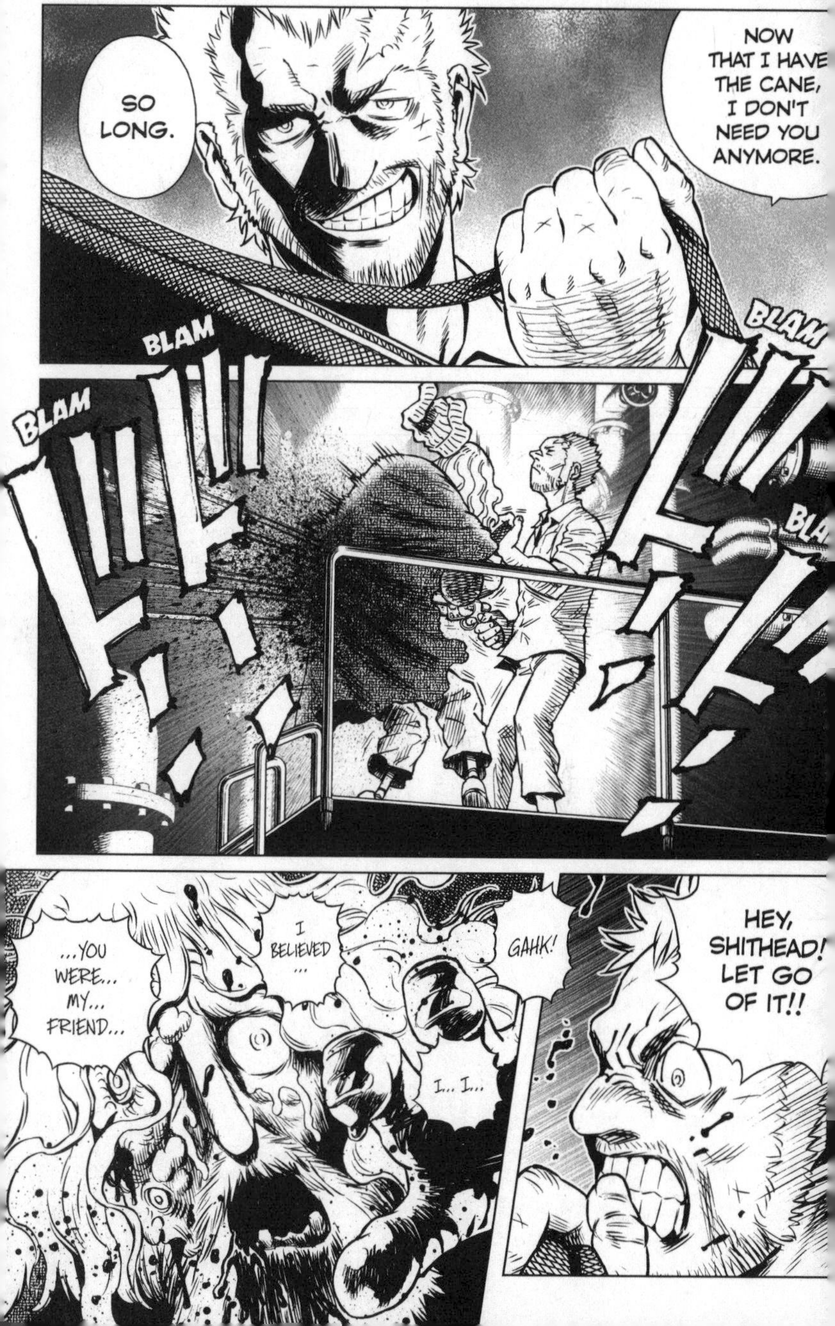
NOW THAT I HAVE THE CANE, I DON'T NEED YOU ANYMORE.
SO LONG.
BLAM
BLAM
BLAM
BLAM
HEY, SHITHEAD! LET GO OF IT!!
GAHK!
I BELIEVED ...
...YOU WERE... MY... FRIEND...
I... I...

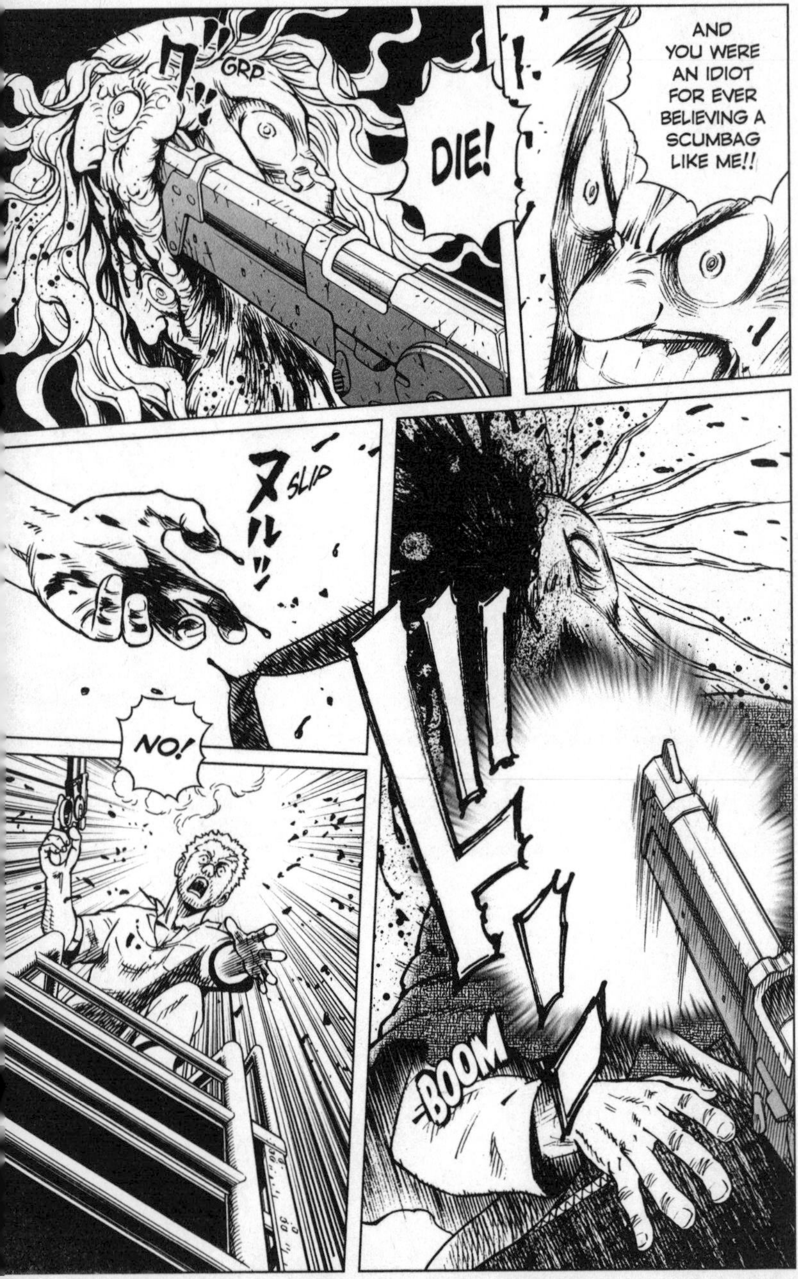

AND YOU WERE AN IDIOT FOR EVER BELIEVING A SCUMBAG LIKE ME!!
GRP
DIE!
BOOM
ヌルッ
SLIP
NO!

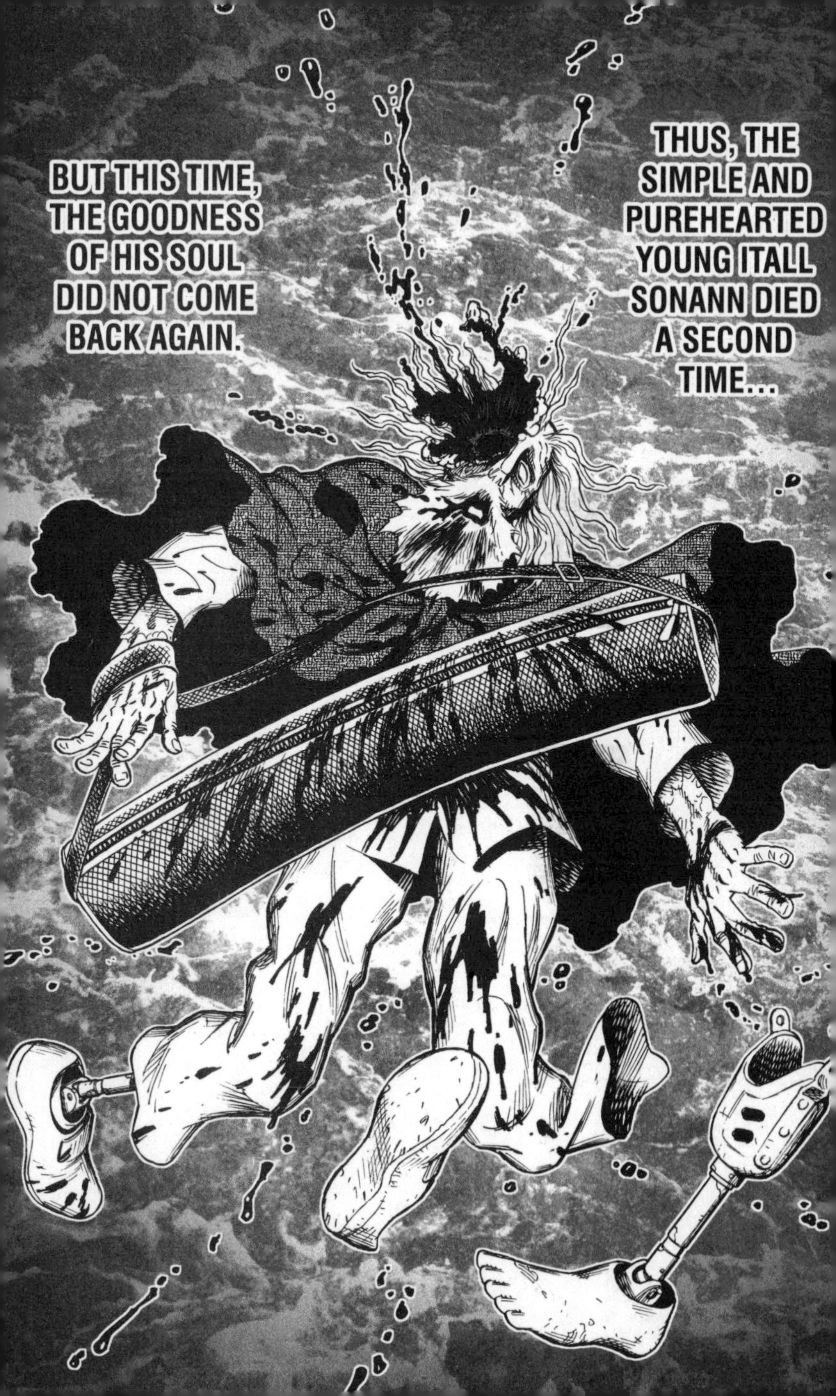
THUS, THE SIMPLE AND PUREHEARTED YOUNG ITALL SONANN DIED A SECOND TIME...
BUT THIS TIME, THE GOODNESS OF HIS SOUL DID NOT COME BACK AGAIN.

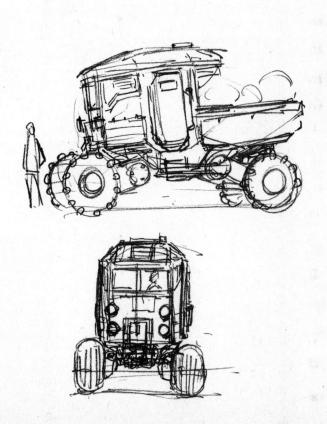

Author's Note:

The following
story is not a direct
recollection of Muster's,
but it is included here
as a demonstration of
how the dreaded Baron
Muster came to be...

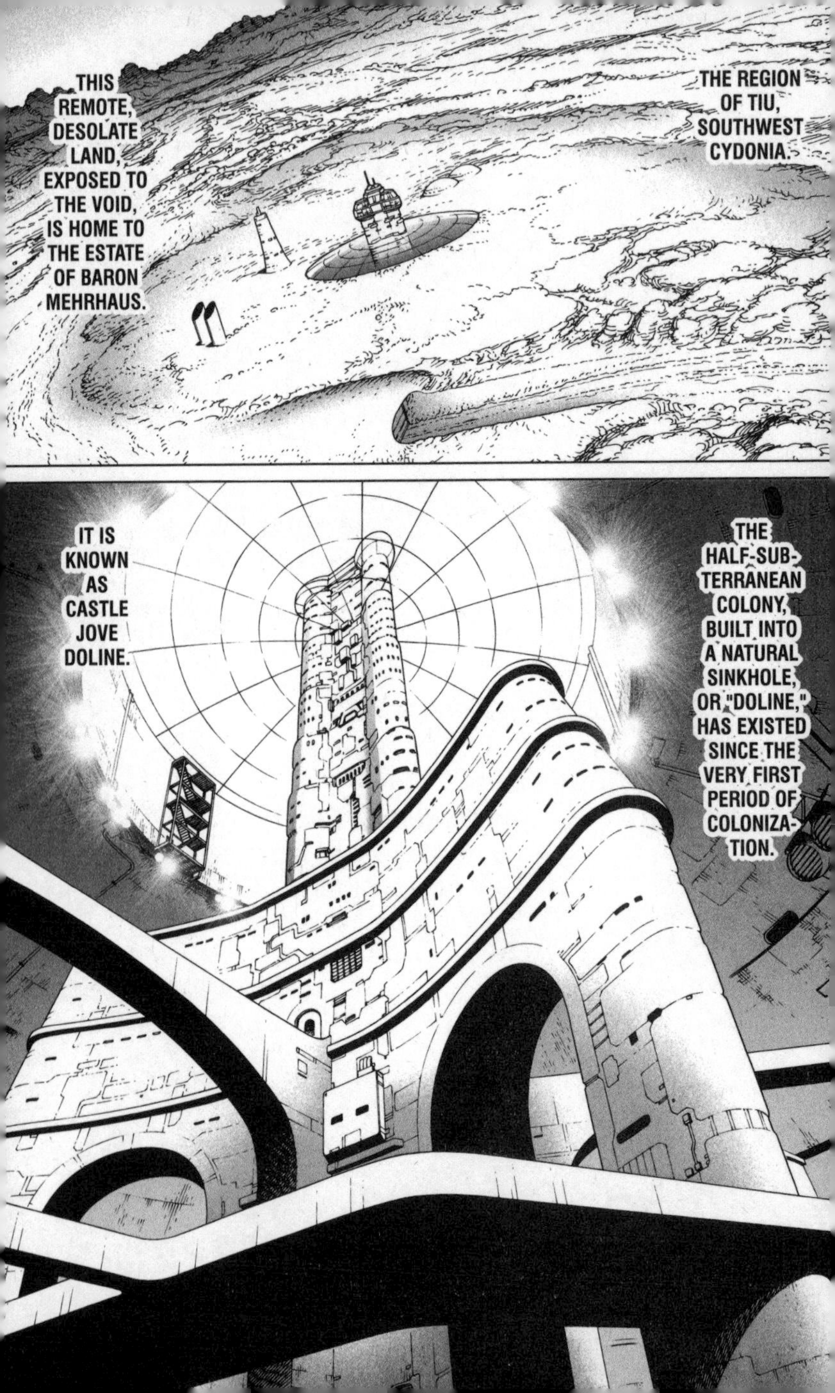
THE REGION OF TIU, SOUTHWEST CYDONIA.
THIS REMOTE, DESOLATE LAND, EXPOSED TO THE VOID, IS HOME TO THE ESTATE OF BARON MEHRHAUS.
THE HALF-SUB-TERRANEAN COLONY, BUILT INTO A NATURAL SINKHOLE, OR "DOLINE," HAS EXISTED SINCE THE VERY FIRST PERIOD OF COLONIZA-TION.
IT IS KNOWN AS CASTLE JOVE DOLINE.

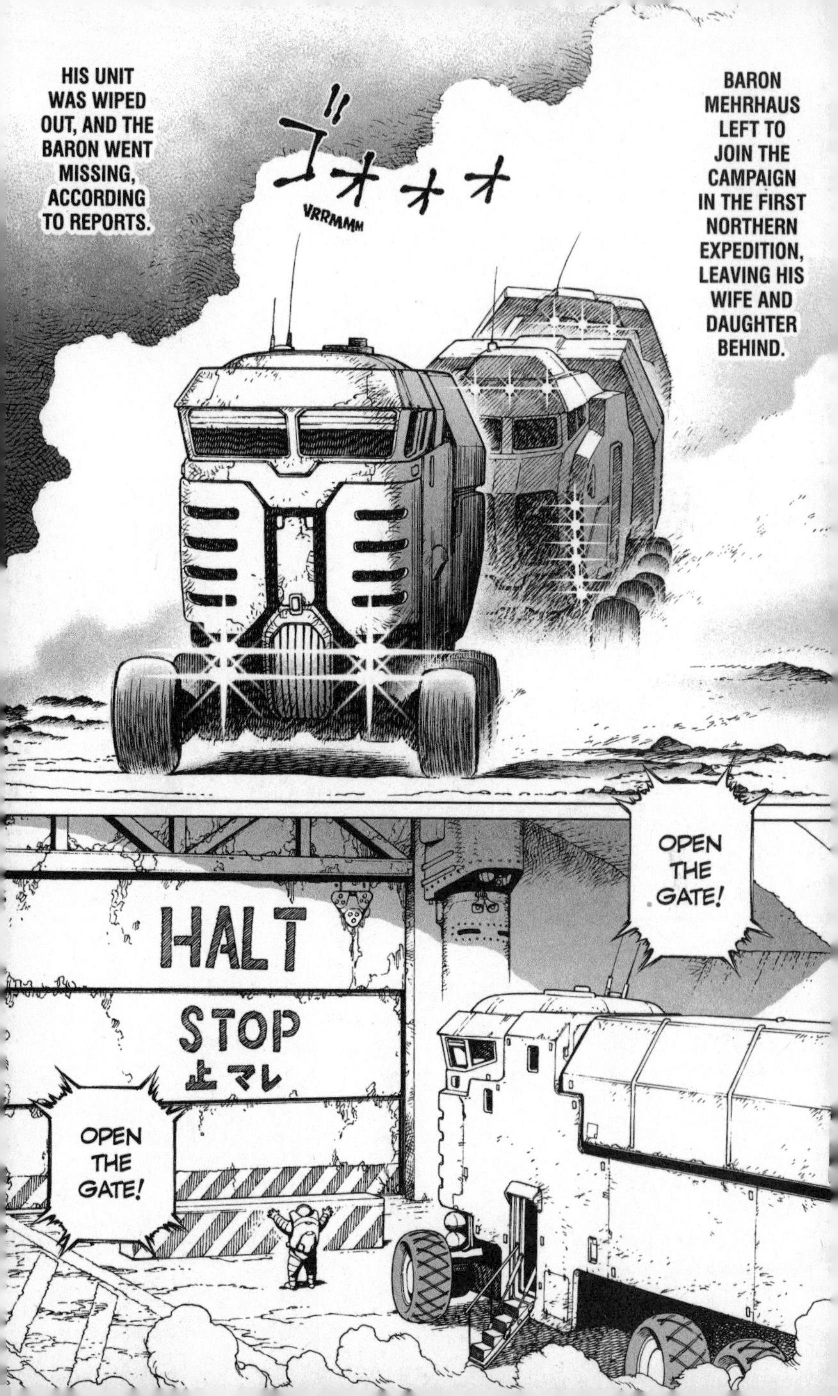
BARON MEHRHAUS LEFT TO JOIN THE CAMPAIGN IN THE FIRST NORTHERN EXPEDITION, LEAVING HIS WIFE AND DAUGHTER BEHIND.
ゴォォォ
VRRMMM
HIS UNIT WAS WIPED OUT, AND THE BARON WENT MISSING, ACCORDING TO REPORTS.
OPEN THE GATE!
HALT
STOP
止マレ
OPEN THE GATE!

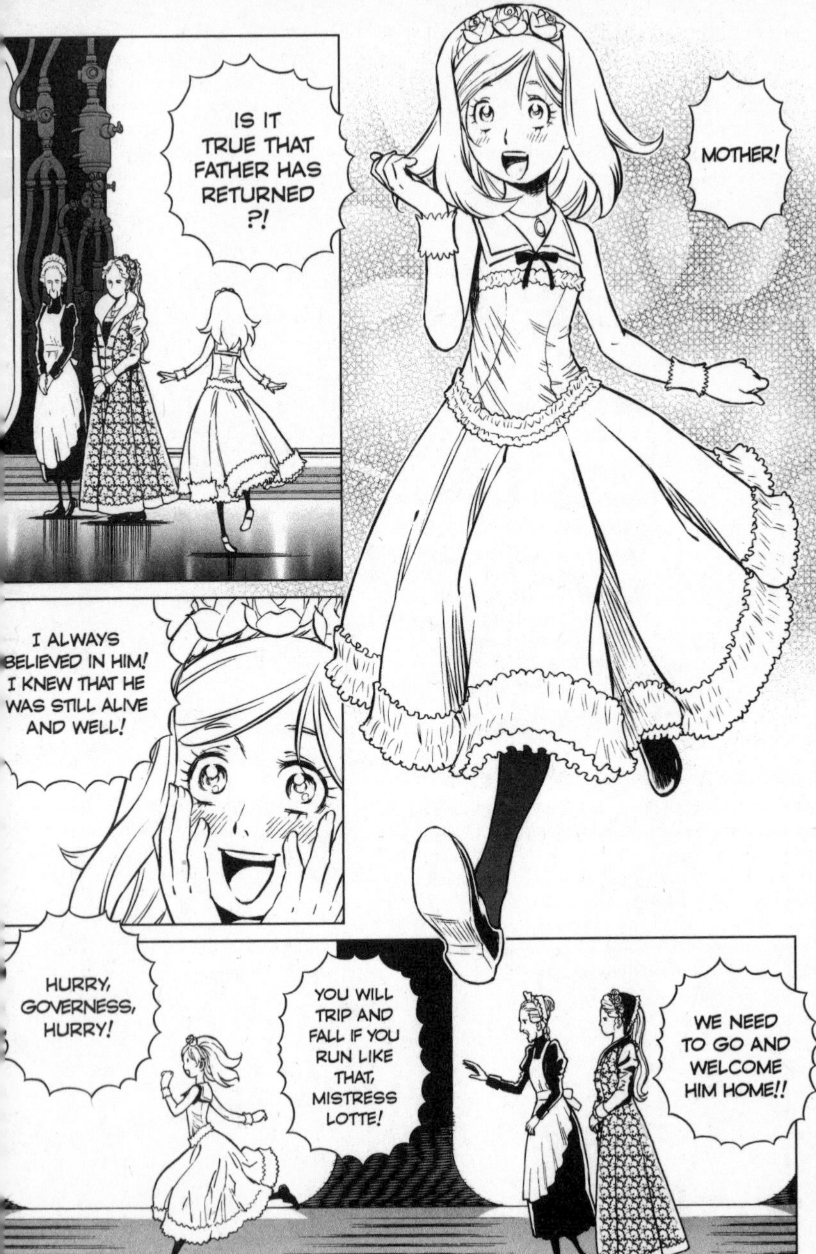
MOTHER!
IS IT TRUE THAT FATHER HAS RETURNED ?!
I ALWAYS BELIEVED IN HIM! I KNEW THAT HE WAS STILL ALIVE AND WELL!
WE NEED TO GO AND WELCOME HIM HOME!!
YOU WILL TRIP AND FALL IF YOU RUN LIKE THAT, MISTRESS LOTTE!
HURRY, GOVERNESS, HURRY!

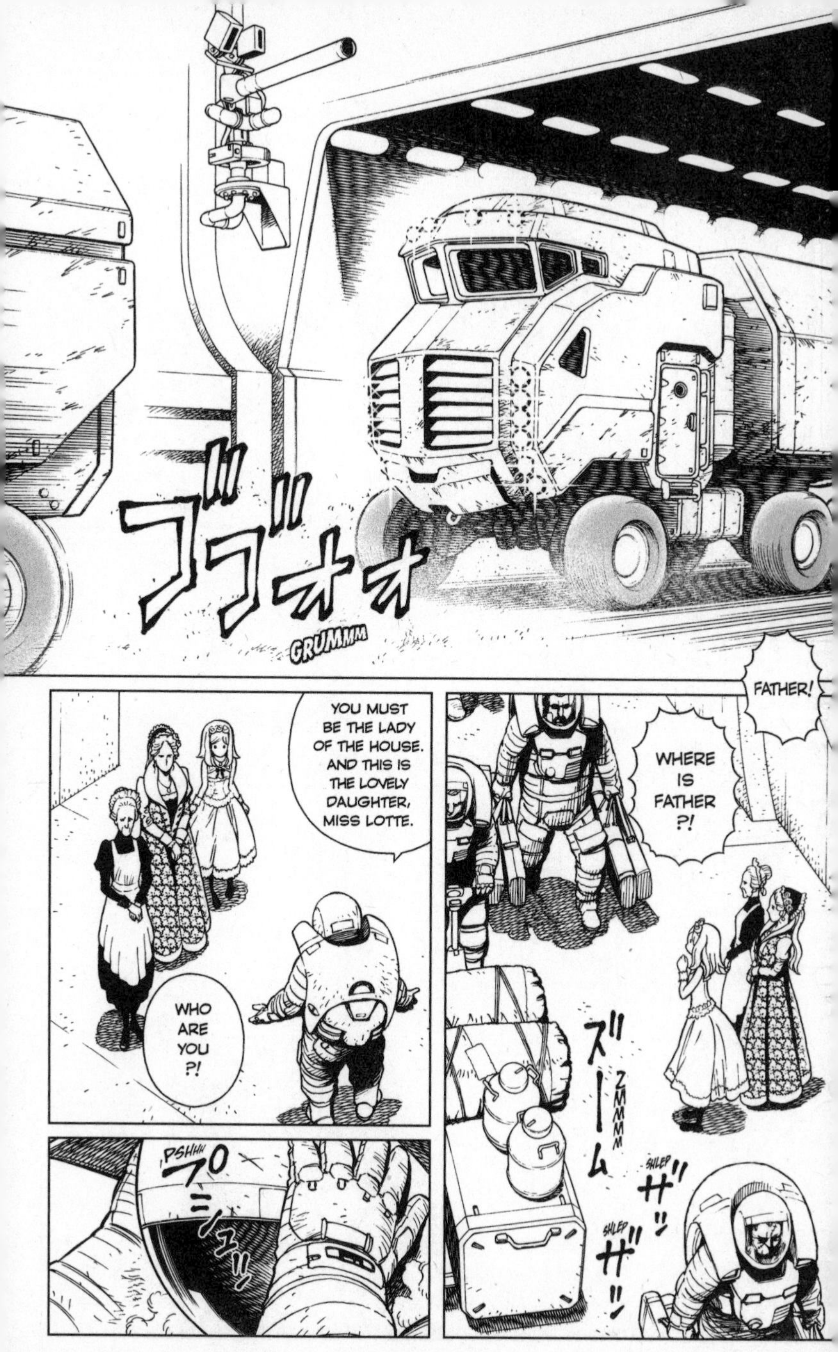

ゴゴオオ
GRUMMM
FATHER!
WHERE IS FATHER ?!
ズーム
ZMMMM
ザッ!!
SHLEP
ザッ!!
SHLEP
YOU MUST BE THE LADY OF THE HOUSE. AND THIS IS THE LOVELY DAUGHTER, MISS LOTTE.
WHO ARE YOU ?!
プシュ!!
PSHHH

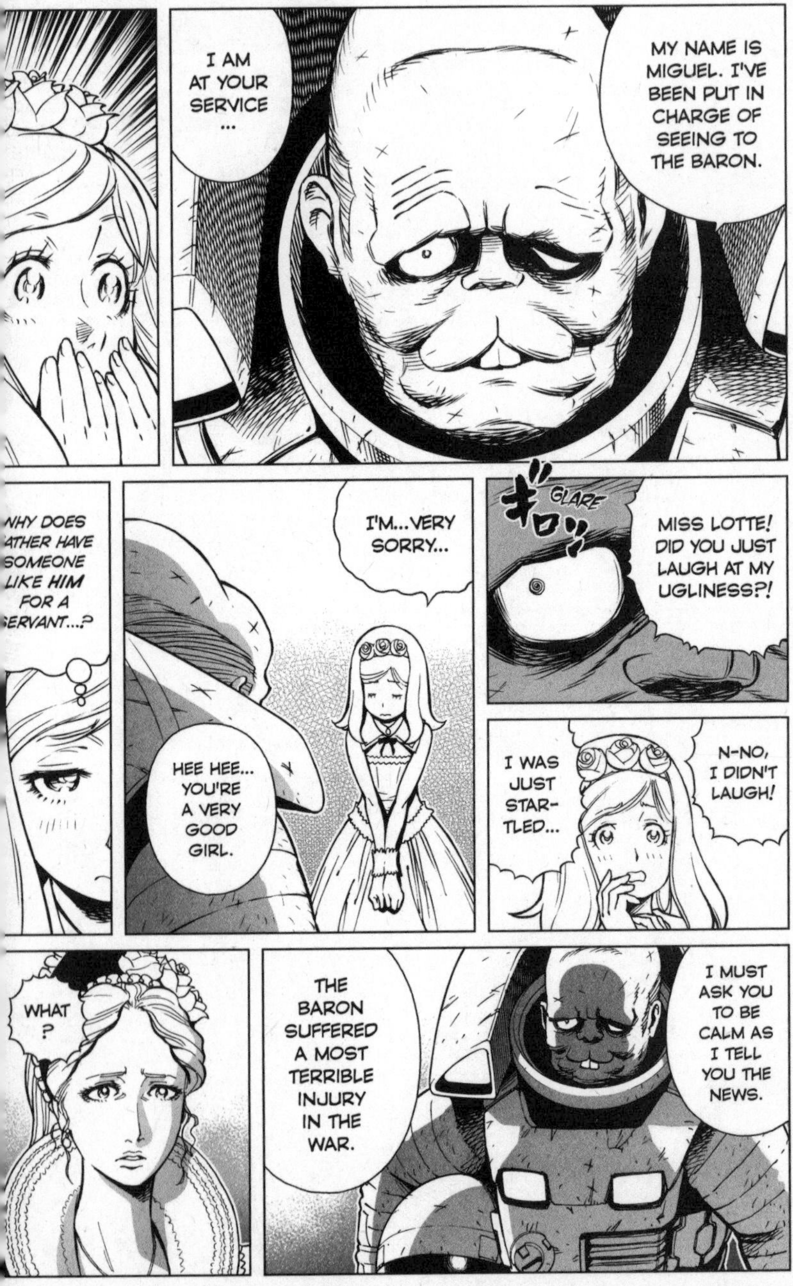
MY NAME IS MIGUEL. I'VE BEEN PUT IN CHARGE OF SEEING TO THE BARON.
I AM AT YOUR SERVICE ...
ギロッ
GLARE
MISS LOTTE! DID YOU JUST LAUGH AT MY UGLINESS?!
N-NO, I DIDN'T LAUGH!
I WAS JUST STAR-TLED...
I'M...VERY SORRY...
HEE HEE... YOU'RE A VERY GOOD GIRL.
NHY DOES ATHER HAVE SOMEONE LIKE HIM FOR A ERVANT...?
I MUST ASK YOU TO BE CALM AS I TELL YOU THE NEWS.
THE BARON SUFFERED A MOST TERRIBLE INJURY IN THE WAR.
WHAT ?

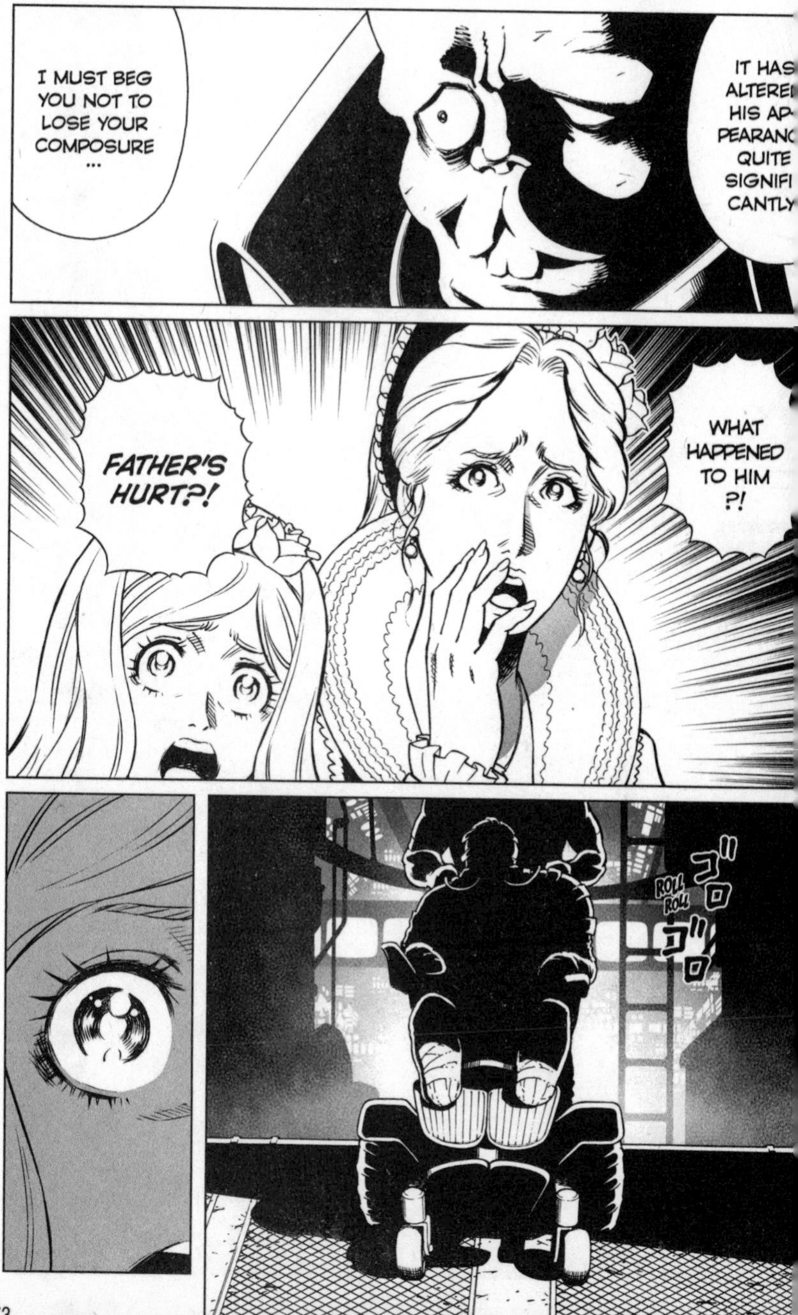
IT HAS ALTERE HIS AP- PEARANC QUITE SIGNIFI CANTLY
I MUST BEG YOU NOT TO LOSE YOUR COMPOSURE ...
WHAT HAPPENED TO HIM ?!
FATHER'S HURT?!
ゴロ ゴロ
ROLL ROLL

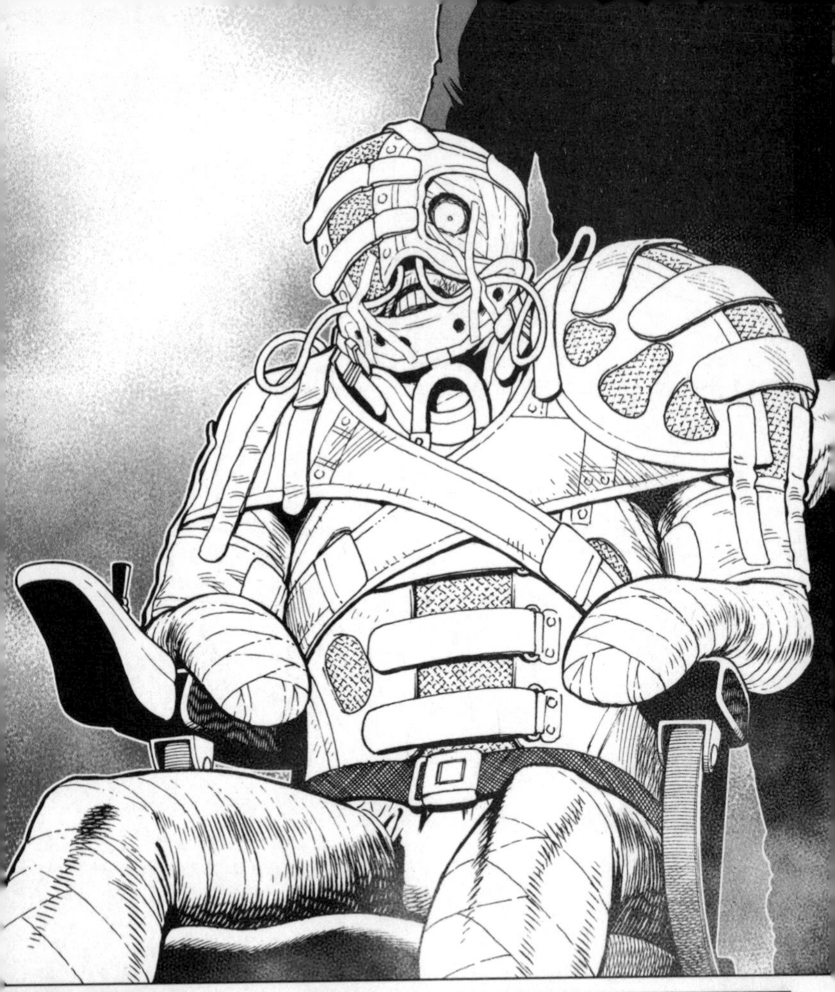

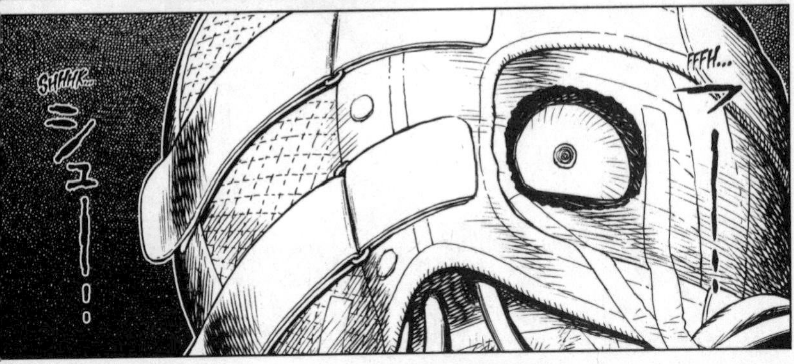
FFFH...
フー!!
SHHHK...
シュー…

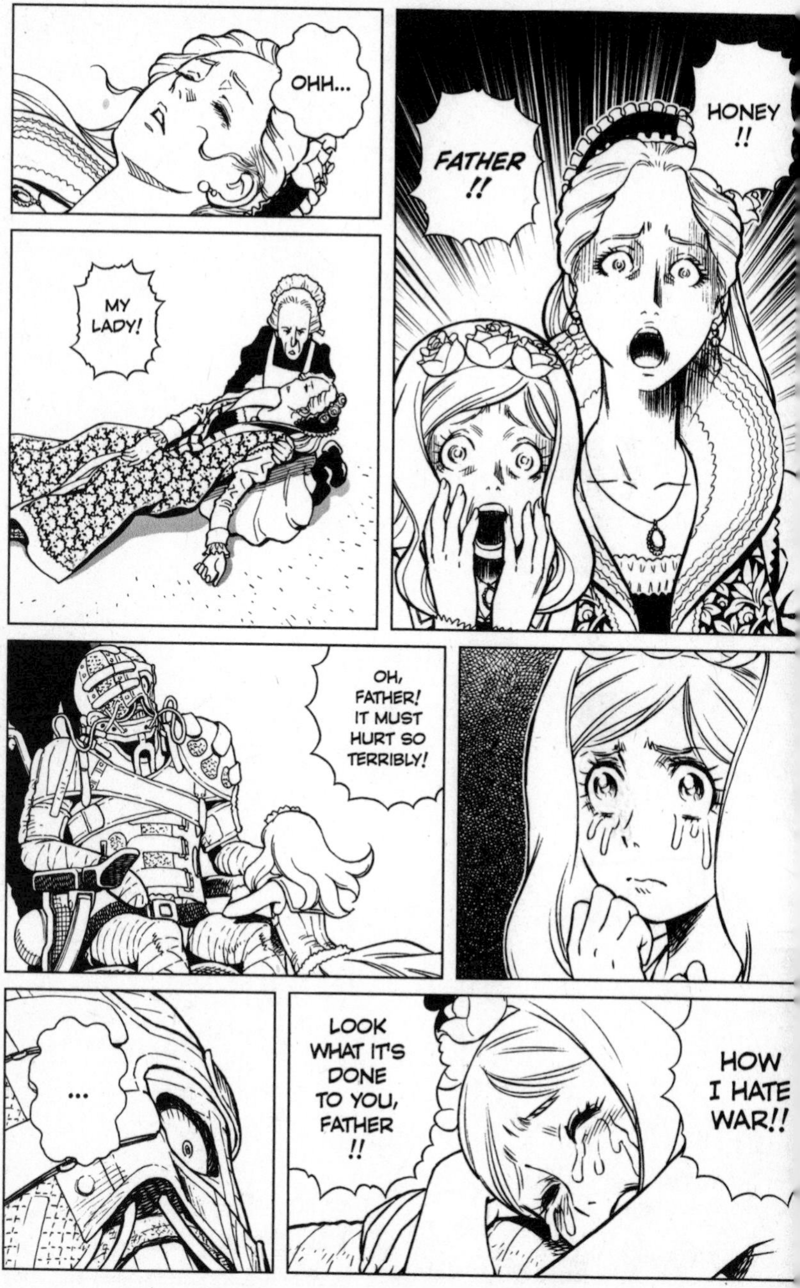
HONEY !!
FATHER !!
OHH...
MY LADY!
OH, FATHER! IT MUST HURT SO TERRIBLY!
HOW I HATE WAR!!
LOOK WHAT IT'S DONE TO YOU, FATHER !!
...

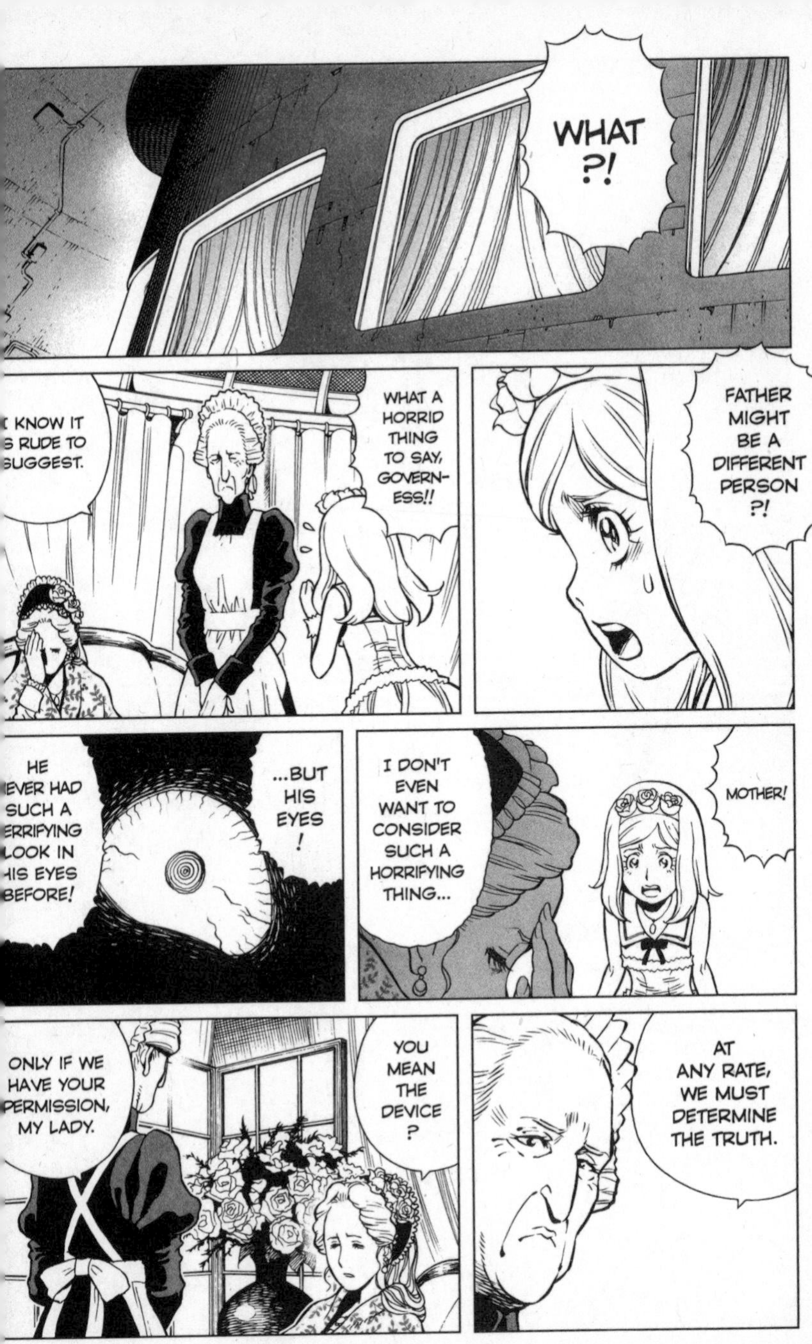
WHAT ?!
FATHER MIGHT BE A DIFFERENT PERSON ?!
WHAT A HORRID THING TO SAY, GOVERNESS!!
KNOW IT S RUDE TO SUGGEST.
MOTHER!
I DON'T EVEN WANT TO CONSIDER SUCH A HORRIFYING THING...
...BUT HIS EYES!
HE EVER HAD SUCH A ERRIFYING LOOK IN IS EYES BEFORE!
AT ANY RATE, WE MUST DETERMINE THE TRUTH.
YOU MEAN THE DEVICE?
ONLY IF WE HAVE YOUR ERMISSION, MY LADY.

IT IS THE MEHRHAUS FAMILY'S IDENTIFICATION DEVICE.

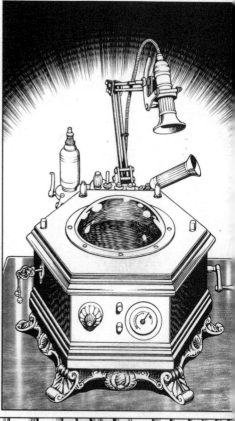

UPON VERIFYING THE MASTER'S PALM AND RETINAL SCANS, THIS SERVES AS THE MASTER KEY FOR ALL OF THE CASTLE'S SAFES AND VITAL FACILITIES.

THOUGH I HARDLY NEED EXPLAIN THIS TO YOU, MASTER.

IF THE PROCESS IS TOO TAXING, WE CAN POSTPONE IT UNTIL ANOTHER DAY.

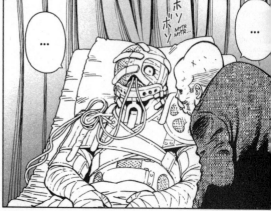

...

ボソ
ボソ
MMTR
MMTR...

...

77

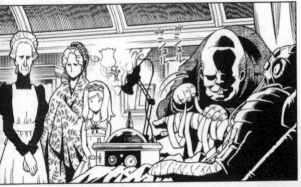

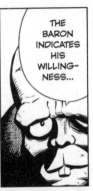

THE BARON INDICATES HIS WILLING-NESS...
slip
slip
HIS HAND LOOKS HIDEOUS !!
KSHIK
VWEEEE
TIKA
TIKA

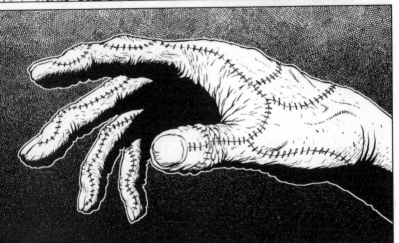

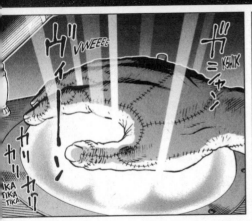

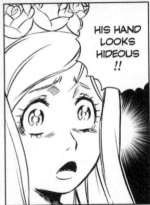

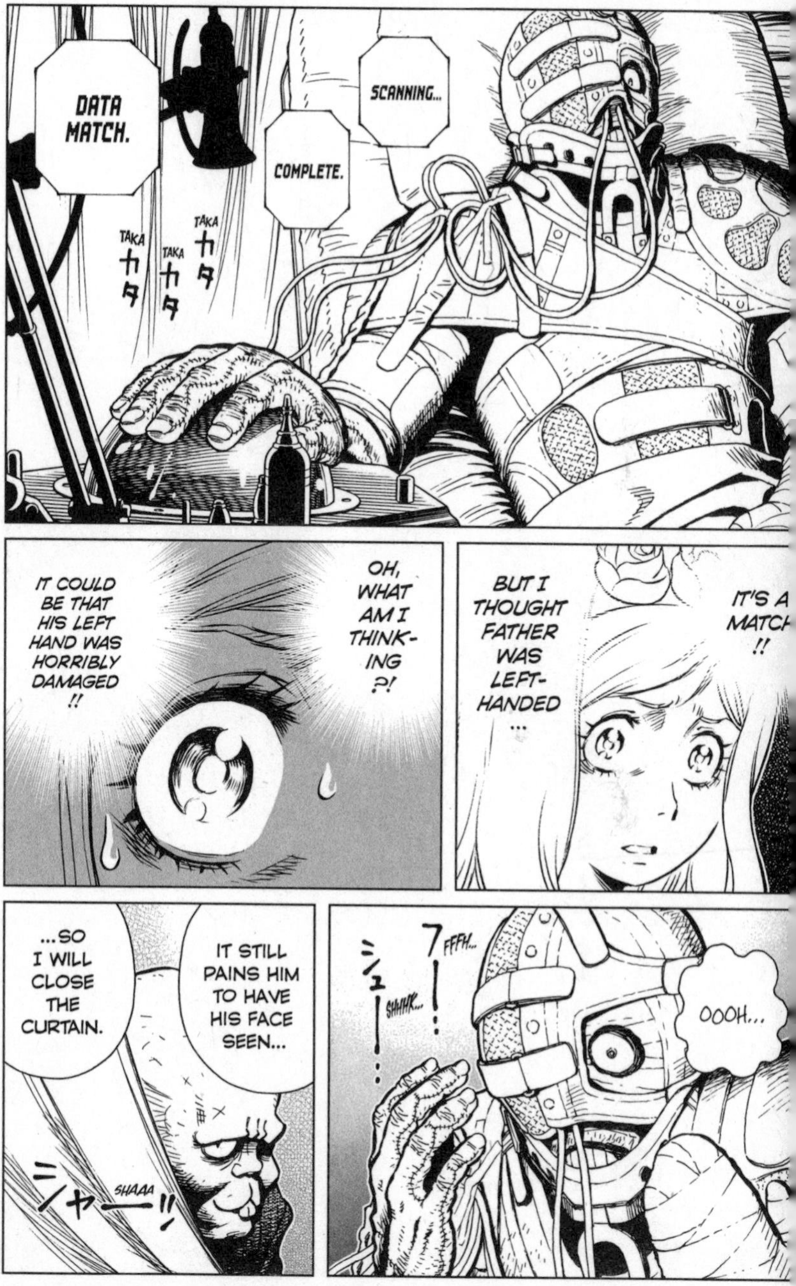
SCANNING...
COMPLETE.
DATA MATCH.
カタ TAKA
カタ TAKA
カタ TAKA
IT'S A MATCH !!
BUT I THOUGHT FATHER WAS LEFT-HANDED ...
OH, WHAT AM I THINKING?!
IT COULD BE THAT HIS LEFT HAND WAS HORRIBLY DAMAGED !!
OOOH...
フー!! FFFH...
シュー... SHHHK...
IT STILL PAINS HIM TO HAVE HIS FACE SEEN...
...SO I WILL CLOSE THE CURTAIN.
シャー!! SHAAA

SCANNING...

COMPLETE.

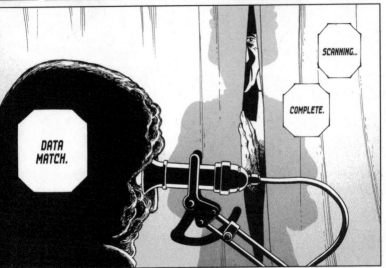

DATA MATCH.

AIEEEEE!!

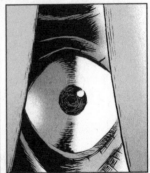

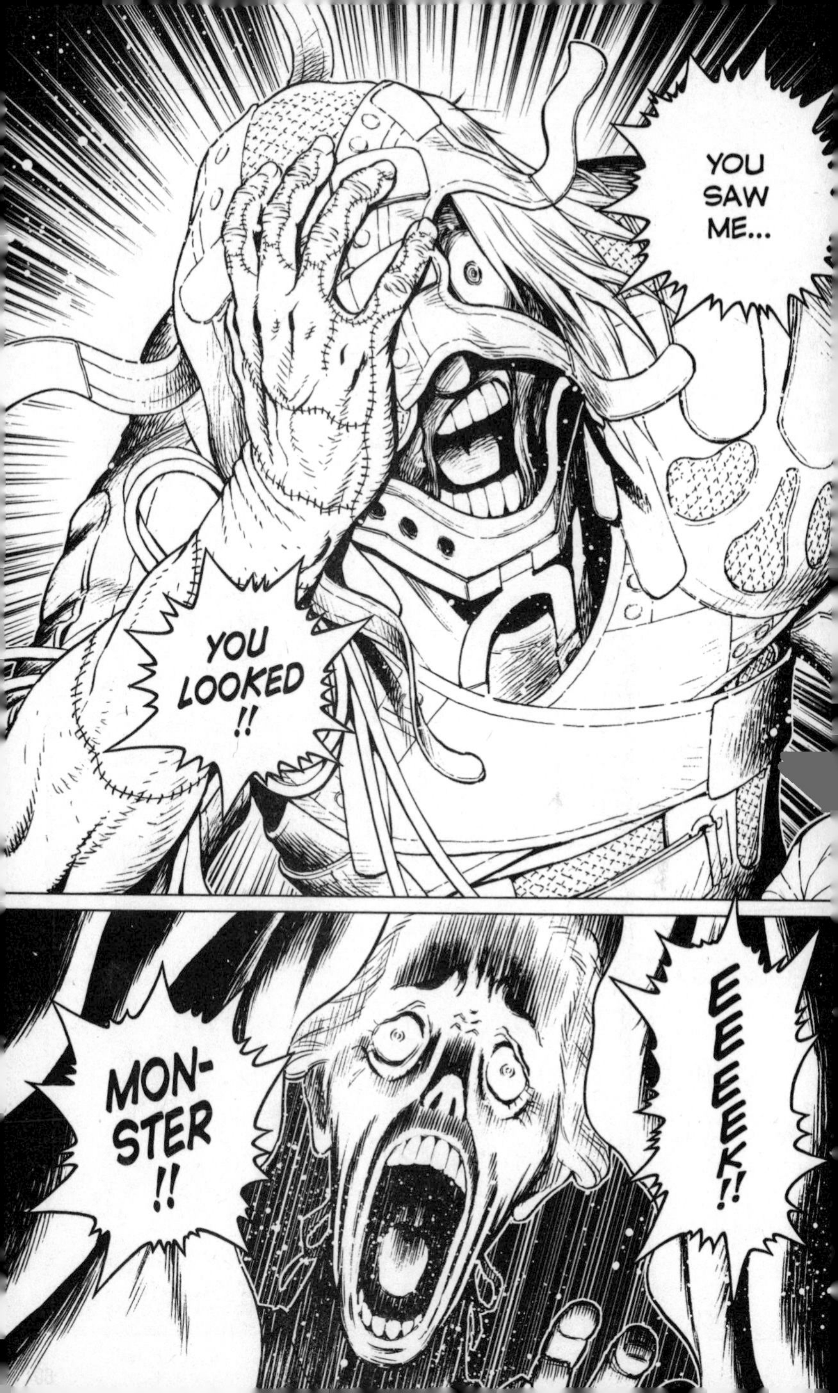
YOU SAW ME...
YOU LOOKED !!
EEEEEK!!
MON-STER !!

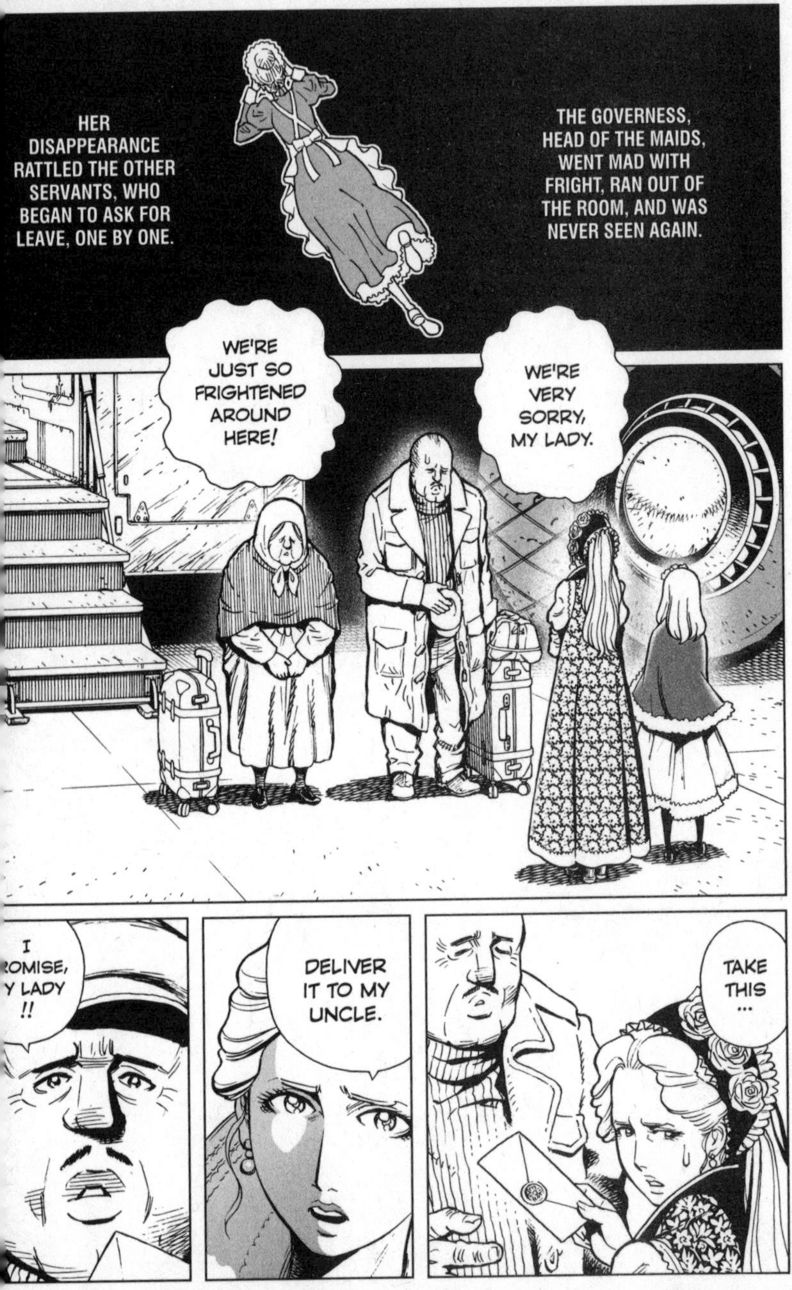
THE GOVERNESS, HEAD OF THE MAIDS, WENT MAD WITH FRIGHT, RAN OUT OF THE ROOM, AND WAS NEVER SEEN AGAIN.
HER DISAPPEARANCE RATTLED THE OTHER SERVANTS, WHO BEGAN TO ASK FOR LEAVE, ONE BY ONE.
WE'RE VERY SORRY, MY LADY.
WE'RE JUST SO FRIGHTENED AROUND HERE!
TAKE THIS ...
DELIVER IT TO MY UNCLE.
I ROMISE, Y LADY !!

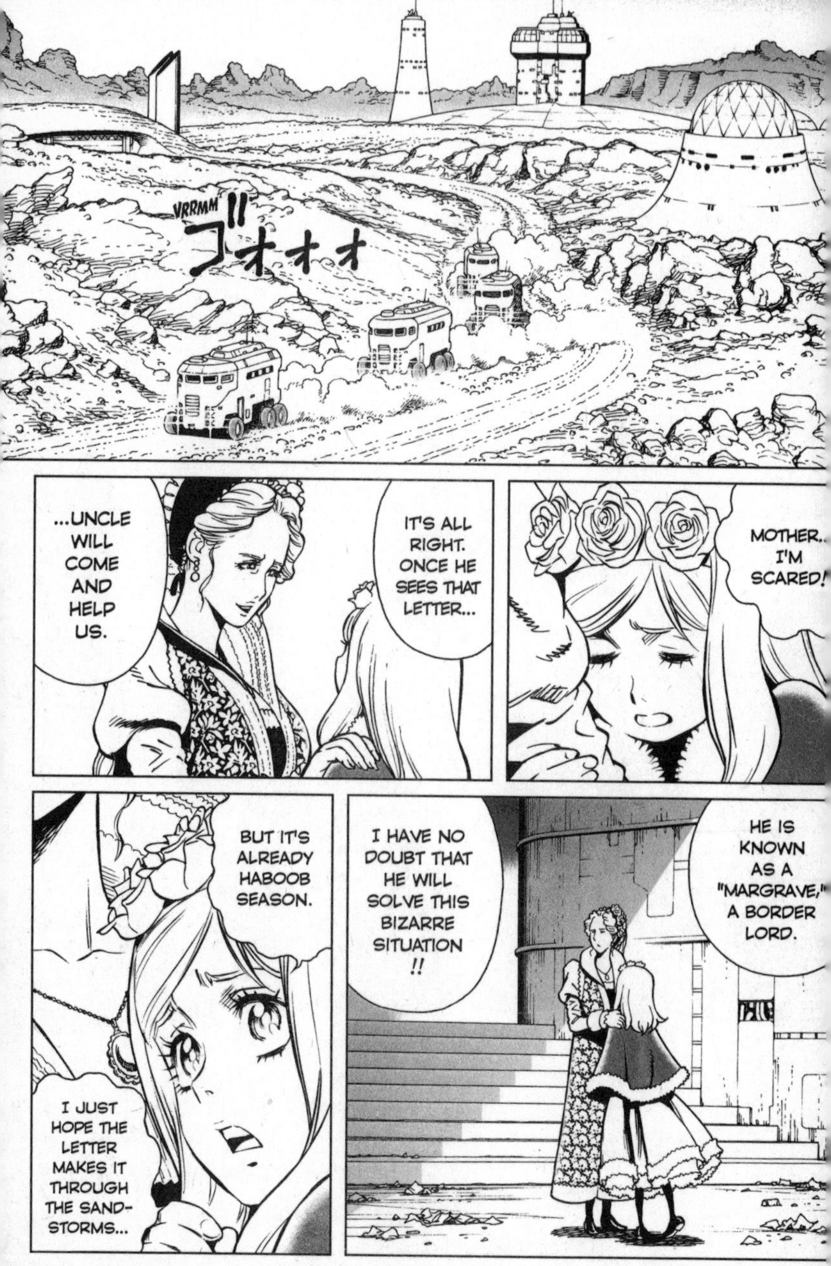
VRRMM!!
ゴオオオ
MOTHER.. I'M SCARED!
IT'S ALL RIGHT. ONCE HE SEES THAT LETTER...
...UNCLE WILL COME AND HELP US.
HE IS KNOWN AS A "MARGRAVE," A BORDER LORD.
I HAVE NO DOUBT THAT HE WILL SOLVE THIS BIZARRE SITUATION !!
BUT IT'S ALREADY HABOOB SEASON.
I JUST HOPE THE LETTER MAKES IT THROUGH THE SAND-STORMS...

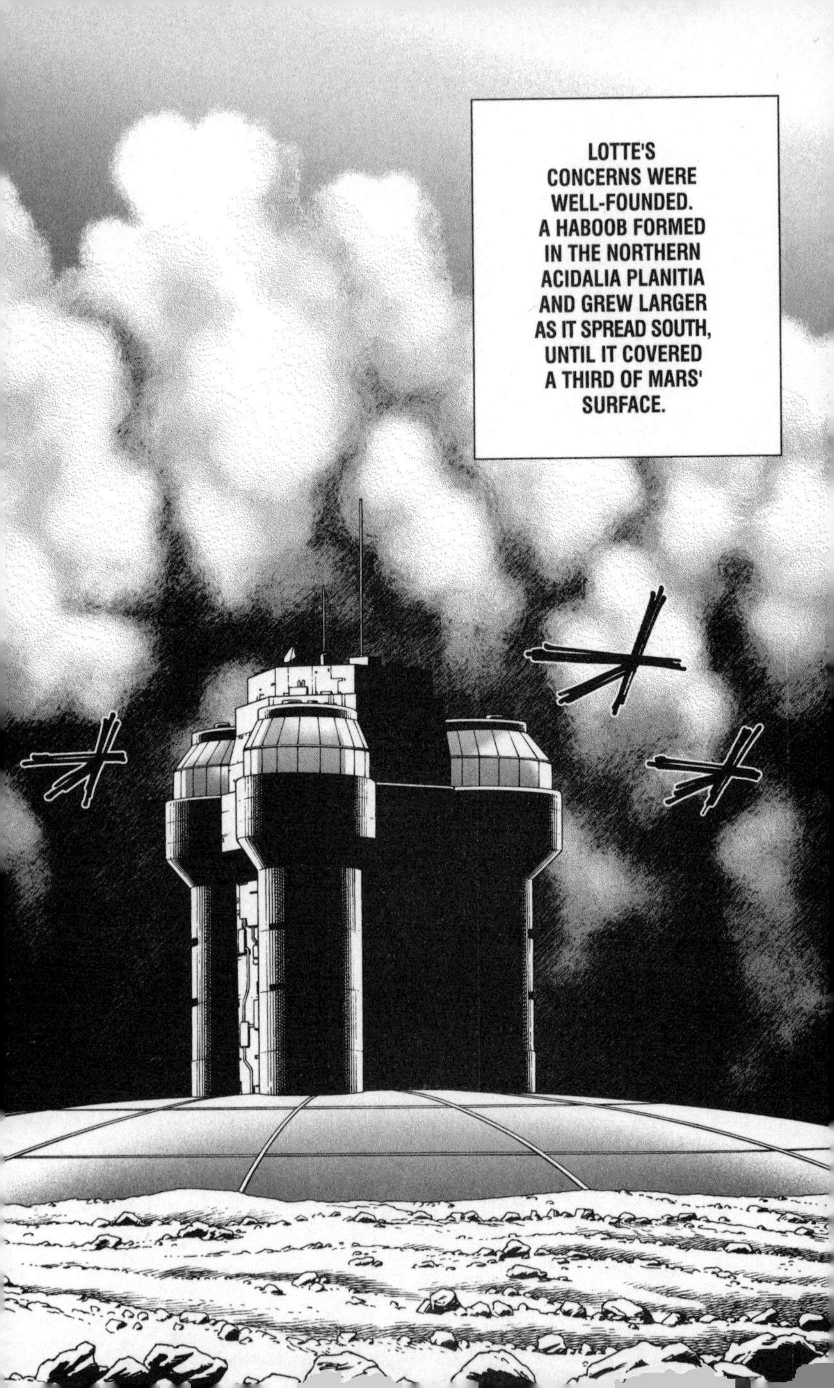
LOTTE'S CONCERNS WERE WELL-FOUNDED. A HABOOB FORMED IN THE NORTHERN ACIDALIA PLANITIA AND GREW LARGER AS IT SPREAD SOUTH, UNTIL IT COVERED A THIRD OF MARS' SURFACE.

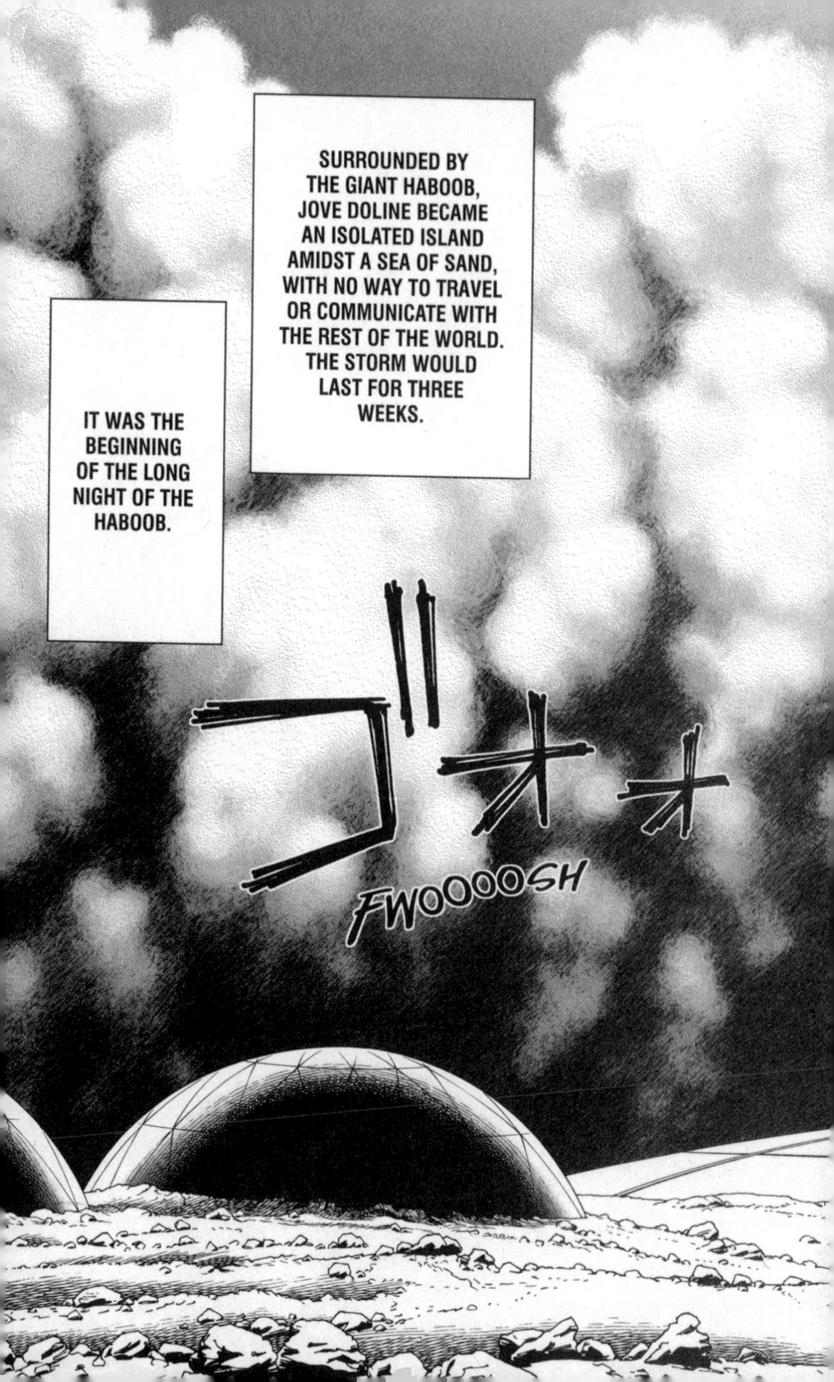
SURROUNDED BY THE GIANT HABOOB, JOVE DOLINE BECAME AN ISOLATED ISLAND AMIDST A SEA OF SAND, WITH NO WAY TO TRAVEL OR COMMUNICATE WITH THE REST OF THE WORLD. THE STORM WOULD LAST FOR THREE WEEKS.
IT WAS THE BEGINNING OF THE LONG NIGHT OF THE HABOOB.
ゴオォ
FWOOOOSH

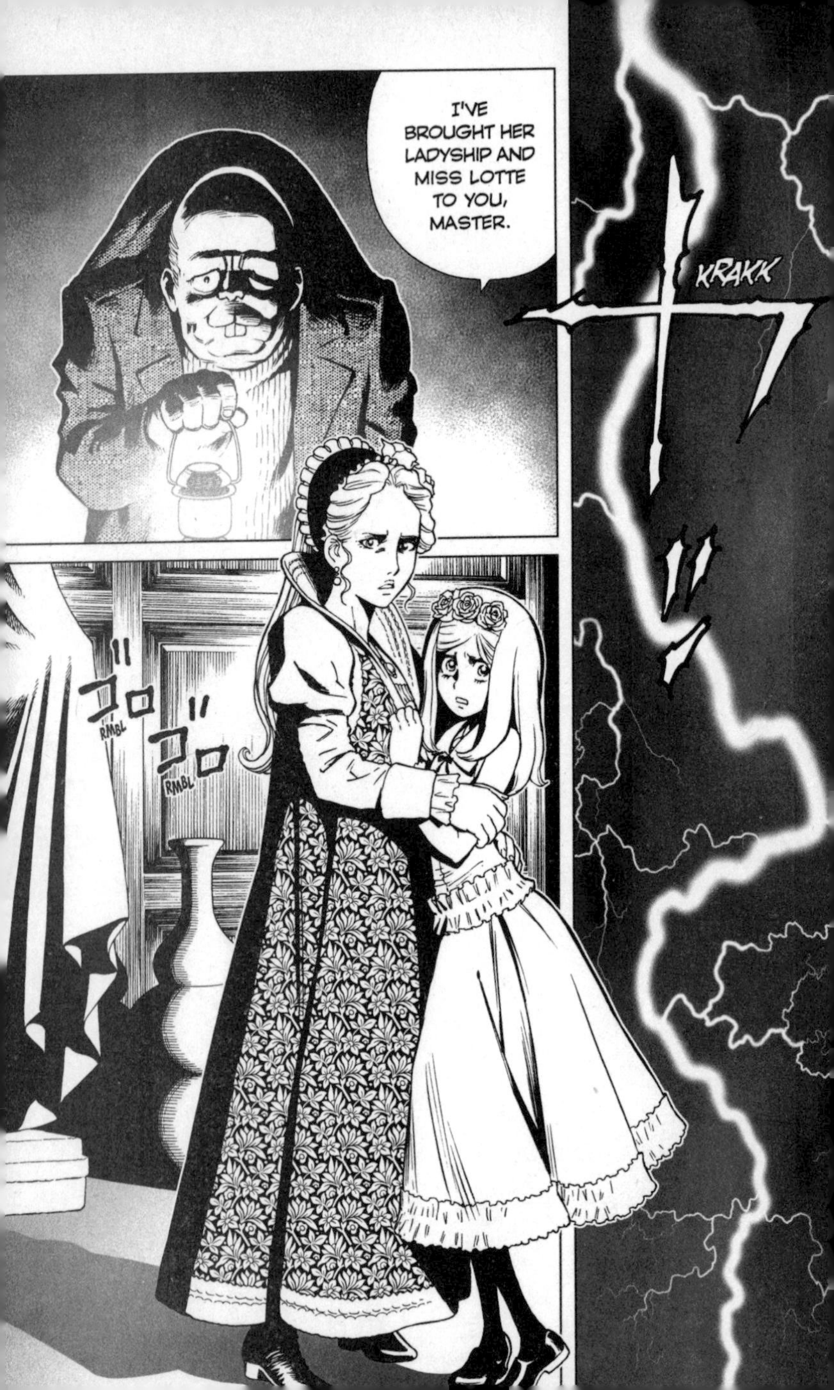
KRAKK
I'VE BROUGHT HER LADYSHIP AND MISS LOTTE TO YOU, MASTER.
ゴロ
RMBL
ゴロ
RMBL

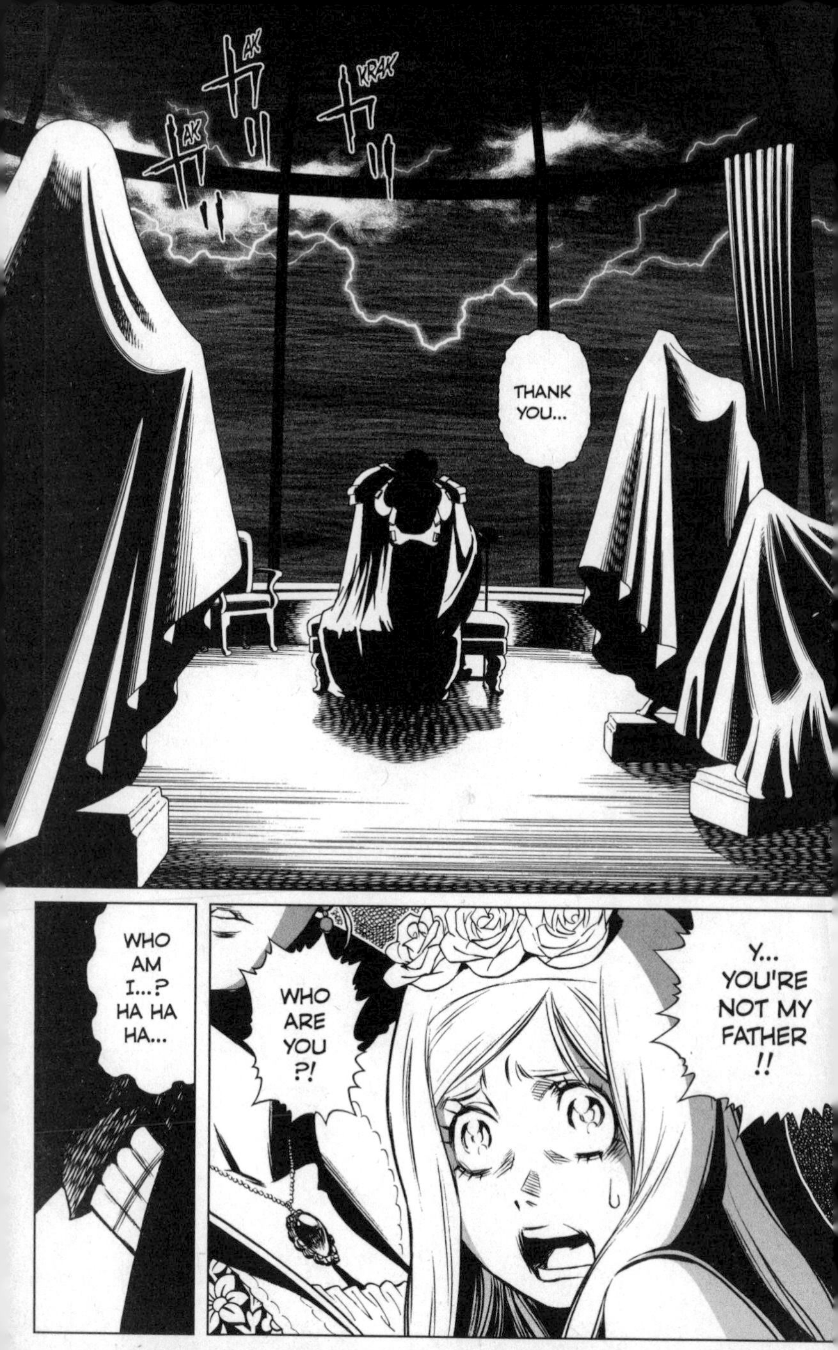
KRAK
AK
AK
THANK YOU...
Y... YOU'RE NOT MY FATHER !!
WHO ARE YOU ?!
WHO AM I...? HA HA HA...

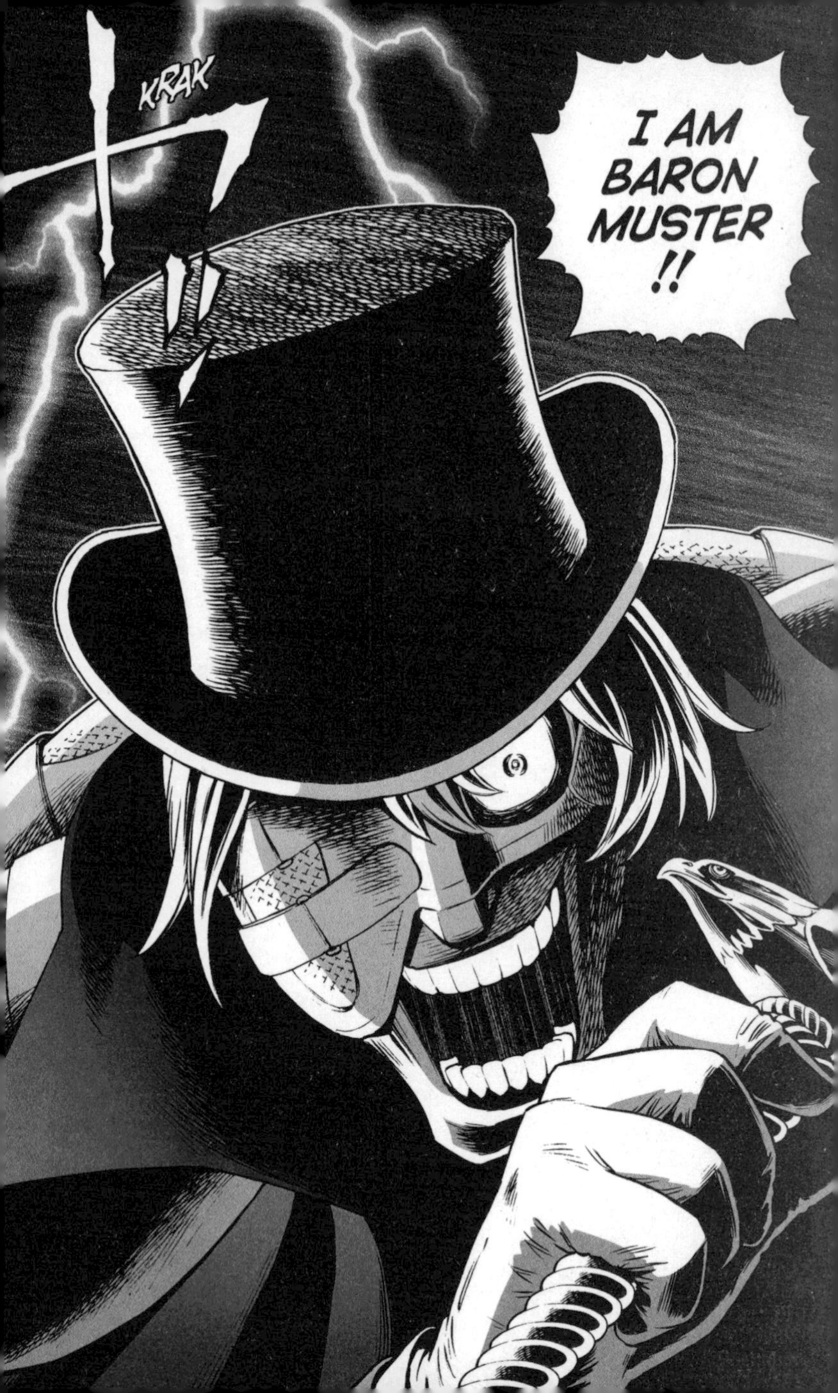
KRAK
I AM BARON MUSTER !!

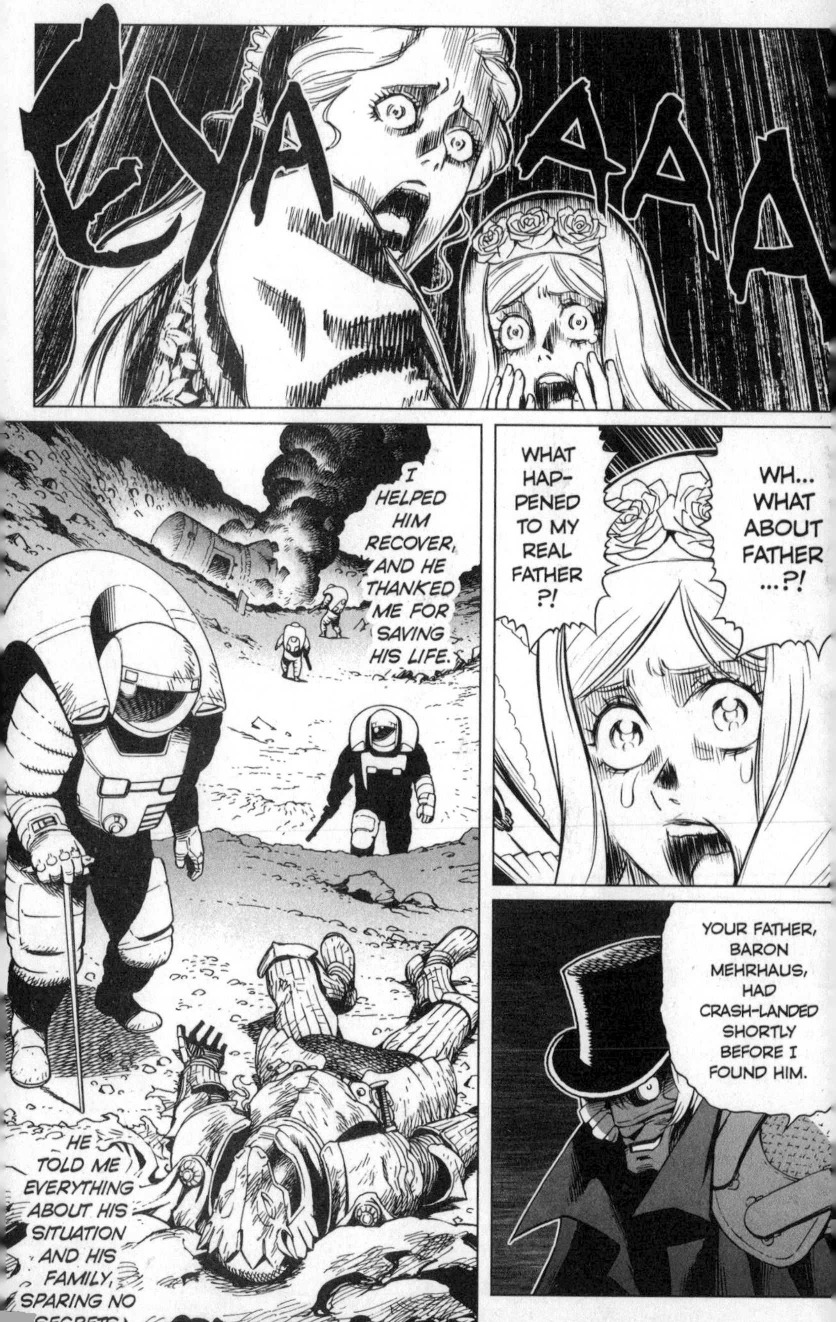
KYAAAA
WH... WHAT ABOUT FATHER ...?!
WHAT HAP-PENED TO MY REAL FATHER ?!
YOUR FATHER, BARON MEHRHAUS, HAD CRASH-LANDED SHORTLY BEFORE I FOUND HIM.
I HELPED HIM RECOVER, AND HE THANKED ME FOR SAVING HIS LIFE.
HE TOLD ME EVERYTHING ABOUT HIS SITUATION AND HIS FAMILY, SPARING NO SECRETS.

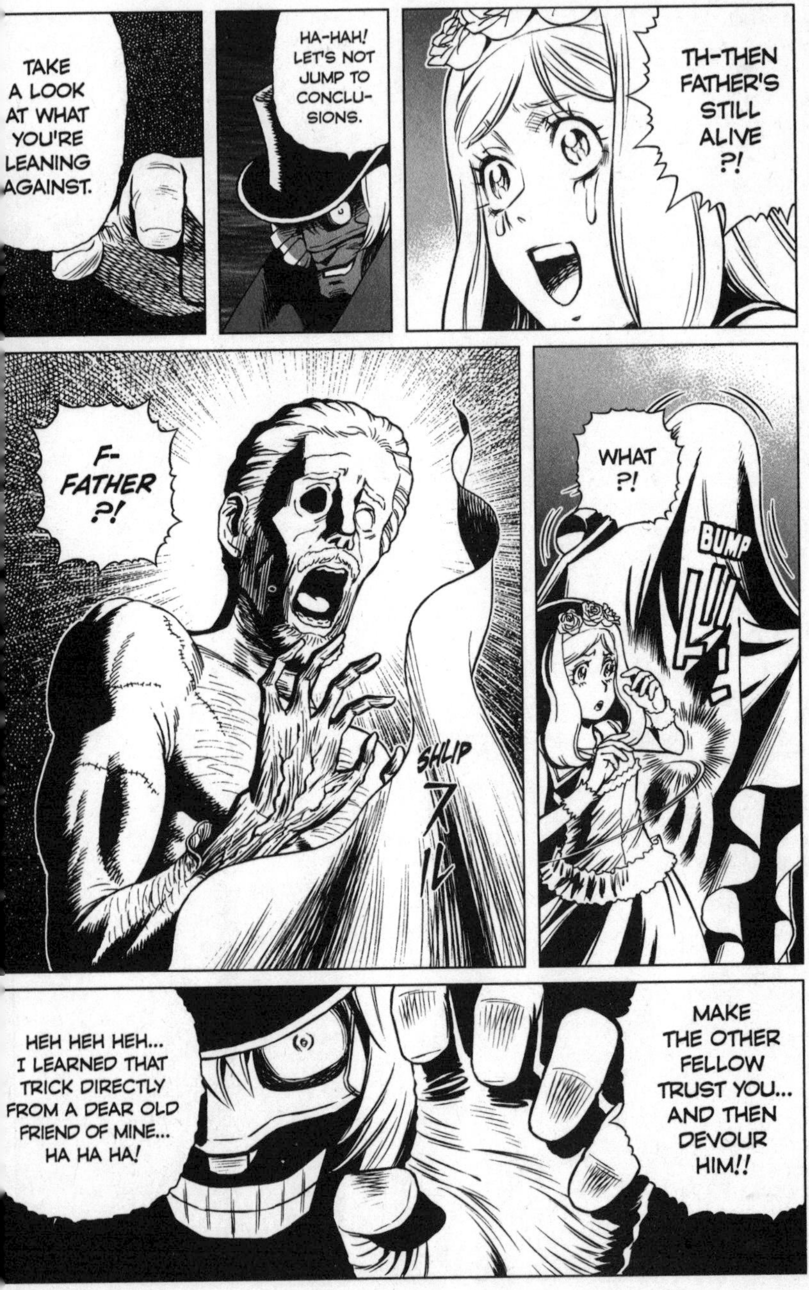
TH-THEN FATHER'S STILL ALIVE ?!
HA-HAH! LET'S NOT JUMP TO CONCLU-SIONS.
TAKE A LOOK AT WHAT YOU'RE LEANING AGAINST.
WHAT ?!
BUMP
F-FATHER ?!
SHLIP
MAKE THE OTHER FELLOW TRUST YOU... AND THEN DEVOUR HIM!!
HEH HEH HEH... I LEARNED THAT TRICK DIRECTLY FROM A DEAR OLD FRIEND OF MINE... HA HA HA!

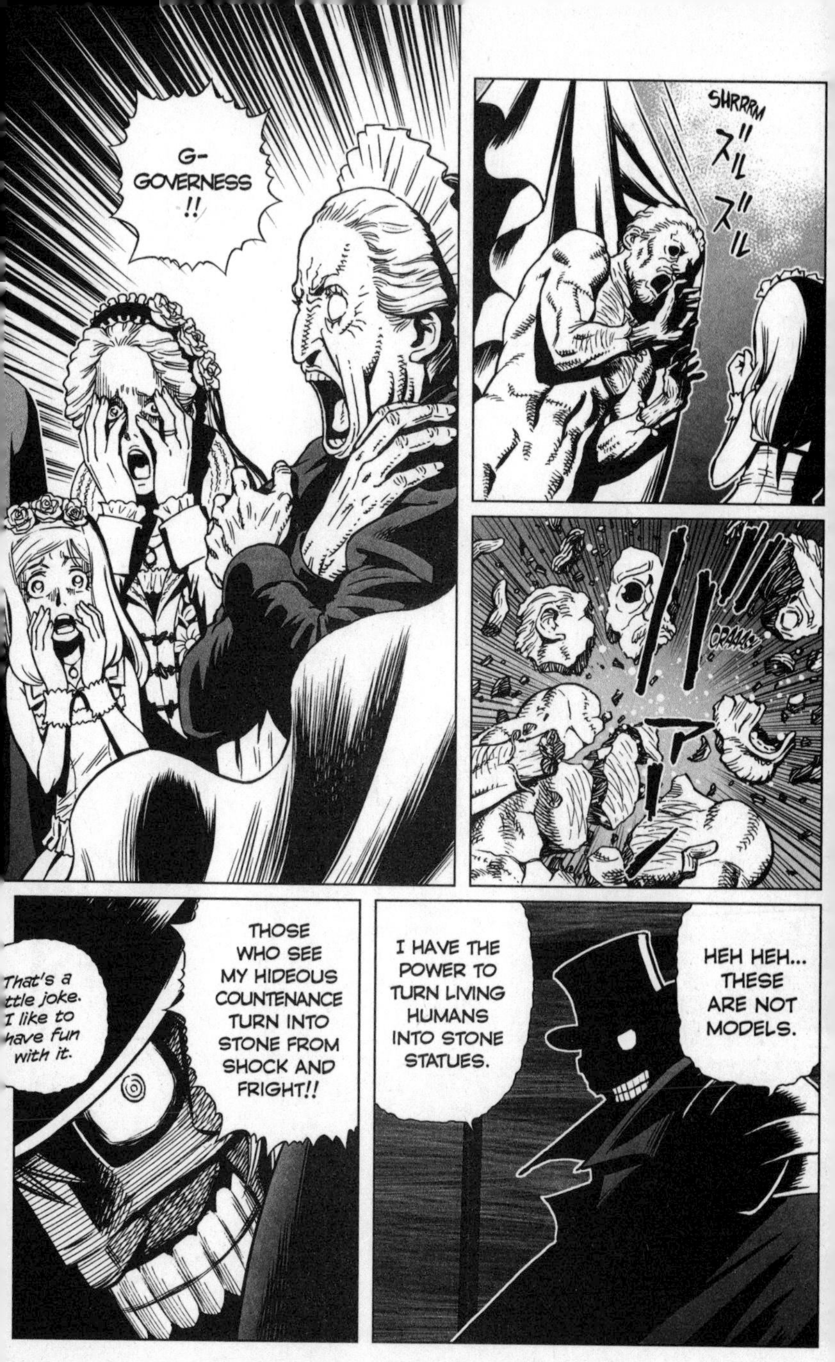
SHRRRM
ズルズル
CRAAAA
G-GOVERNESS!!
HEH HEH... THESE ARE NOT MODELS.
I HAVE THE POWER TO TURN LIVING HUMANS INTO STONE STATUES.
THOSE WHO SEE MY HIDEOUS COUNTENANCE TURN INTO STONE FROM SHOCK AND FRIGHT!!
That's a ttle joke. I like to have fun with it.

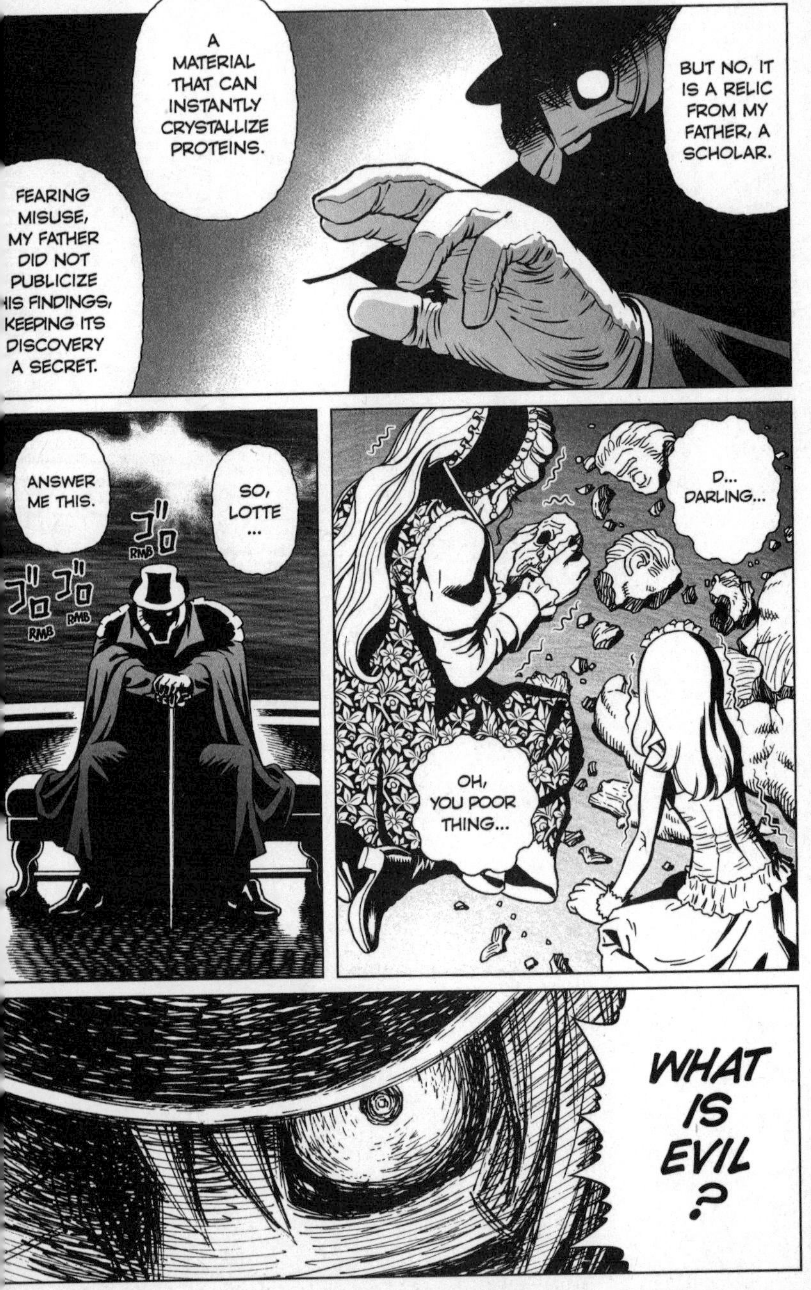
BUT NO, IT IS A RELIC FROM MY FATHER, A SCHOLAR.
A MATERIAL THAT CAN INSTANTLY CRYSTALLIZE PROTEINS.
FEARING MISUSE, MY FATHER DID NOT PUBLICIZE IS FINDINGS, KEEPING ITS DISCOVERY A SECRET.
D... DARLING...
OH, YOU POOR THING...
SO, LOTTE ...
ANSWER ME THIS.
ゴロ RMB
ゴロ RMB
ゴロ RMB
WHAT IS EVIL ?

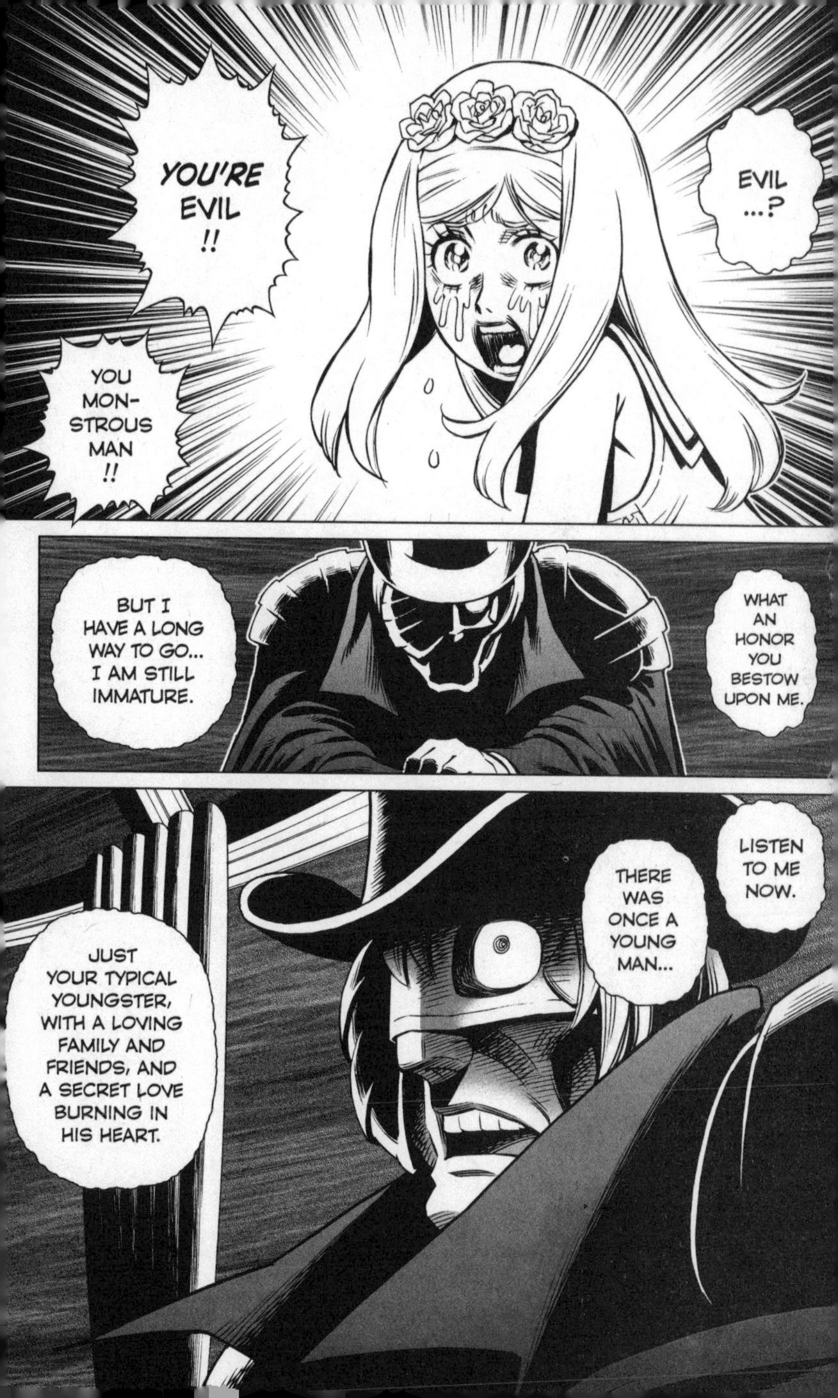
EVIL ...?
YOU'RE EVIL !!
YOU MONSTROUS MAN !!
WHAT AN HONOR YOU BESTOW UPON ME.
BUT I HAVE A LONG WAY TO GO... I AM STILL IMMATURE.
LISTEN TO ME NOW.
THERE WAS ONCE A YOUNG MAN...
JUST YOUR TYPICAL YOUNGSTER, WITH A LOVING FAMILY AND FRIENDS, AND A SECRET LOVE BURNING IN HIS HEART.

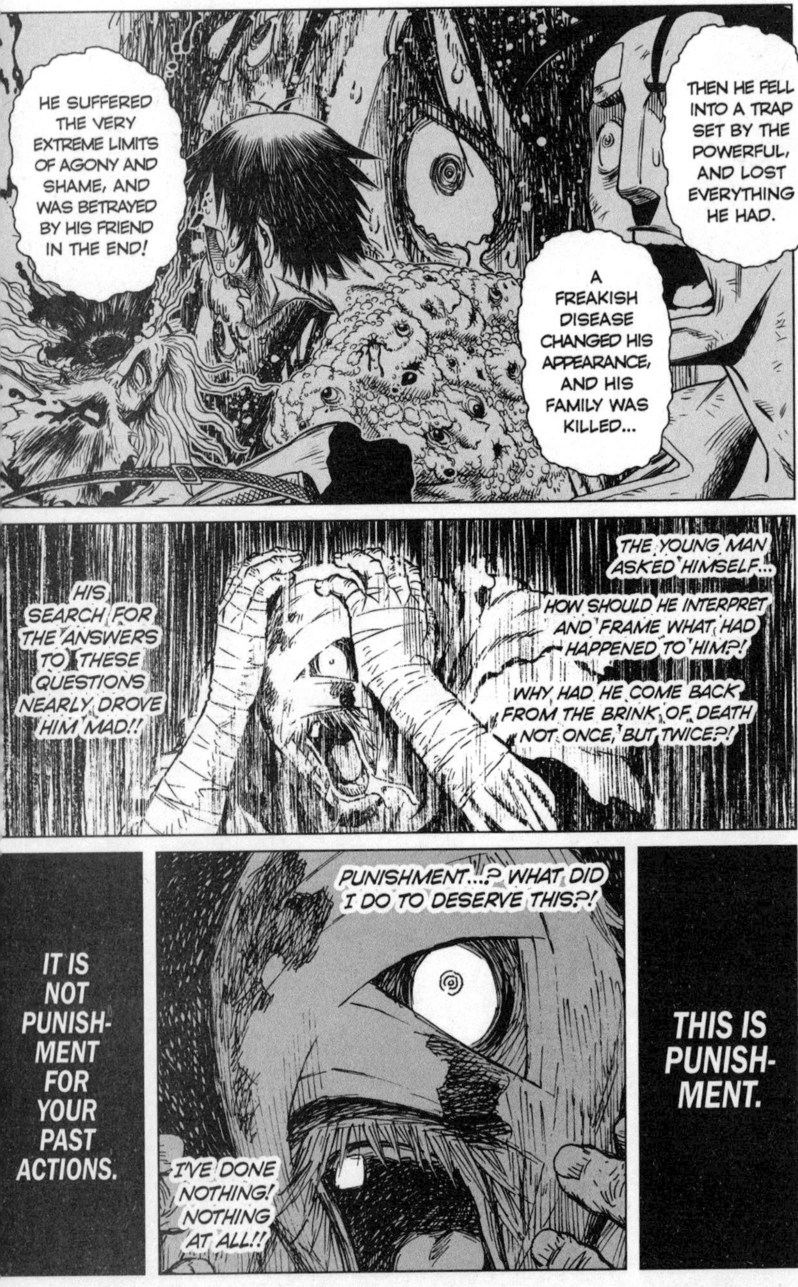
A FREAKISH DISEASE CHANGED HIS APPEARANCE, AND HIS FAMILY WAS KILLED...
THEN HE FELL INTO A TRAP SET BY THE POWERFUL, AND LOST EVERYTHING HE HAD.
HE SUFFERED THE VERY EXTREME LIMITS OF AGONY AND SHAME, AND WAS BETRAYED BY HIS FRIEND IN THE END!
THE YOUNG MAN ASKED HIMSELF...
HOW SHOULD HE INTERPRET AND FRAME WHAT HAD HAPPENED TO HIM?!
WHY HAD HE COME BACK FROM THE BRINK OF DEATH NOT ONCE, BUT TWICE?!
HIS SEARCH FOR THE ANSWERS TO THESE QUESTIONS NEARLY DROVE HIM MAD!!
THIS IS PUNISHMENT.
PUNISHMENT...? WHAT DID I DO TO DESERVE THIS?!
I'VE DONE NOTHING! NOTHING AT ALL!!
IT IS NOT PUNISHMENT FOR YOUR PAST ACTIONS.

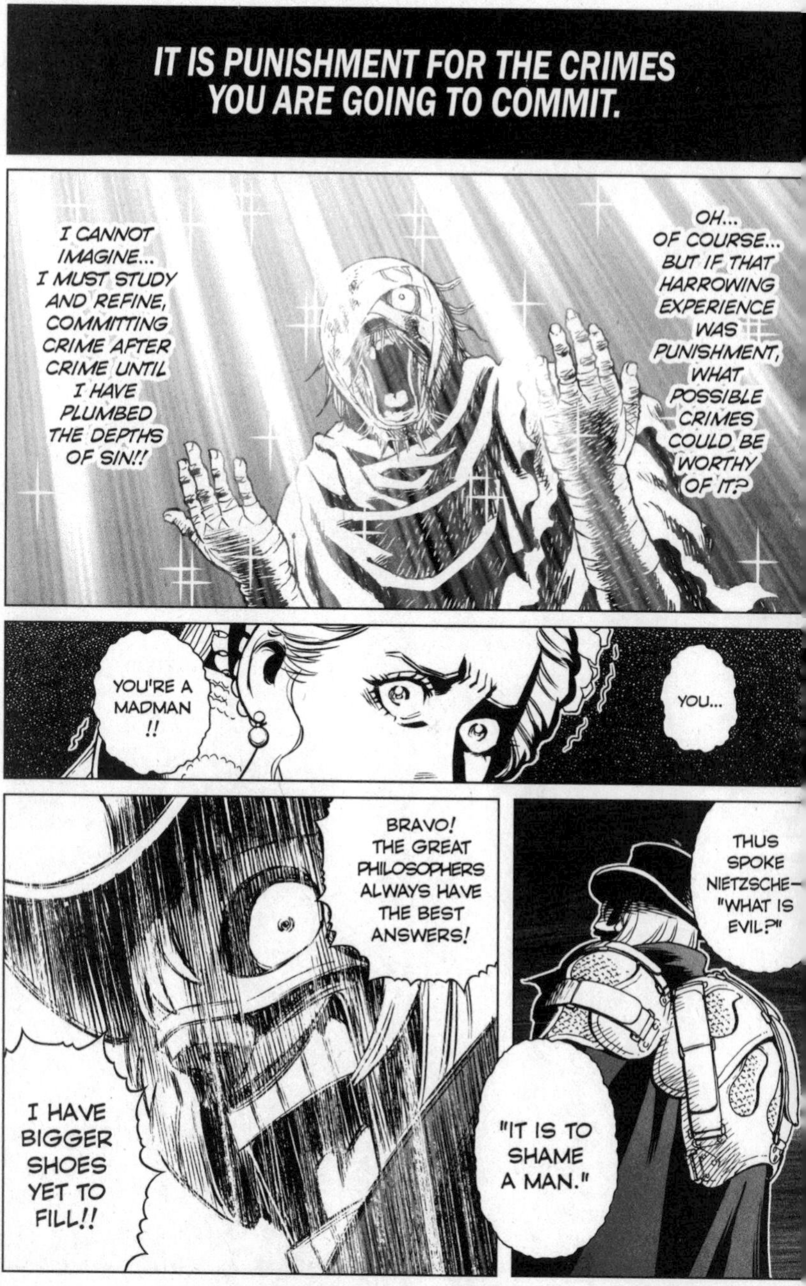
IT IS PUNISHMENT FOR THE CRIMES YOU ARE GOING TO COMMIT.
OH... OF COURSE... BUT IF THAT HARROWING EXPERIENCE WAS PUNISHMENT, WHAT POSSIBLE CRIMES COULD BE WORTHY OF IT?
I CANNOT IMAGINE... I MUST STUDY AND REFINE, COMMITTING CRIME AFTER CRIME UNTIL I HAVE PLUMBED THE DEPTHS OF SIN!!
YOU...
YOU'RE A MADMAN !!
THUS SPOKE NIETZSCHE— "WHAT IS EVIL?"
"IT IS TO SHAME A MAN."
BRAVO! THE GREAT PHILOSOPHERS ALWAYS HAVE THE BEST ANSWERS!
I HAVE BIGGER SHOES YET TO FILL!!

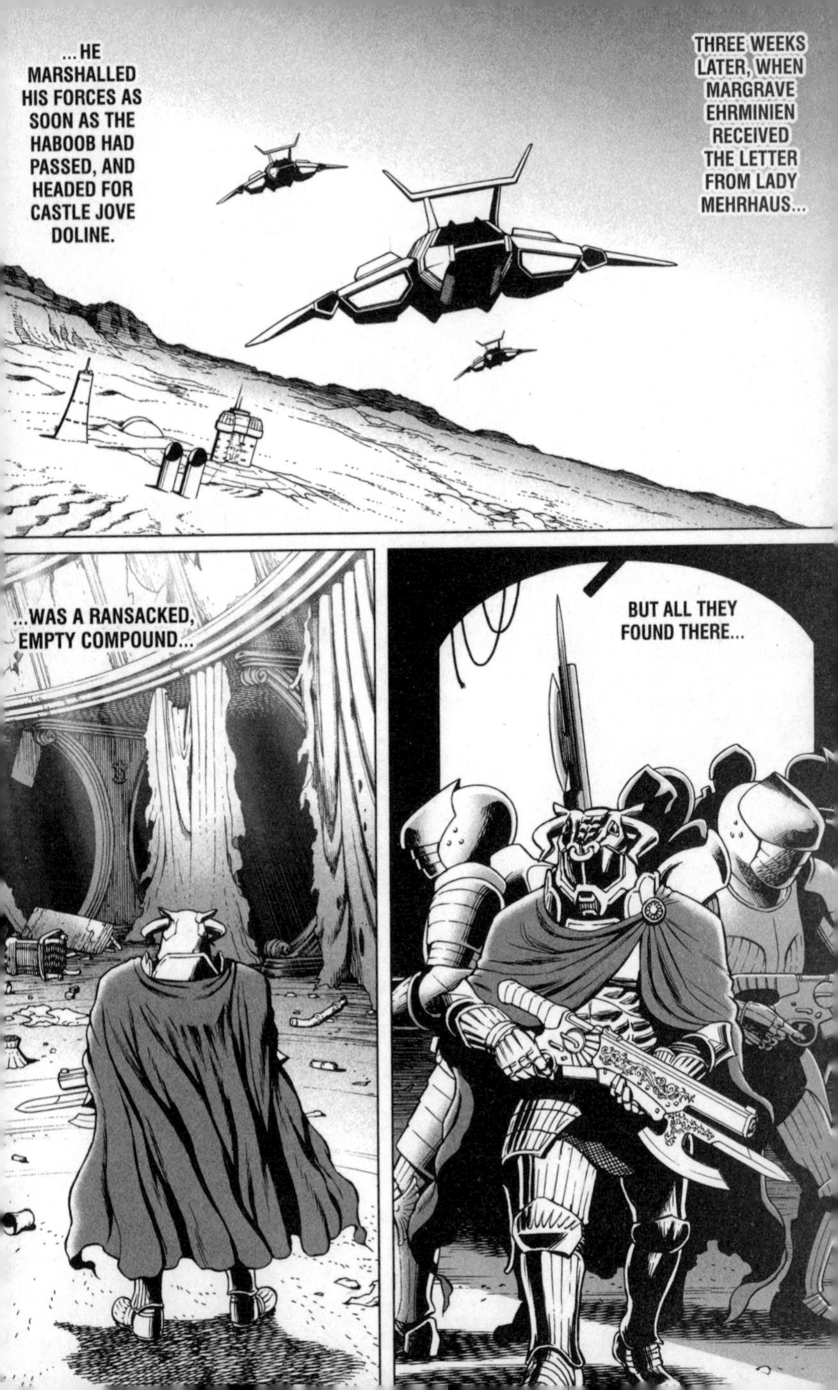
THREE WEEKS LATER, WHEN MARGRAVE EHRMINIEN RECEIVED THE LETTER FROM LADY MEHRHAUS...
...HE MARSHALLED HIS FORCES AS SOON AS THE HABOOB HAD PASSED, AND HEADED FOR CASTLE JOVE DOLINE.
BUT ALL THEY FOUND THERE...
...WAS A RANSACKED, EMPTY COMPOUND...

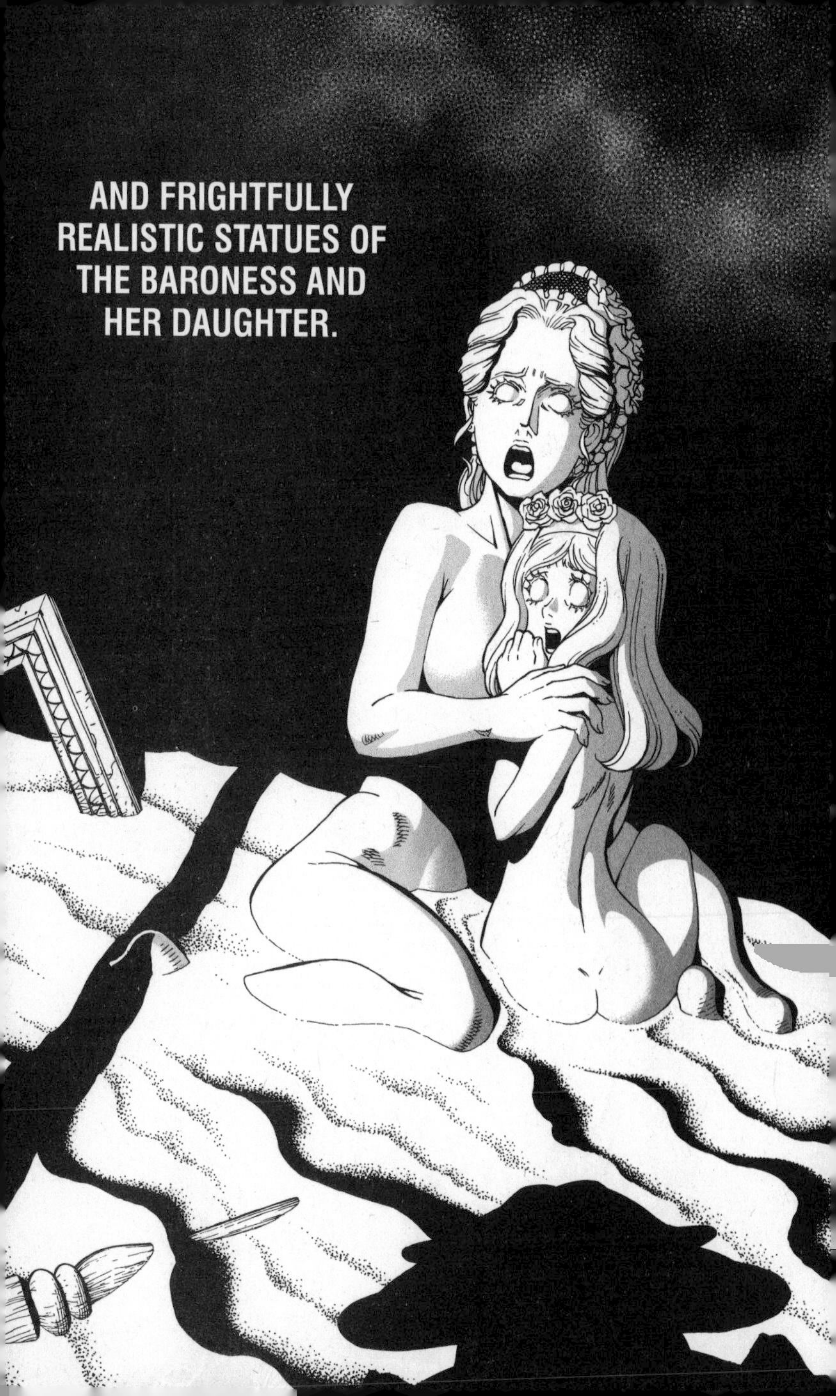
AND FRIGHTFULLY REALISTIC STATUES OF THE BARONESS AND HER DAUGHTER.

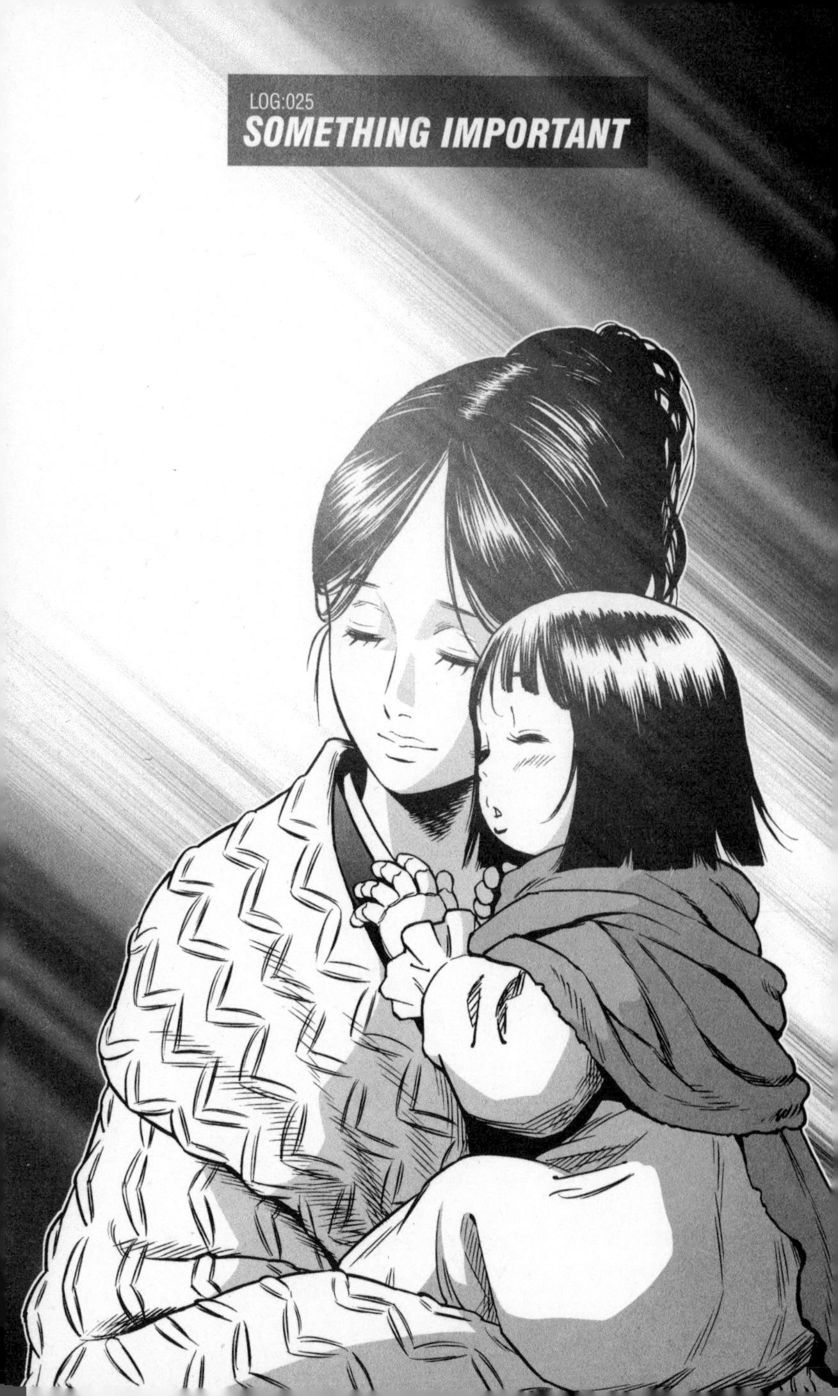
LOG:025
SOMETHING IMPORTANT

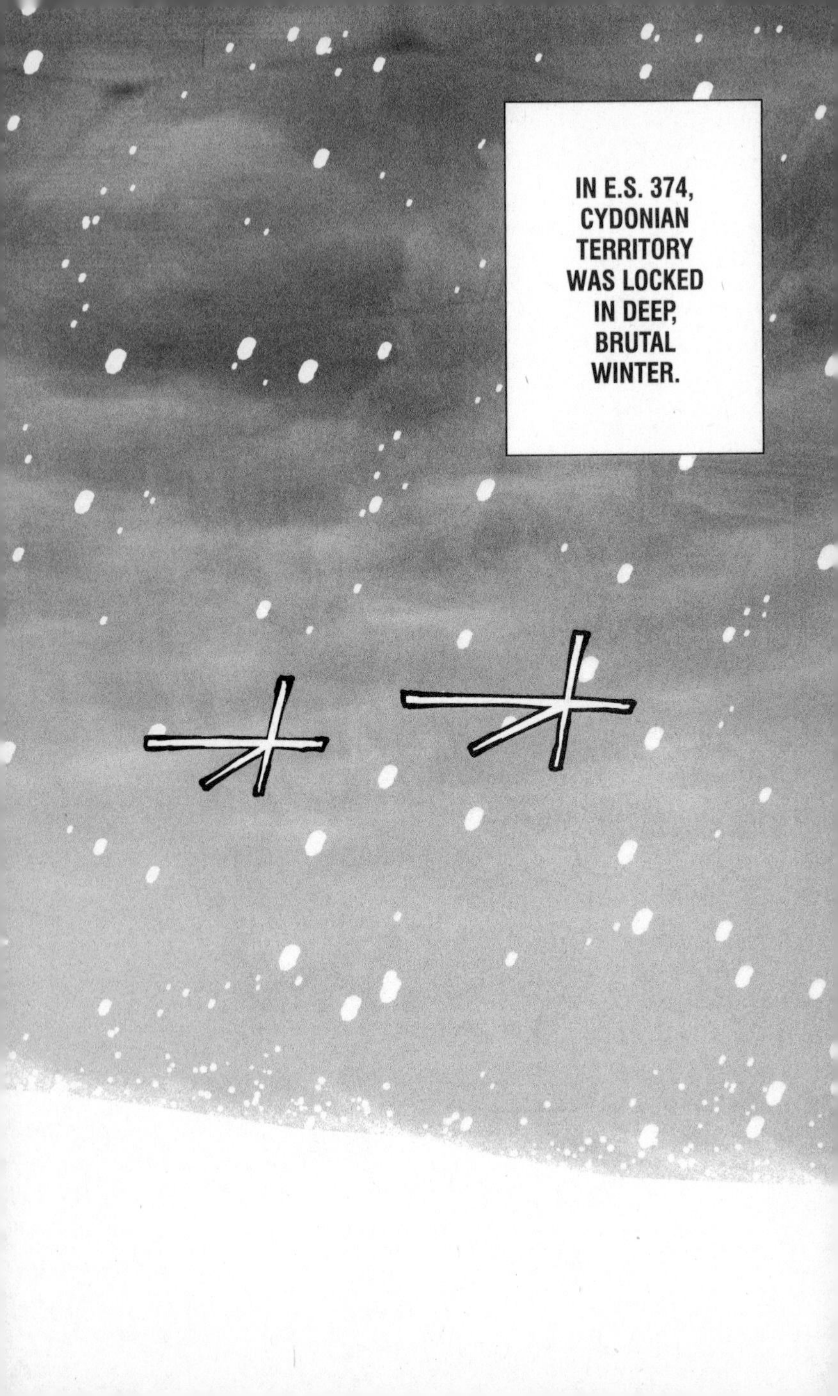
IN E.S. 374, CYDONIAN TERRITORY WAS LOCKED IN DEEP, BRUTAL WINTER.

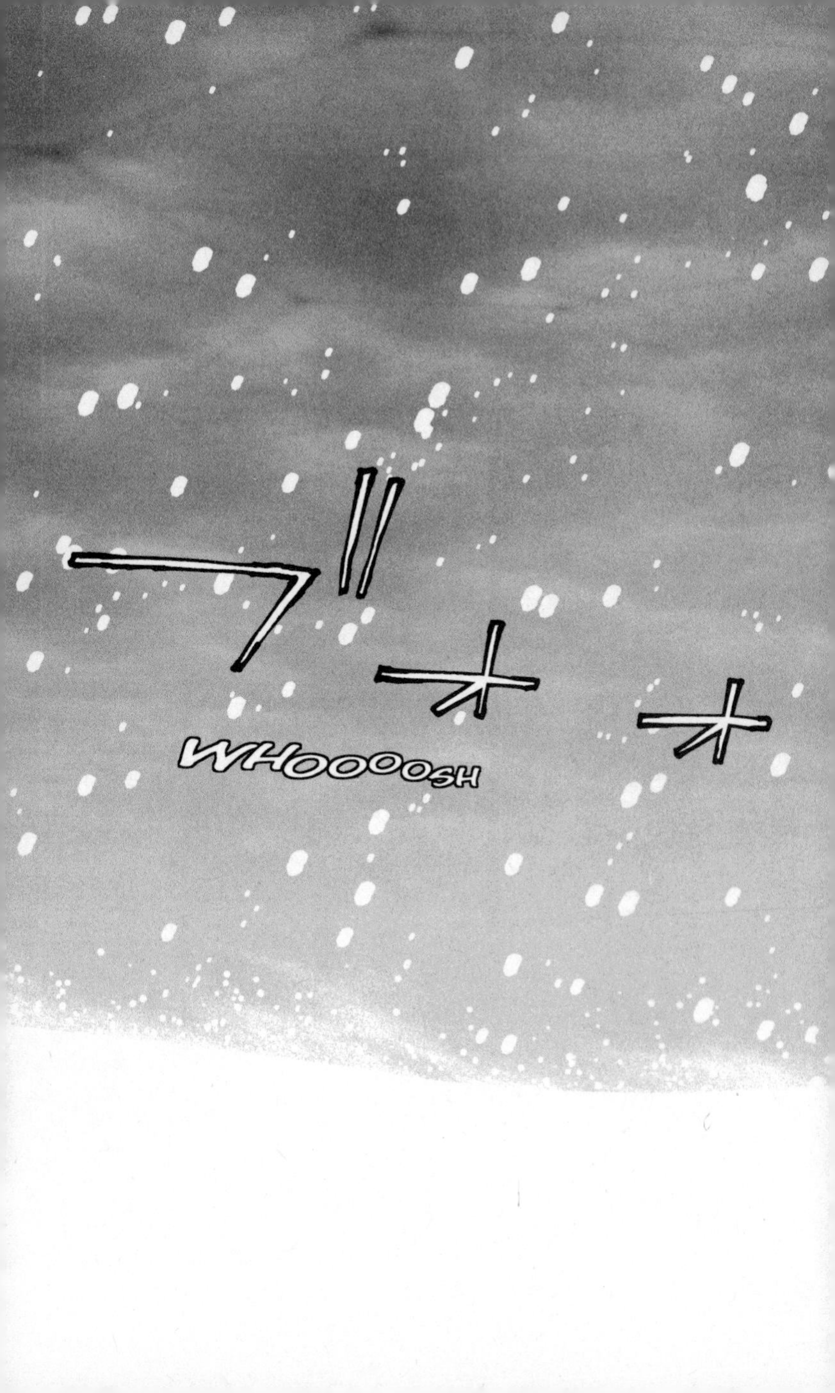
ブオオ
WHOOOOSH

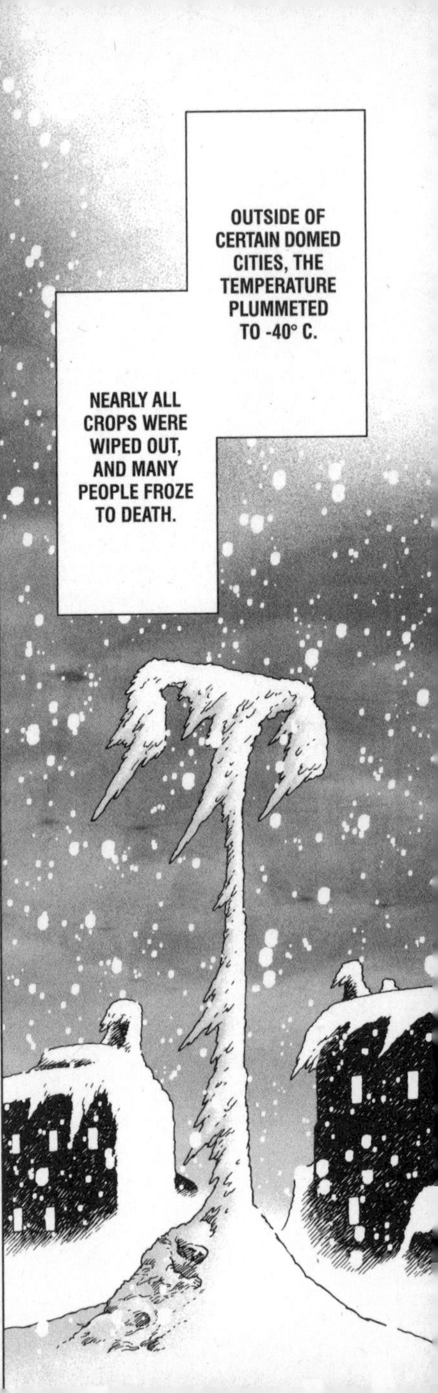
OUTSIDE OF CERTAIN DOMED CITIES, THE TEMPERATURE PLUMMETED TO -40° C.
NEARLY ALL CROPS WERE WIPED OUT, AND MANY PEOPLE FROZE TO DEATH.
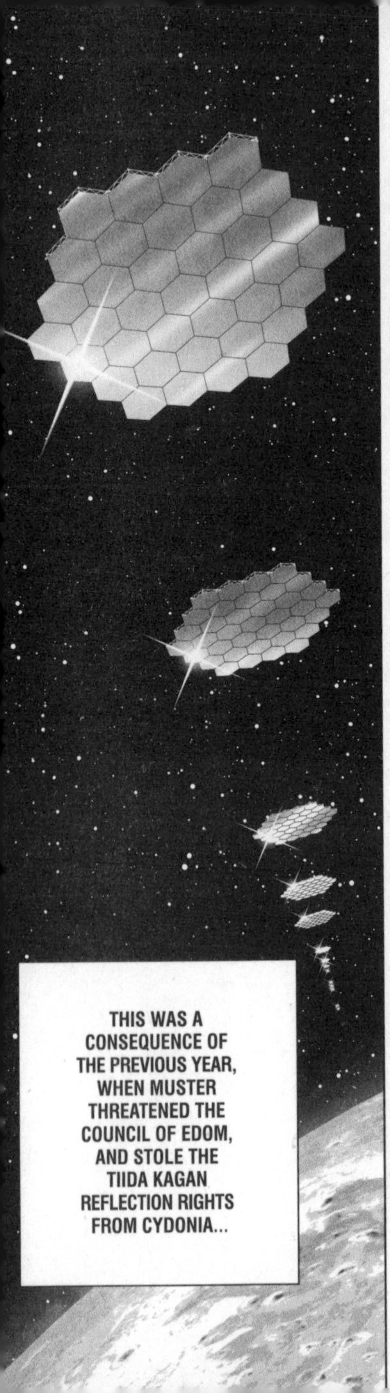
THIS WAS A CONSEQUENCE OF THE PREVIOUS YEAR, WHEN MUSTER THREATENED THE COUNCIL OF EDOM, AND STOLE THE TIIDA KAGAN REFLECTION RIGHTS FROM CYDONIA...

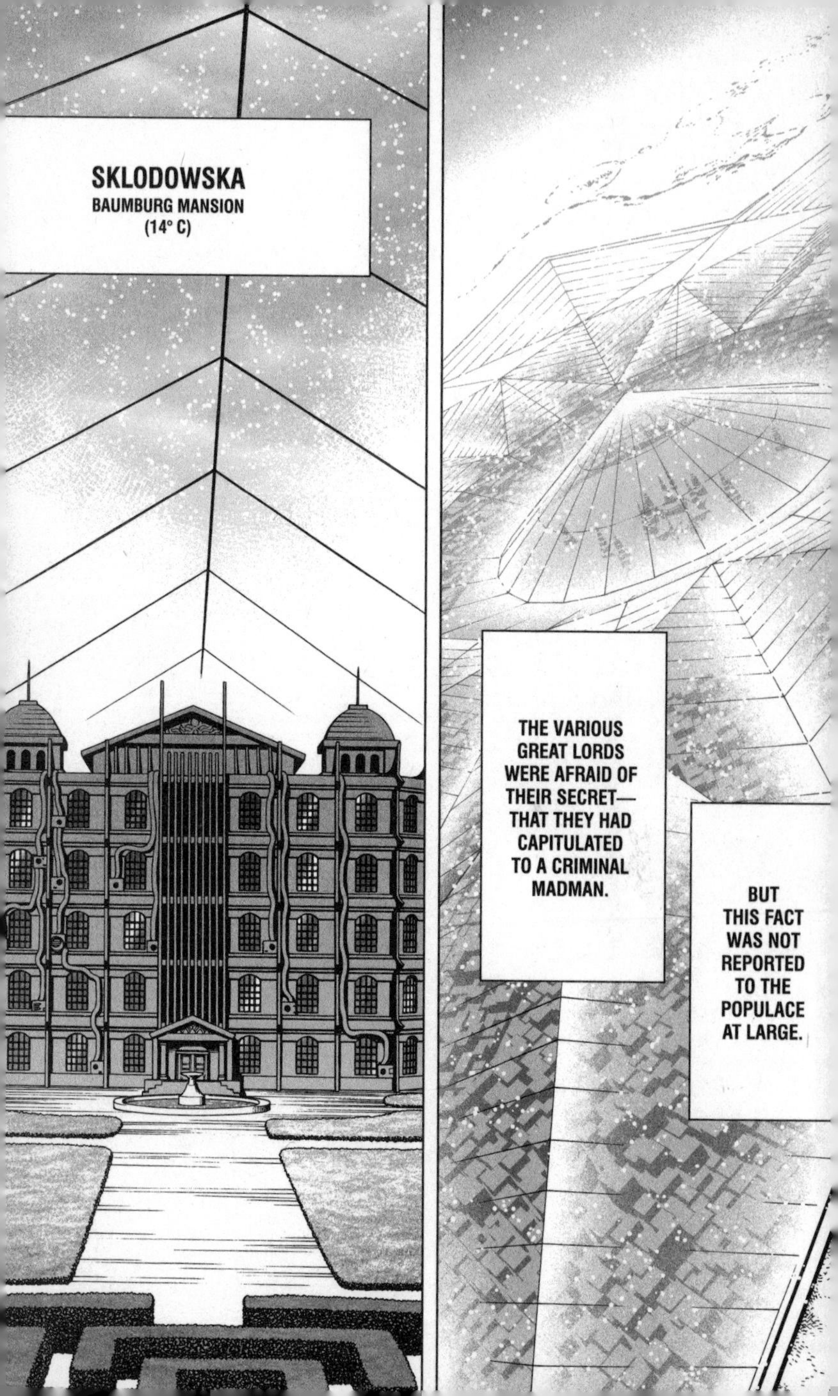
THE VARIOUS GREAT LORDS WERE AFRAID OF THEIR SECRET— THAT THEY HAD CAPITULATED TO A CRIMINAL MADMAN.
BUT THIS FACT WAS NOT REPORTED TO THE POPULACE AT LARGE.
SKLODOWSKA
BAUMBURG MANSION
(14° C)

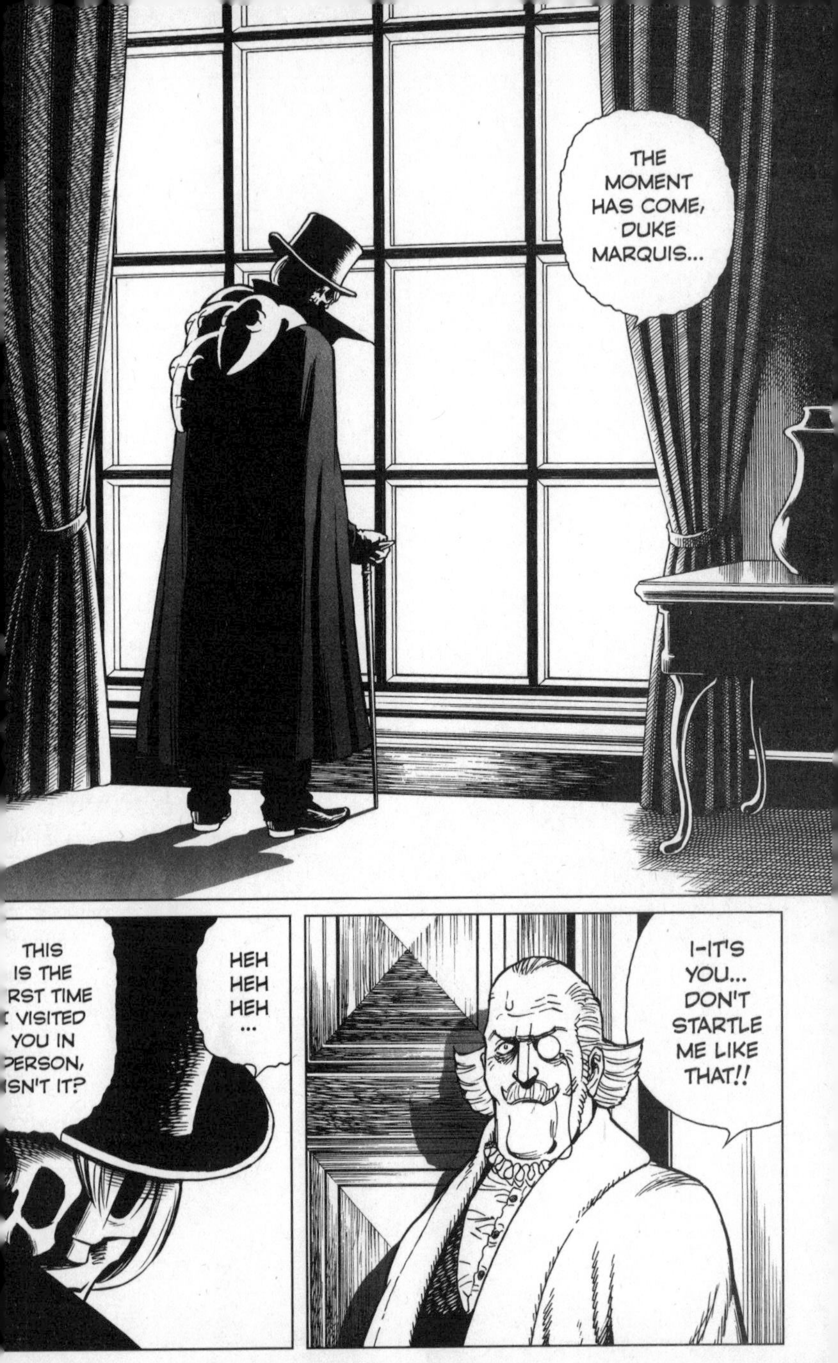
THE MOMENT HAS COME, DUKE MARQUIS...
I-IT'S YOU... DON'T STARTLE ME LIKE THAT!!
HEH HEH HEH ...
THIS IS THE RST TIME VISITED YOU IN PERSON, SN'T IT?

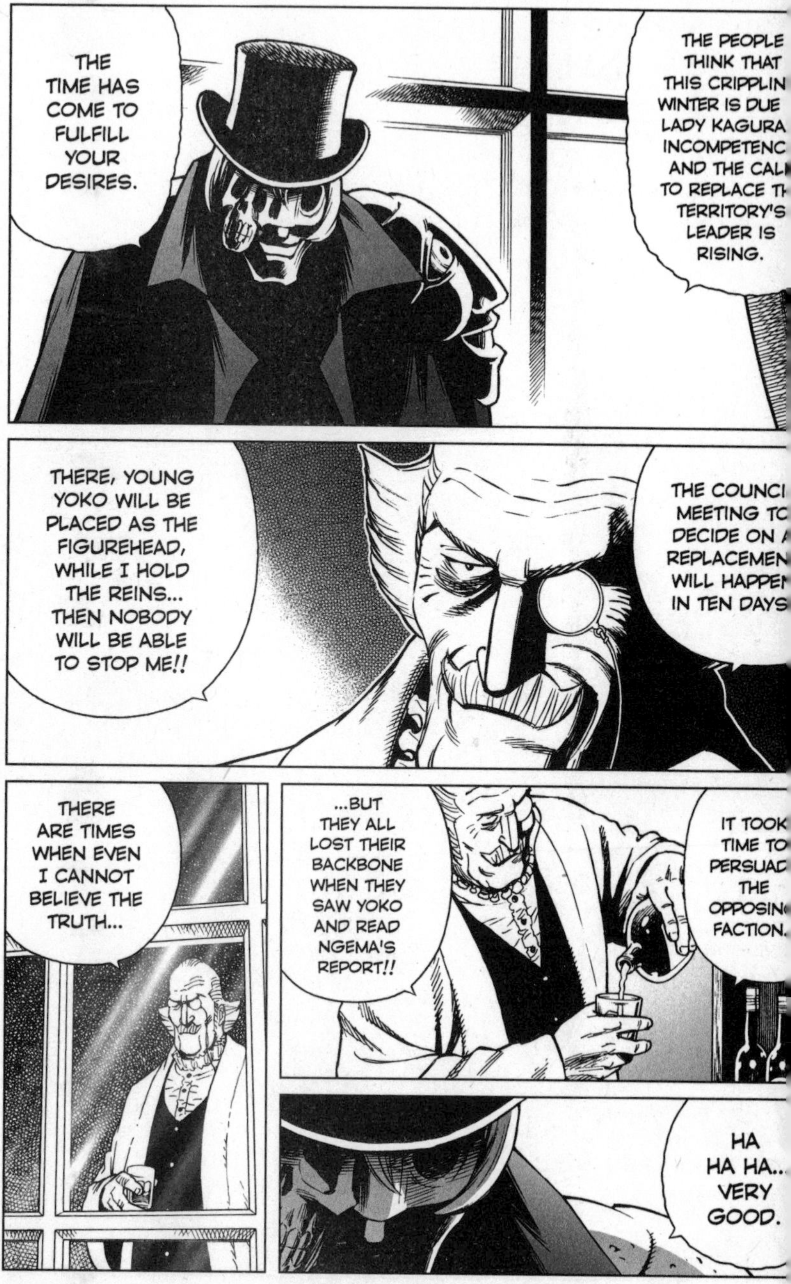
THE PEOPLE THINK THAT THIS CRIPPLIN WINTER IS DUE LADY KAGURA INCOMPETENC AND THE CAL TO REPLACE TH TERRITORY'S LEADER IS RISING.
THE TIME HAS COME TO FULFILL YOUR DESIRES.
THE COUNCI MEETING TO DECIDE ON REPLACEMEN WILL HAPPE IN TEN DAYS
THERE, YOUNG YOKO WILL BE PLACED AS THE FIGUREHEAD, WHILE I HOLD THE REINS... THEN NOBODY WILL BE ABLE TO STOP ME!!
IT TOOK TIME TO PERSUAD THE OPPOSIN FACTION.
...BUT THEY ALL LOST THEIR BACKBONE WHEN THEY SAW YOKO AND READ NGEMA'S REPORT!!
HA HA HA... VERY GOOD.
THERE ARE TIMES WHEN EVEN I CANNOT BELIEVE THE TRUTH...

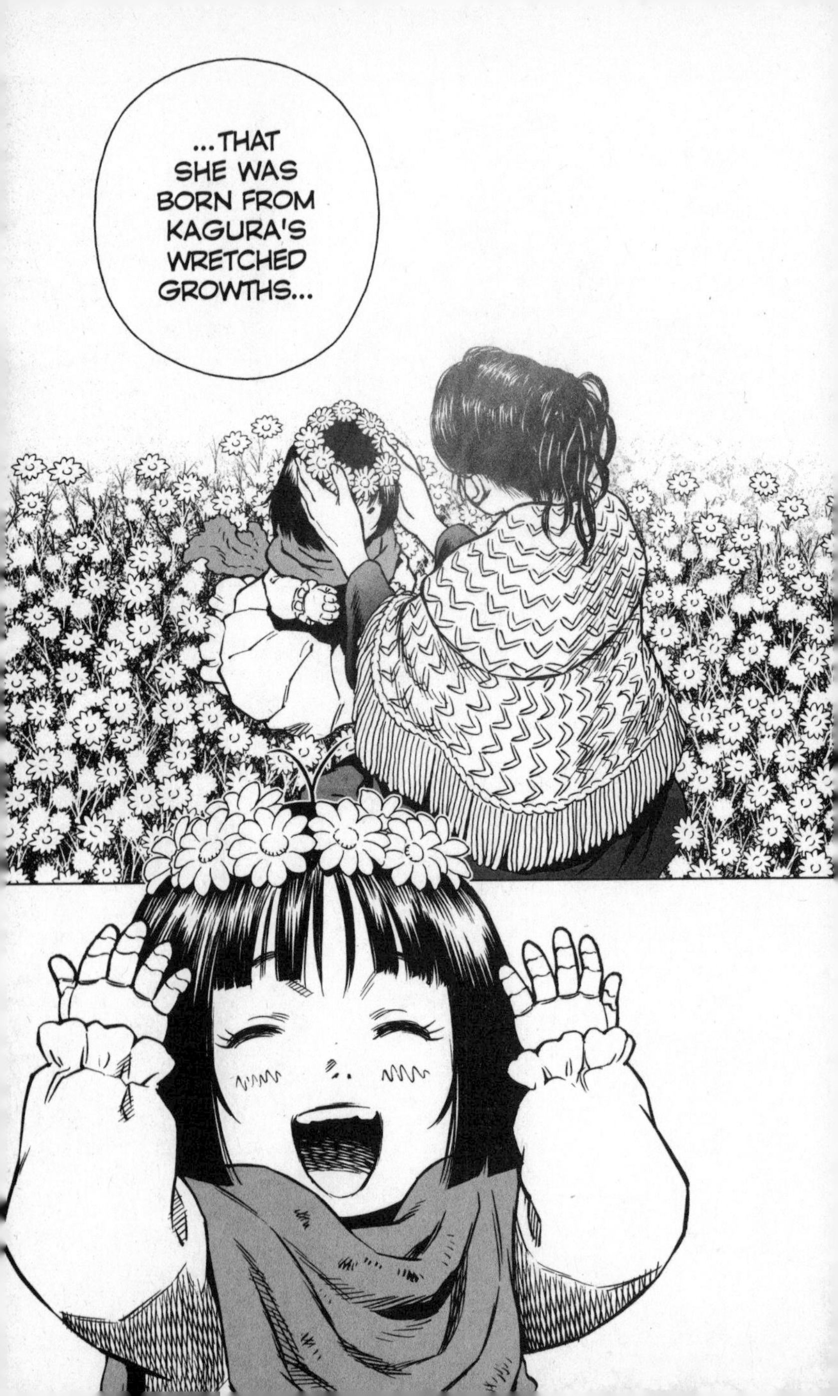
...THAT SHE WAS BORN FROM KAGURA'S WRETCHED GROWTHS...

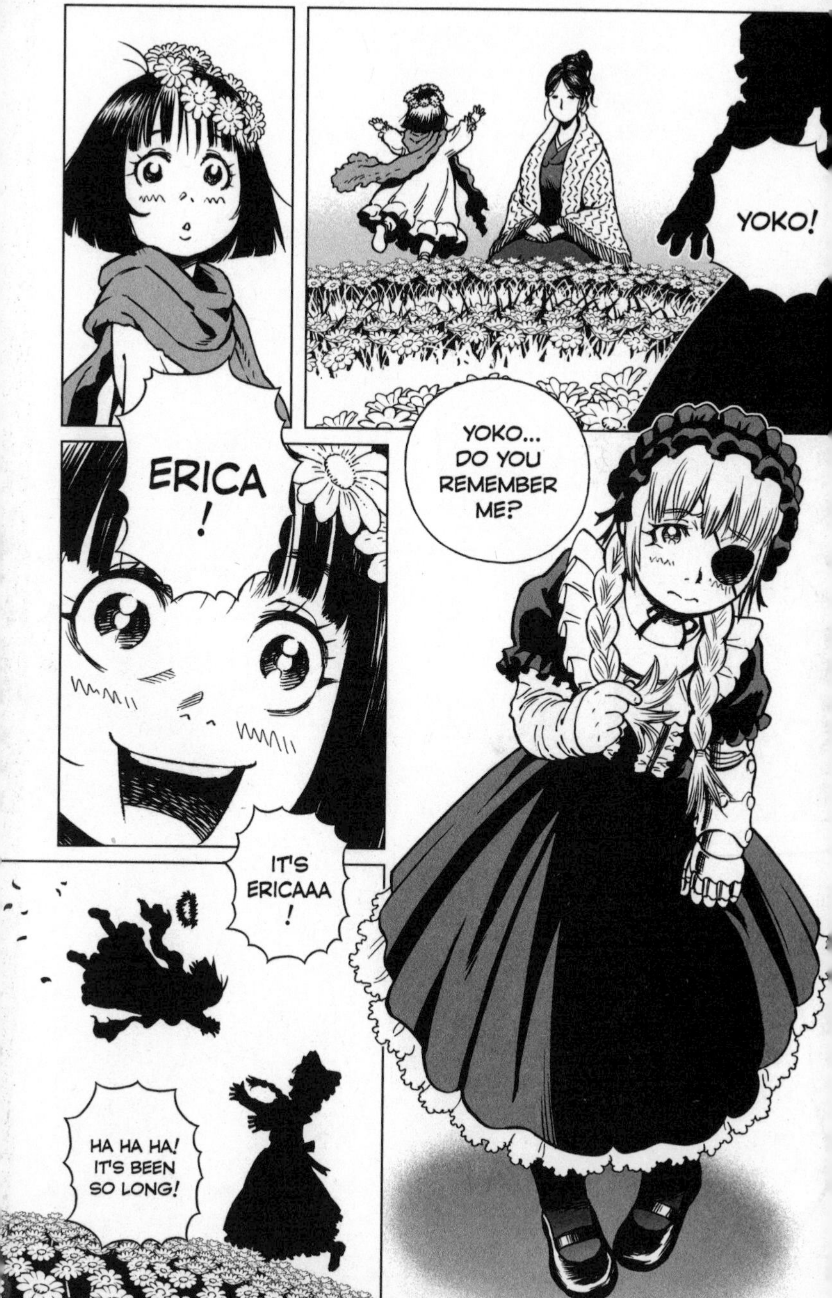
YOKO!
YOKO... DO YOU REMEMBER ME?
ERICA!
IT'S ERICAAA!
HA HA HA! IT'S BEEN SO LONG!

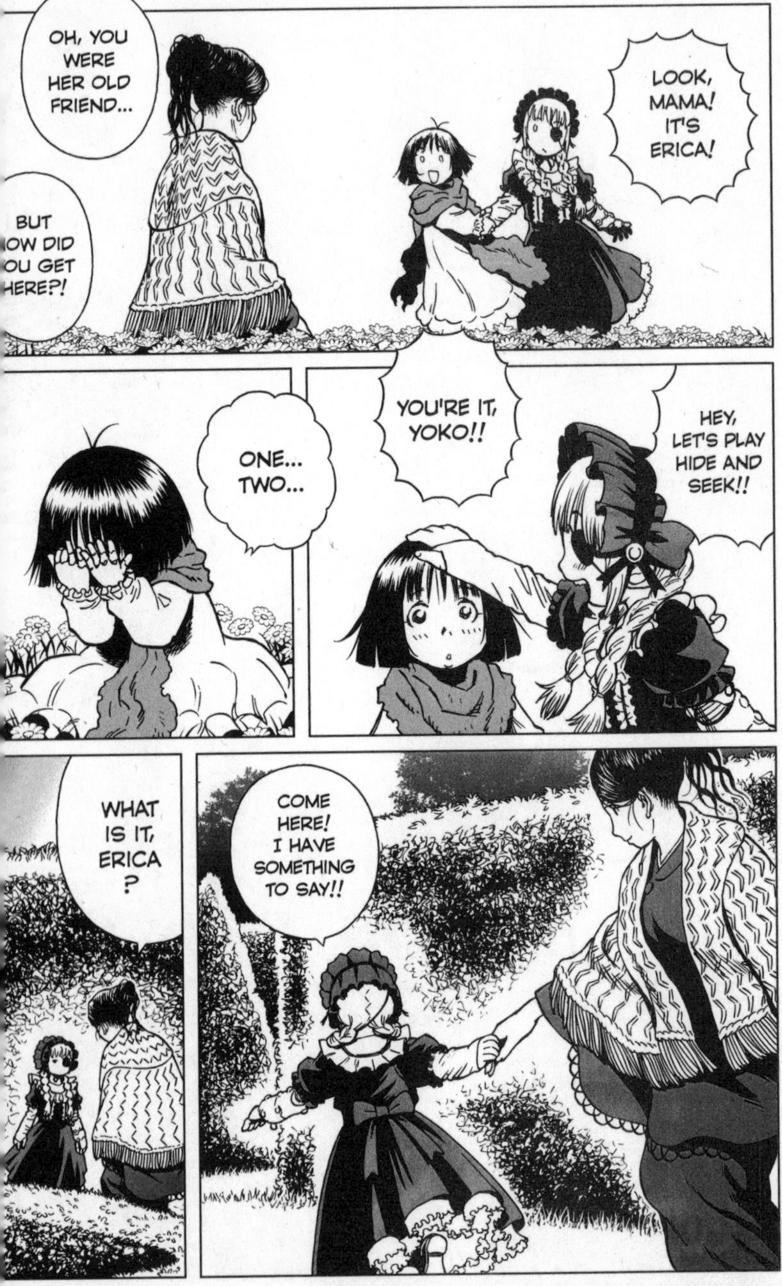

LOOK, MAMA! IT'S ERICA!
OH, YOU WERE HER OLD FRIEND...
BUT OW DID OU GET HERE?!
HEY, LET'S PLAY HIDE AND SEEK!!
YOU'RE IT, YOKO!!
ONE... TWO...
COME HERE! I HAVE SOMETHING TO SAY!!
WHAT IS IT, ERICA?

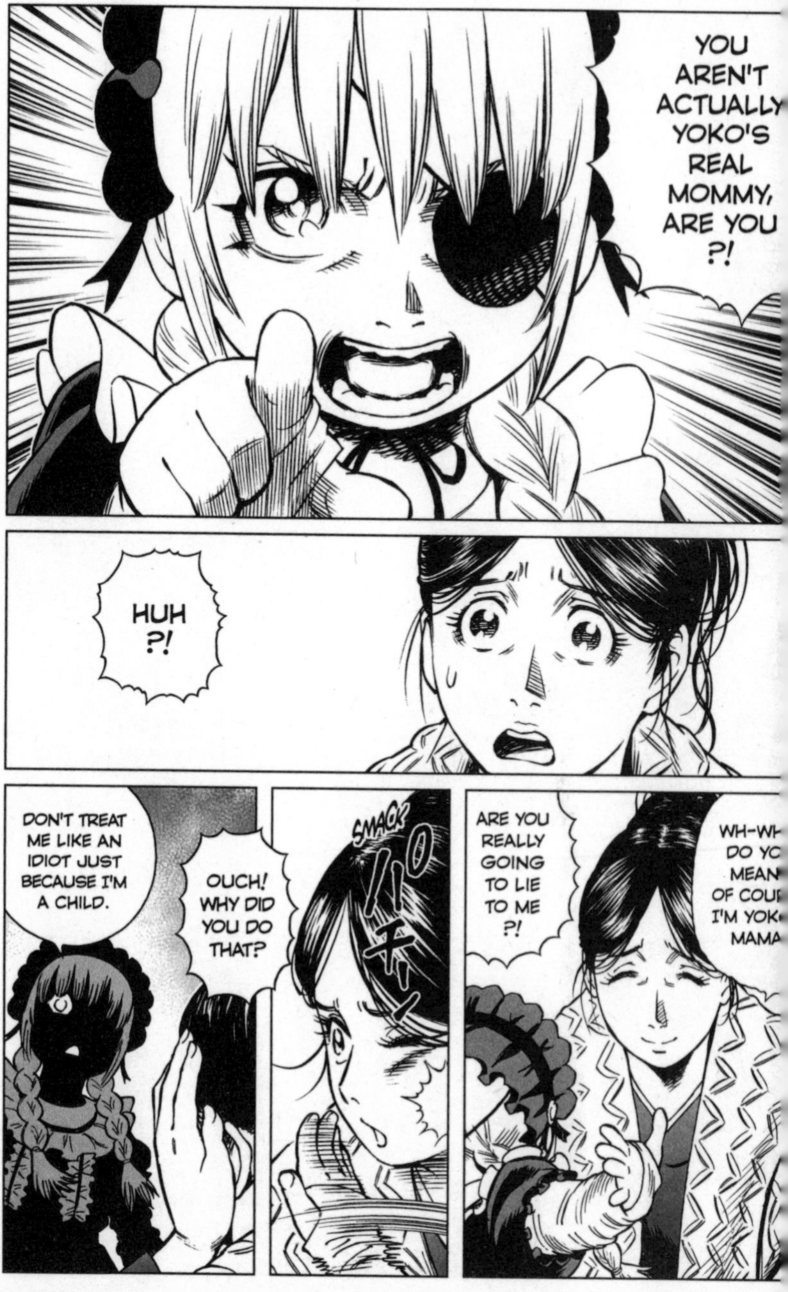

YOU AREN'T ACTUALLY YOKO'S REAL MOMMY, ARE YOU ?!
HUH ?!
WH-WH DO YO MEAN OF COUR I'M YOK MAMA
ARE YOU REALLY GOING TO LIE TO ME ?!
SMACK
OUCH! WHY DID YOU DO THAT?
DON'T TREAT ME LIKE AN IDIOT JUST BECAUSE I'M A CHILD.

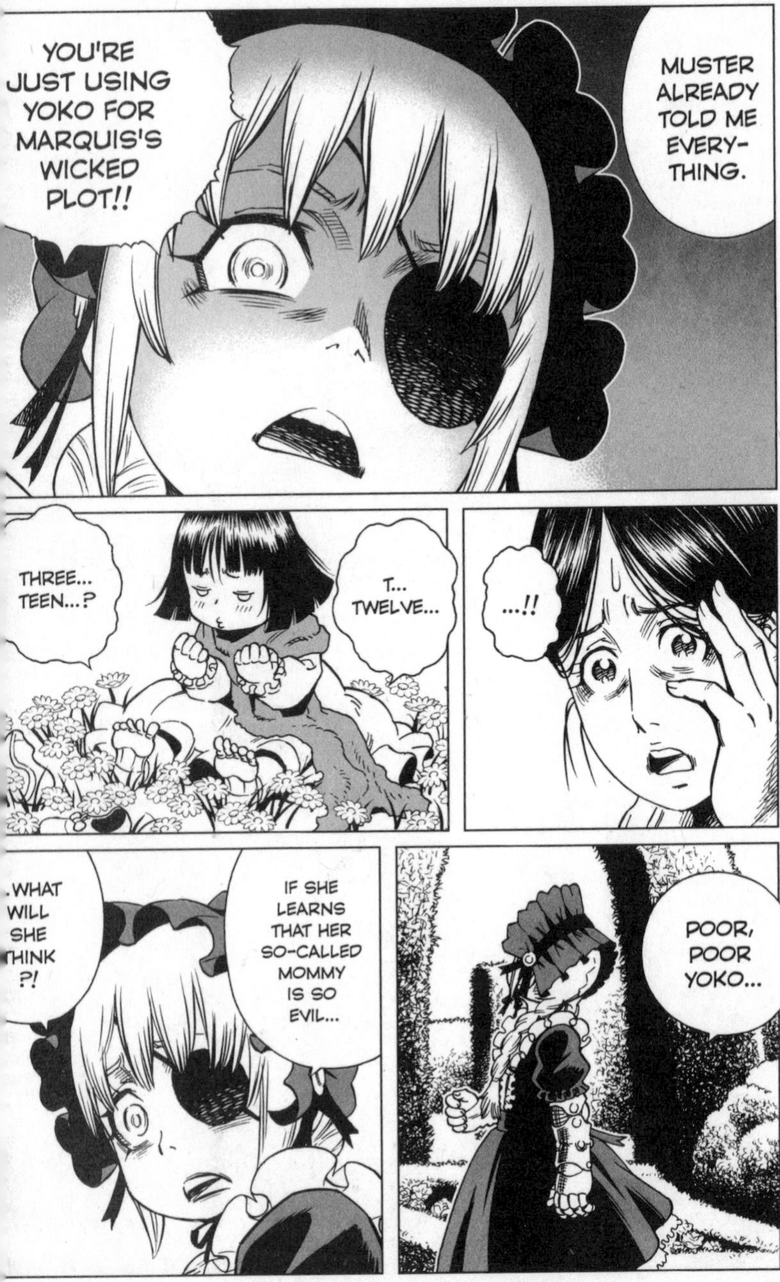
MUSTER ALREADY TOLD ME EVERY-THING.
YOU'RE JUST USING YOKO FOR MARQUIS'S WICKED PLOT!!
...!!
T... TWELVE...
THREE... TEEN...?
POOR, POOR YOKO...
IF SHE LEARNS THAT HER SO-CALLED MOMMY IS SO EVIL...
.WHAT WILL SHE THINK?!

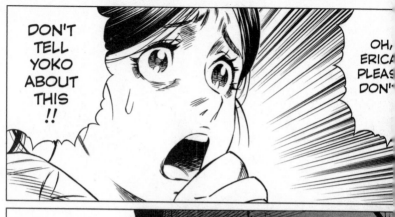

OH, ERICA PLEAS DON'
DON'T TELL YOKO ABOUT THIS !!
HEH
LORD MARQU TOOK M IN AFTER LOST M BABY..
BUT YOU MUST BELIEVE ME, I DIDN'T KNOW ABOUT ANY CONSPI- RACY!!
OH.. SO YO WANT TO KE THIS SECRE ?
WELL, I GUESS THAT DEPENDS, DOESN'T IT?
HOW ABOUT IF I KEEP YOUR SECRET, AS LONG AS YOU DO WHAT I SAY?!
F- FINE ...
IF IT'S WITHIN MY MEANS ...

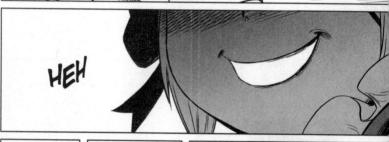

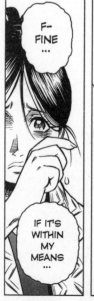

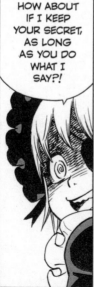

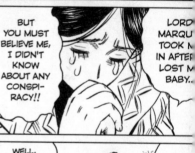

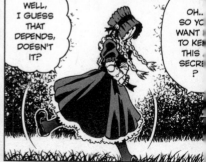

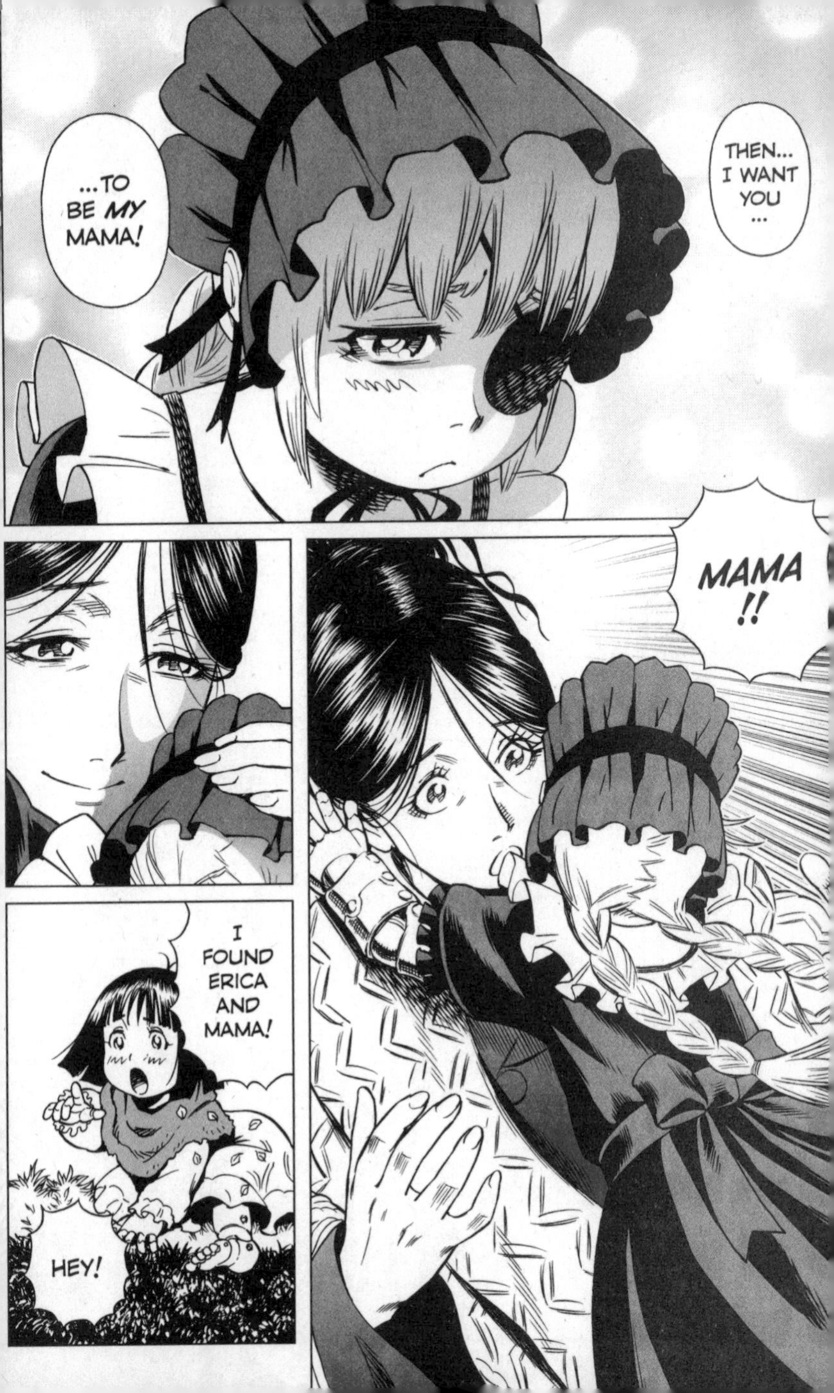
THEN... I WANT YOU ...
...TO BE *MY* MAMA!
MAMA !!
I FOUND ERICA AND MAMA!
HEY!

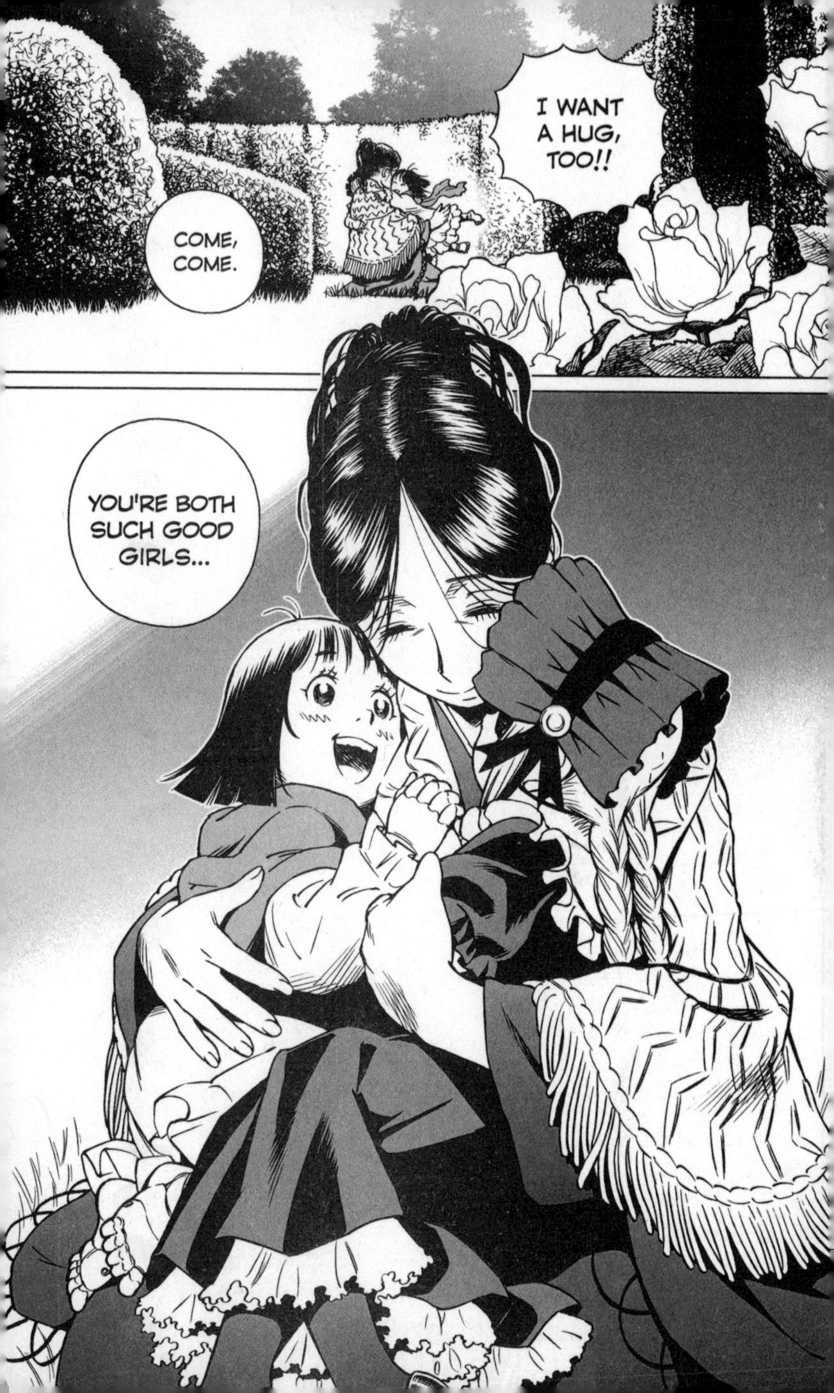
I WANT A HUG, TOO!!
COME, COME.
YOU'RE BOTH SUCH GOOD GIRLS...

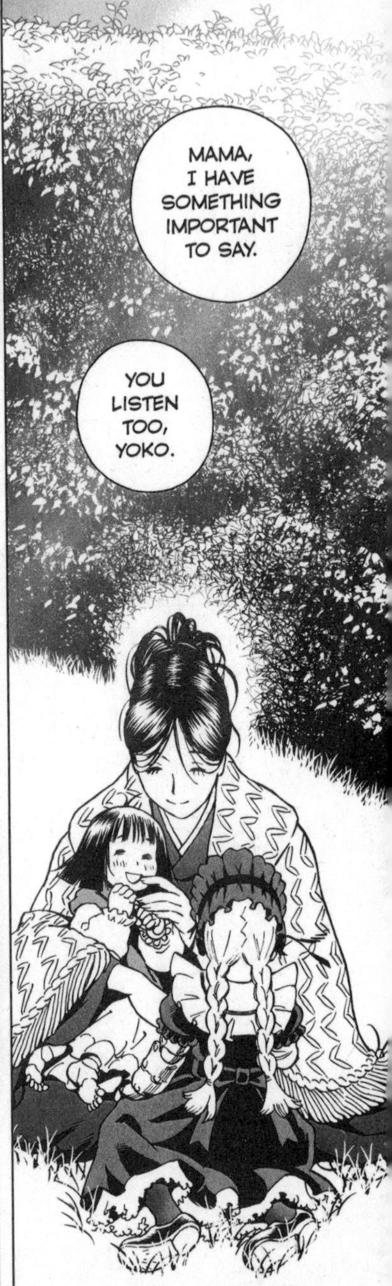
MAMA, I HAVE SOMETHING IMPORTANT TO SAY.
YOU LISTEN TOO, YOKO.

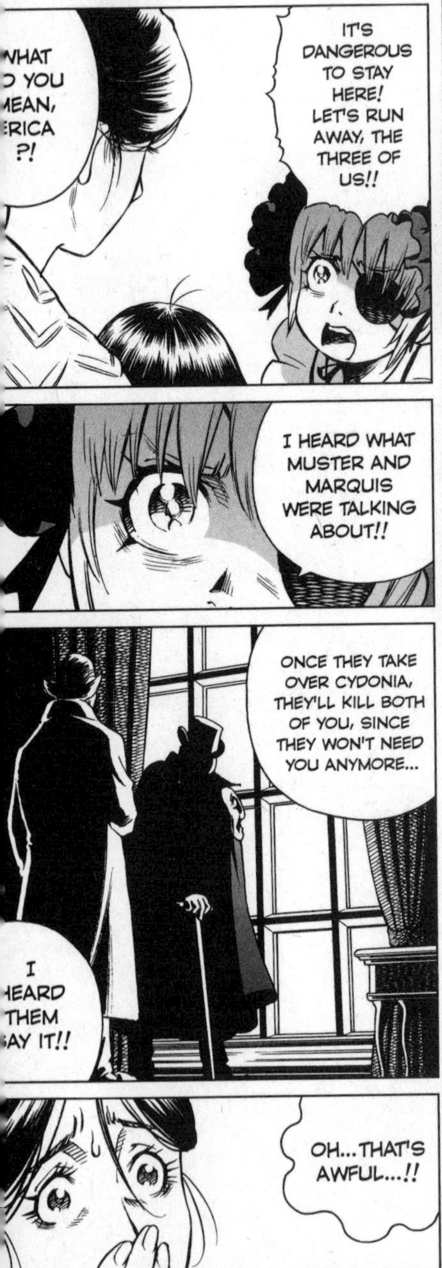
IT'S DANGEROUS TO STAY HERE! LET'S RUN AWAY, THE THREE OF US!!
WHAT D YOU MEAN, ERICA ?!
I HEARD WHAT MUSTER AND MARQUIS WERE TALKING ABOUT!!
ONCE THEY TAKE OVER CYDONIA, THEY'LL KILL BOTH OF YOU, SINCE THEY WON'T NEED YOU ANYMORE...
I HEARD THEM AY IT!!
OH...THAT'S AWFUL...!!

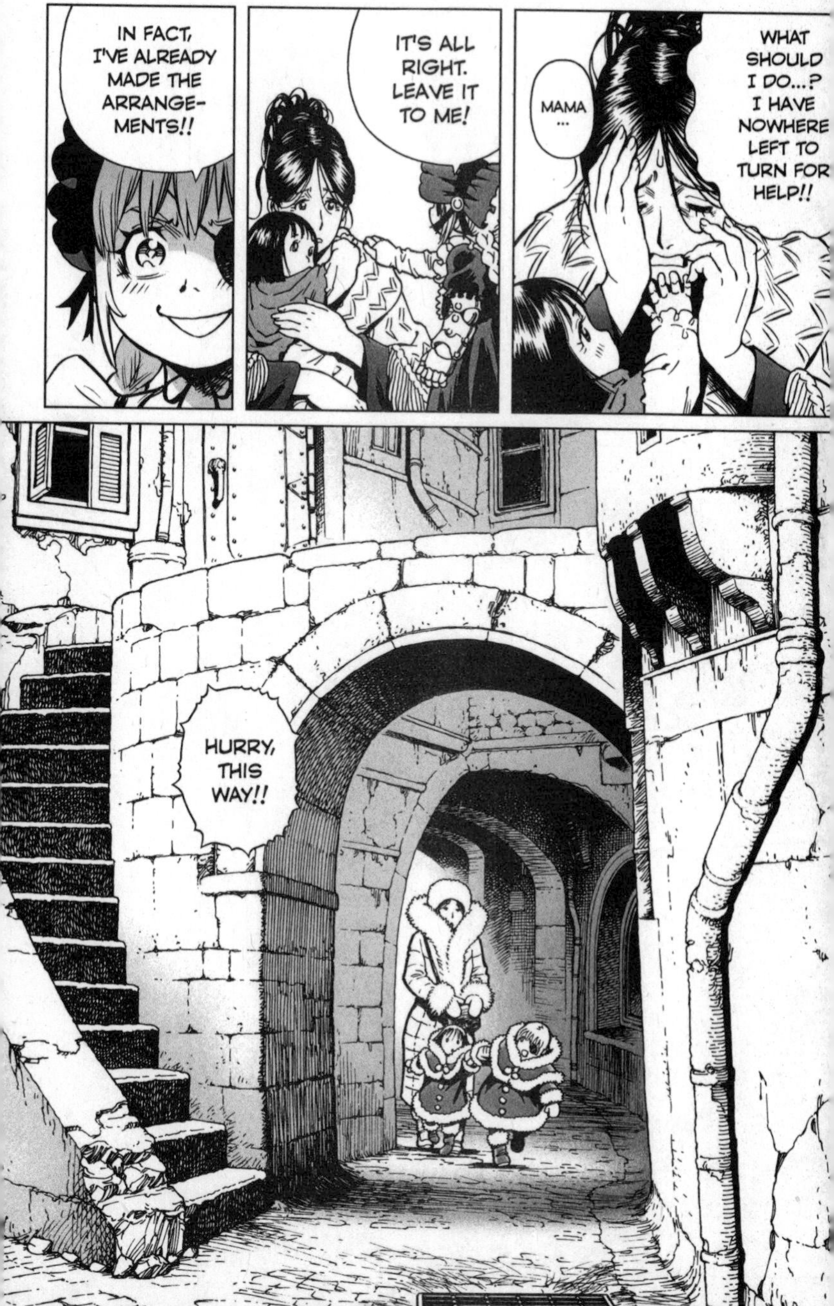
WHAT SHOULD I DO...? I HAVE NOWHERE LEFT TO TURN FOR HELP!!
MAMA ...
IT'S ALL RIGHT. LEAVE IT TO ME!
IN FACT, I'VE ALREADY MADE THE ARRANGE-MENTS!!
HURRY, THIS WAY!!

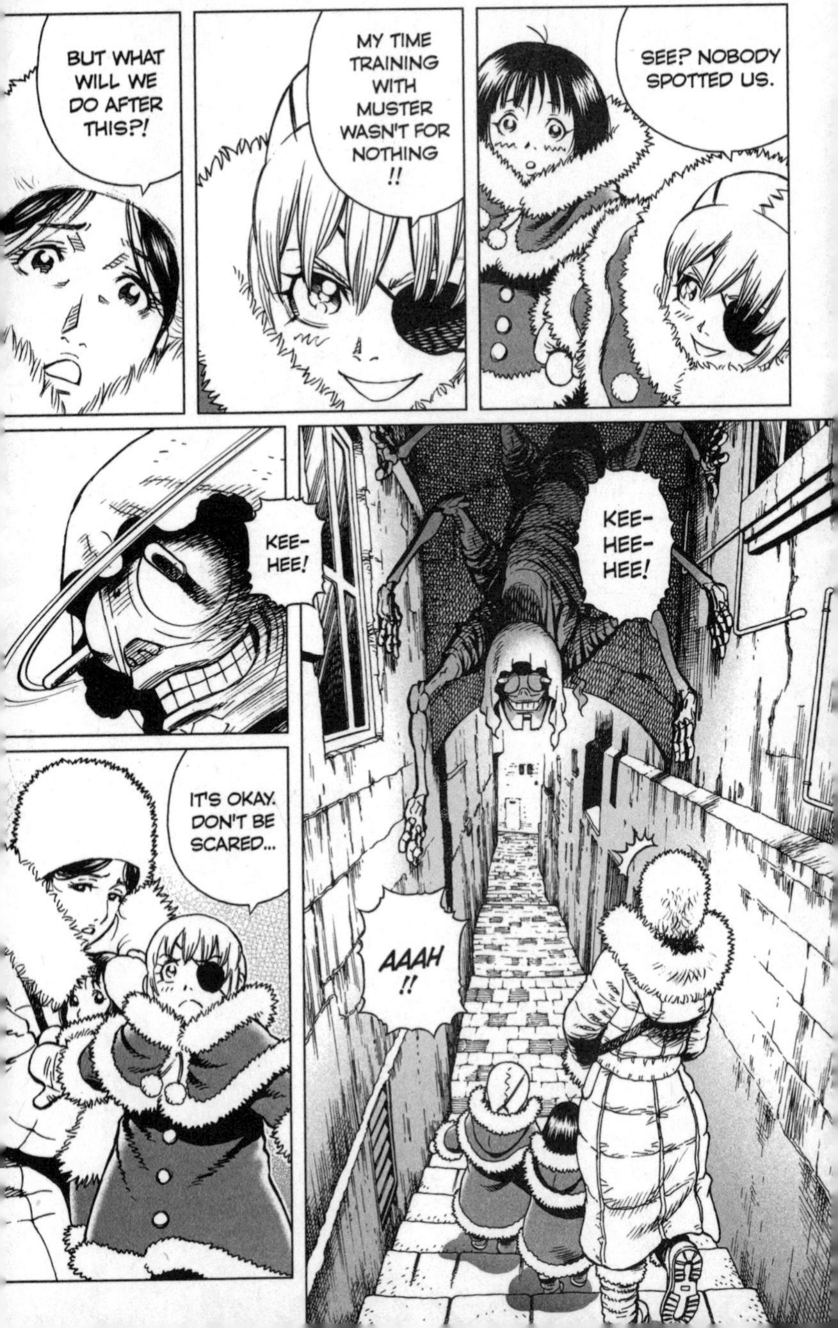
SEE? NOBODY SPOTTED US.
MY TIME TRAINING WITH MUSTER WASN'T FOR NOTHING!!
BUT WHAT WILL WE DO AFTER THIS?!
KEE-HEE-HEE!
AAAH!!
KEE-HEE!
IT'S OKAY. DON'T BE SCARED...

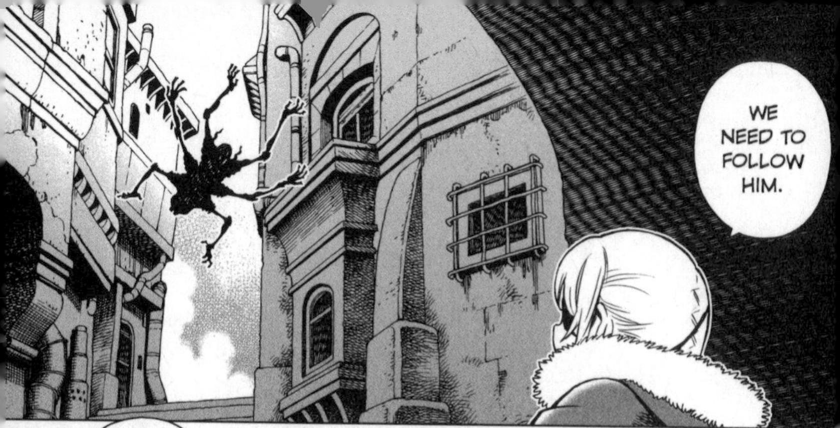
WE NEED TO FOLLOW HIM.
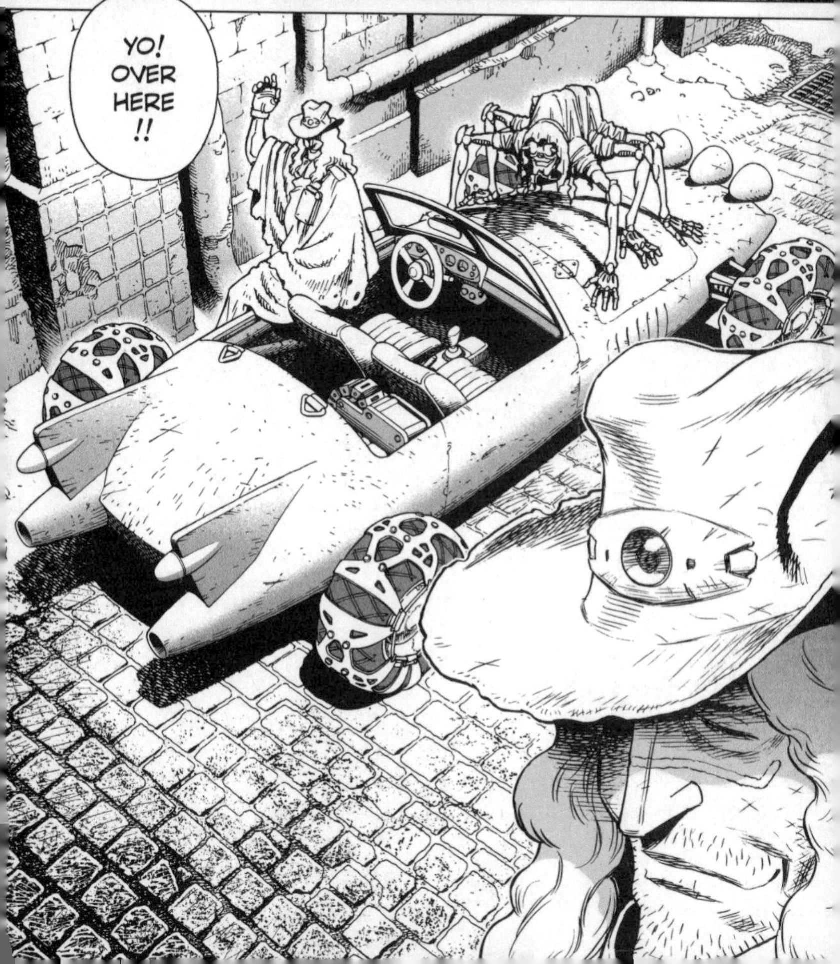
YO! OVER HERE !!

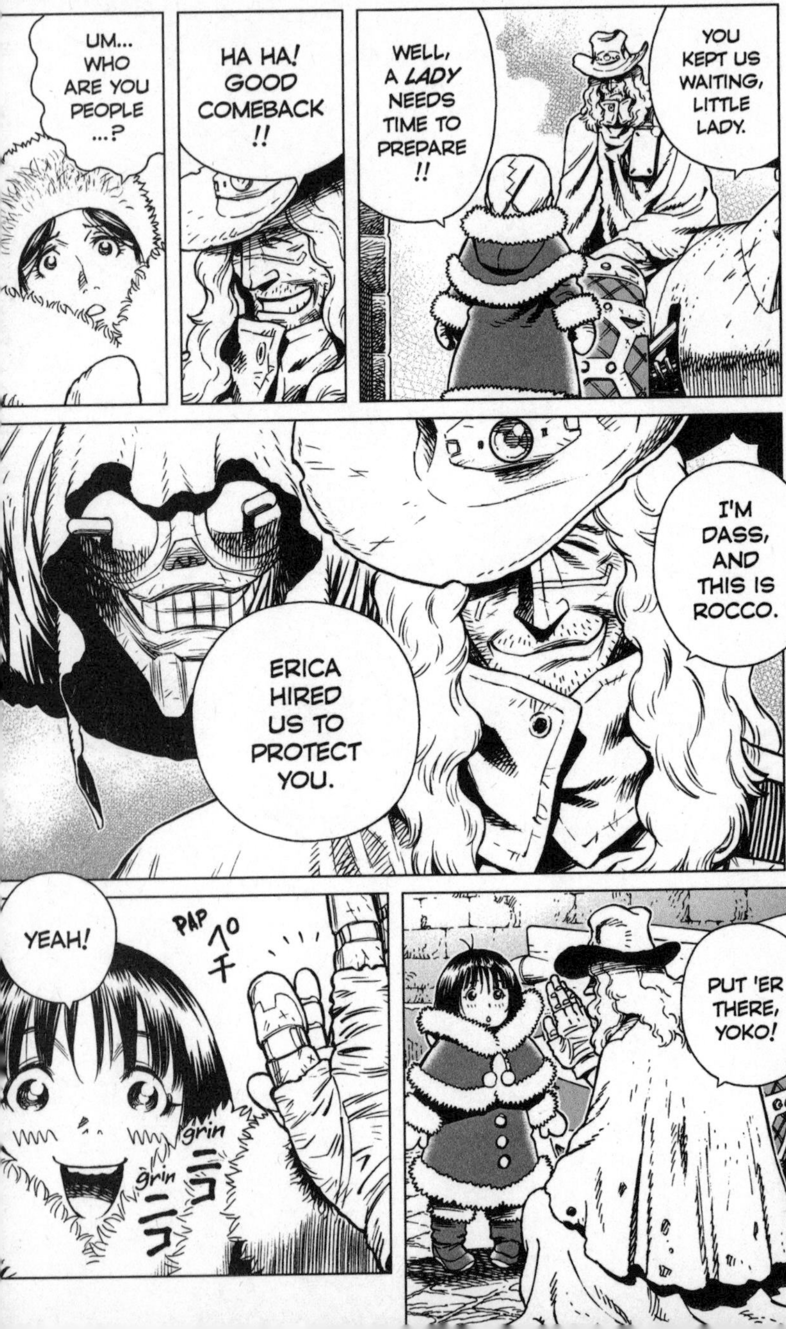
YOU KEPT US WAITING, LITTLE LADY.
WELL, A LADY NEEDS TIME TO PREPARE!!
HA HA! GOOD COMEBACK!!
UM... WHO ARE YOU PEOPLE...?
I'M DASS, AND THIS IS ROCCO.
ERICA HIRED US TO PROTECT YOU.
PUT 'ER THERE, YOKO!
PAP
YEAH!
grin
grin

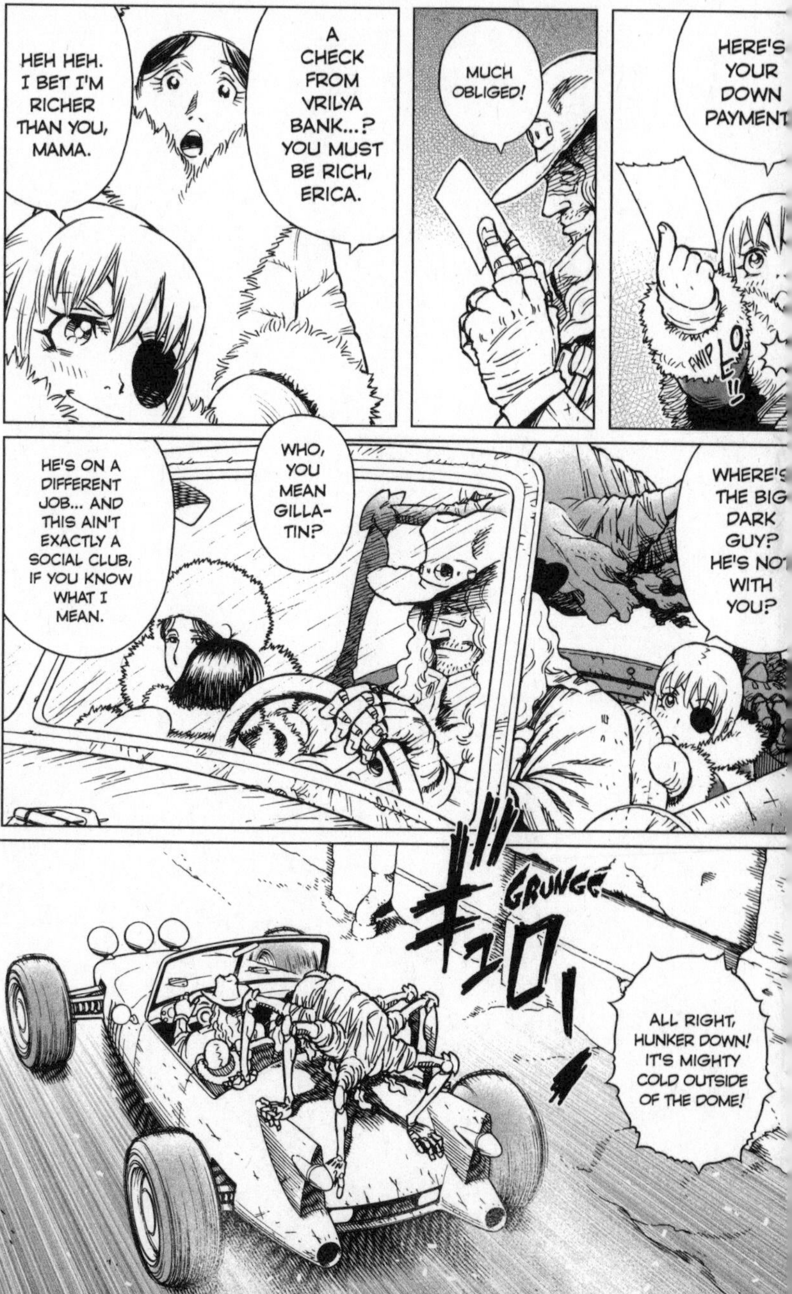
HERE'S YOUR DOWN PAYMENT
FWIP
MUCH OBLIGED!
A CHECK FROM VRILYA BANK...? YOU MUST BE RICH, ERICA.
HEH HEH. I BET I'M RICHER THAN YOU, MAMA.
WHERE'S THE BIG DARK GUY? HE'S NOT WITH YOU?
WHO, YOU MEAN GILLA-TIN?
HE'S ON A DIFFERENT JOB... AND THIS AIN'T EXACTLY A SOCIAL CLUB, IF YOU KNOW WHAT I MEAN.
GRUNGE
ALL RIGHT, HUNKER DOWN! IT'S MIGHTY COLD OUTSIDE OF THE DOME!

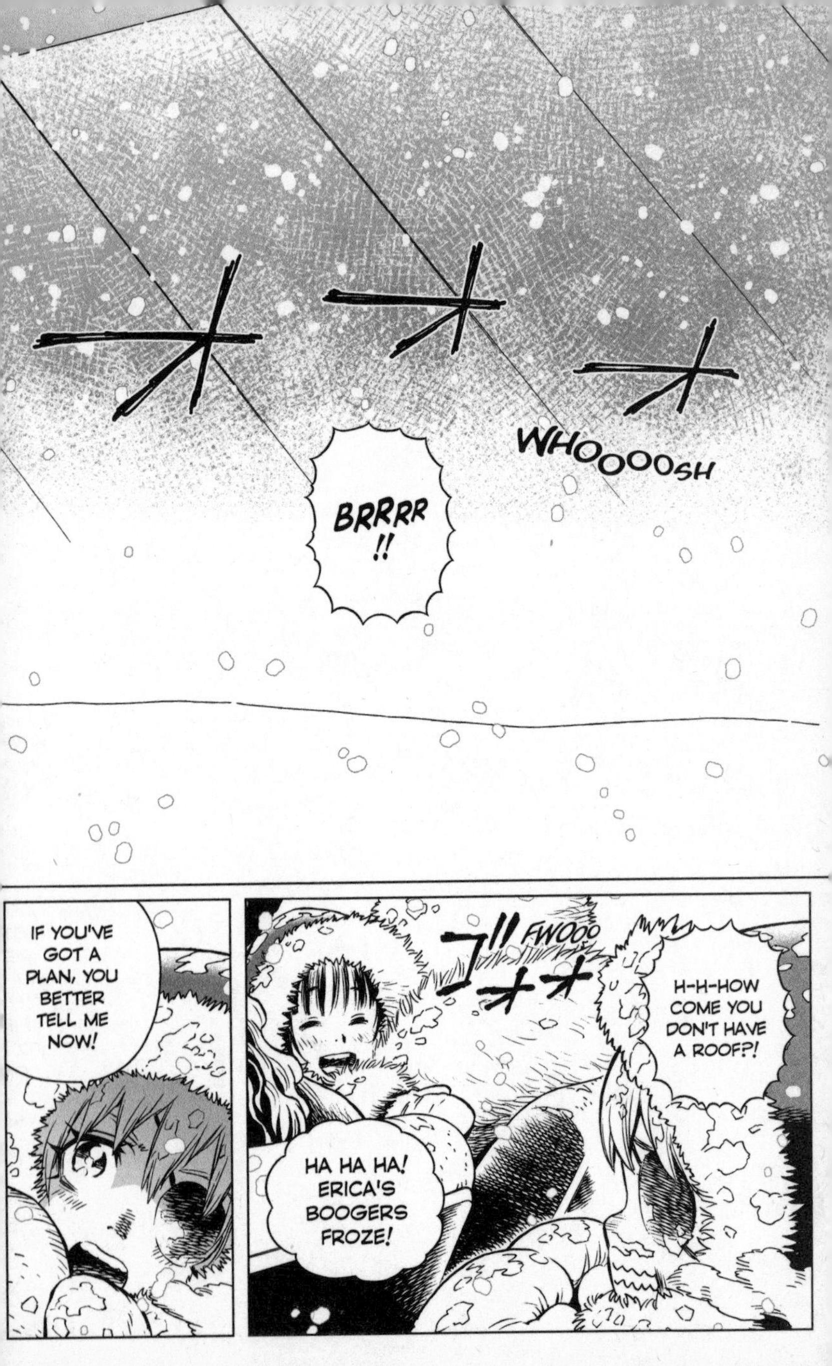
WHOOOOSH
BRRRR !!
H-H-HOW COME YOU DON'T HAVE A ROOF?!
FWOOO
HA HA HA! ERICA'S BOOGERS FROZE!
IF YOU'VE GOT A PLAN, YOU BETTER TELL ME NOW!

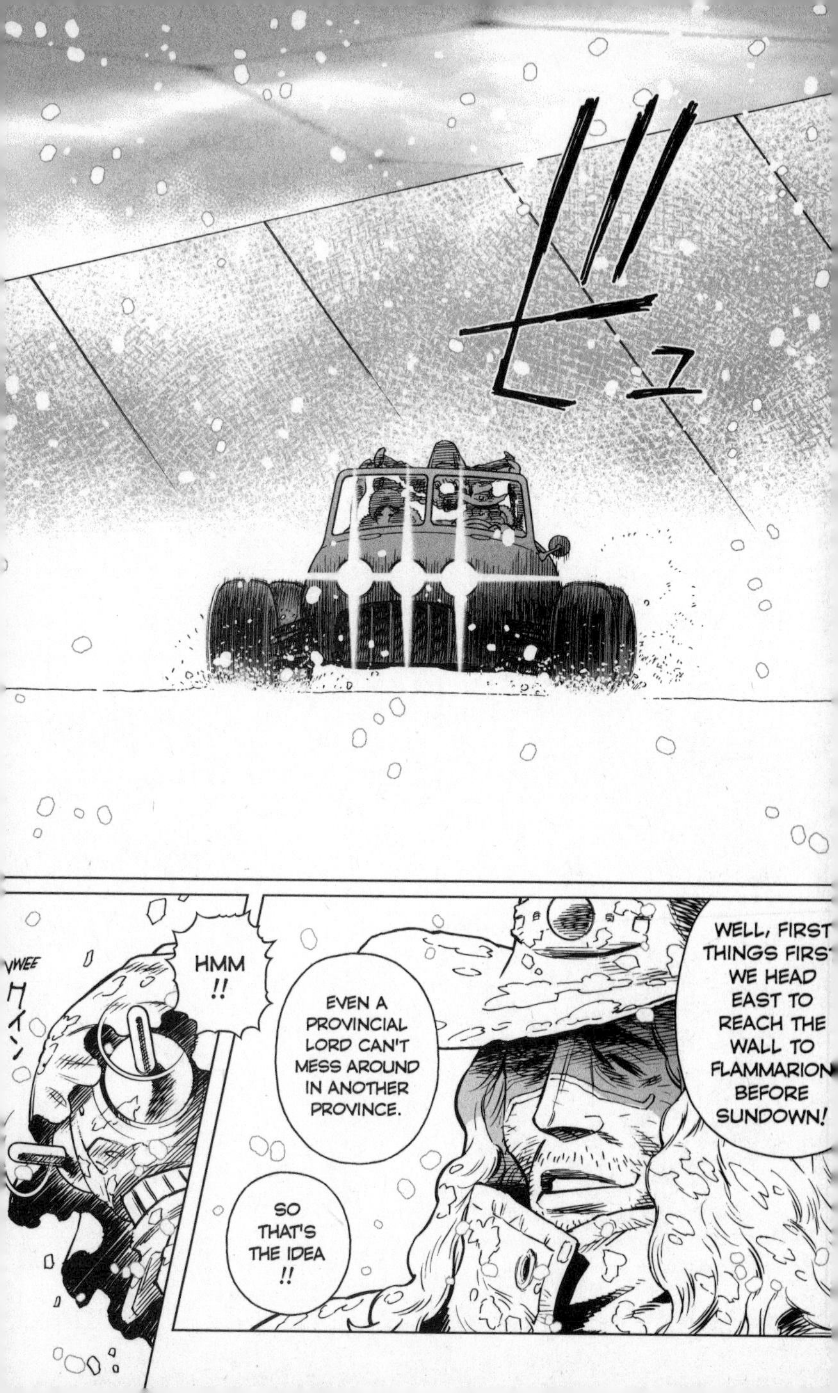

ビュ
WELL, FIRST THINGS FIRST WE HEAD EAST TO REACH THE WALL TO FLAMMARION BEFORE SUNDOWN!
EVEN A PROVINCIAL LORD CAN'T MESS AROUND IN ANOTHER PROVINCE.
SO THAT'S THE IDEA!!
HMM!!
VWEE
ウイン

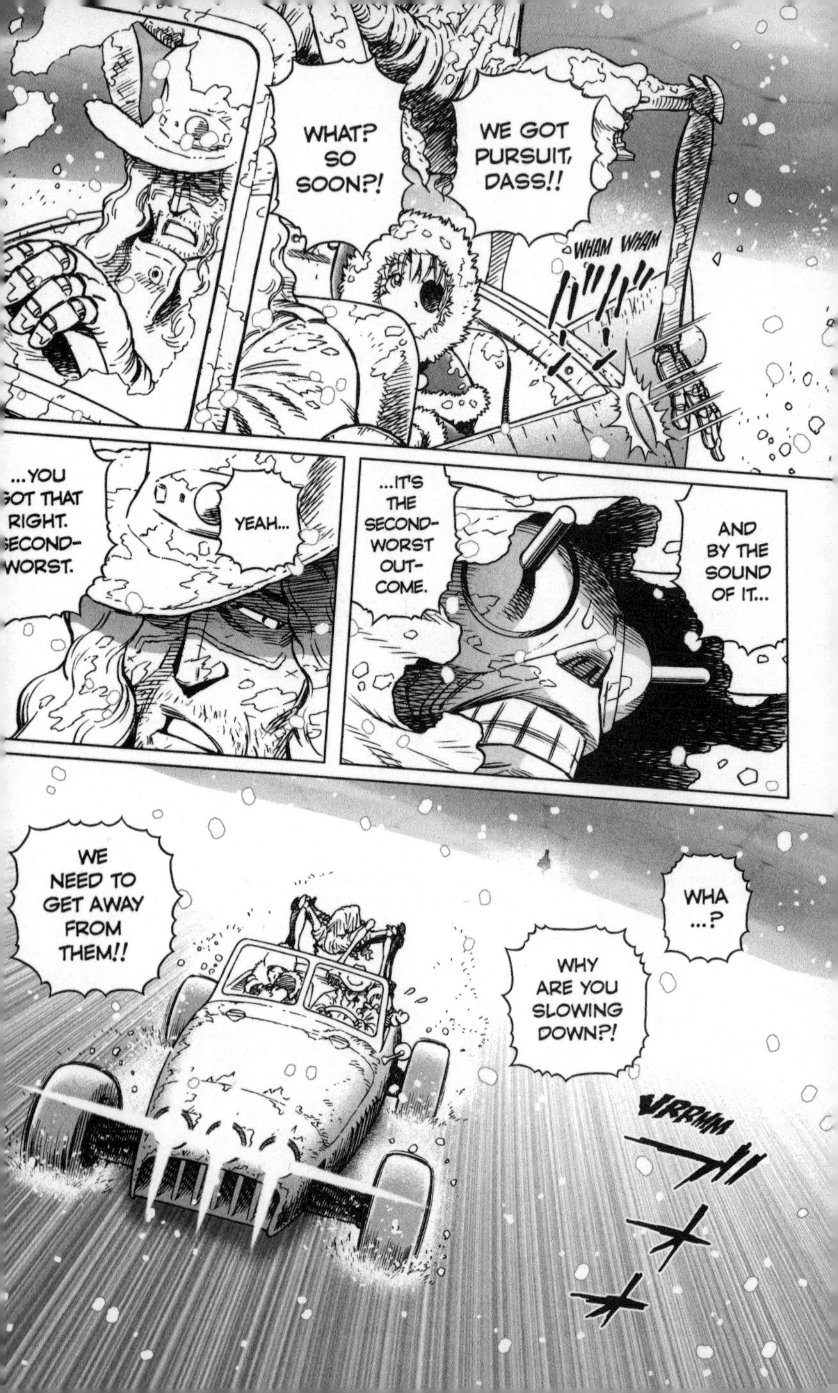
WE GOT PURSUIT, DASS!!
WHAT? SO SOON?!
WHAM WHAM
AND BY THE SOUND OF IT...
...IT'S THE SECOND-WORST OUT-COME.
YEAH...
...YOU GOT THAT RIGHT. SECOND-WORST.
WHA...?
WHY ARE YOU SLOWING DOWN?!
WE NEED TO GET AWAY FROM THEM!!
VRRMM

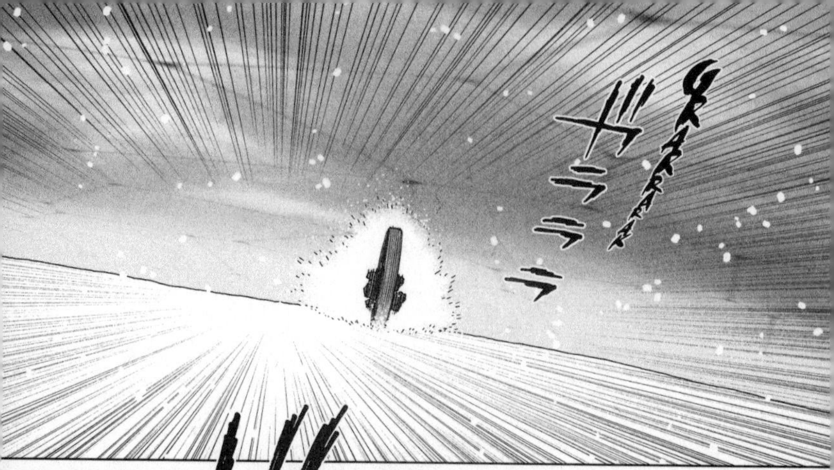
ザラララ
GRARARARA
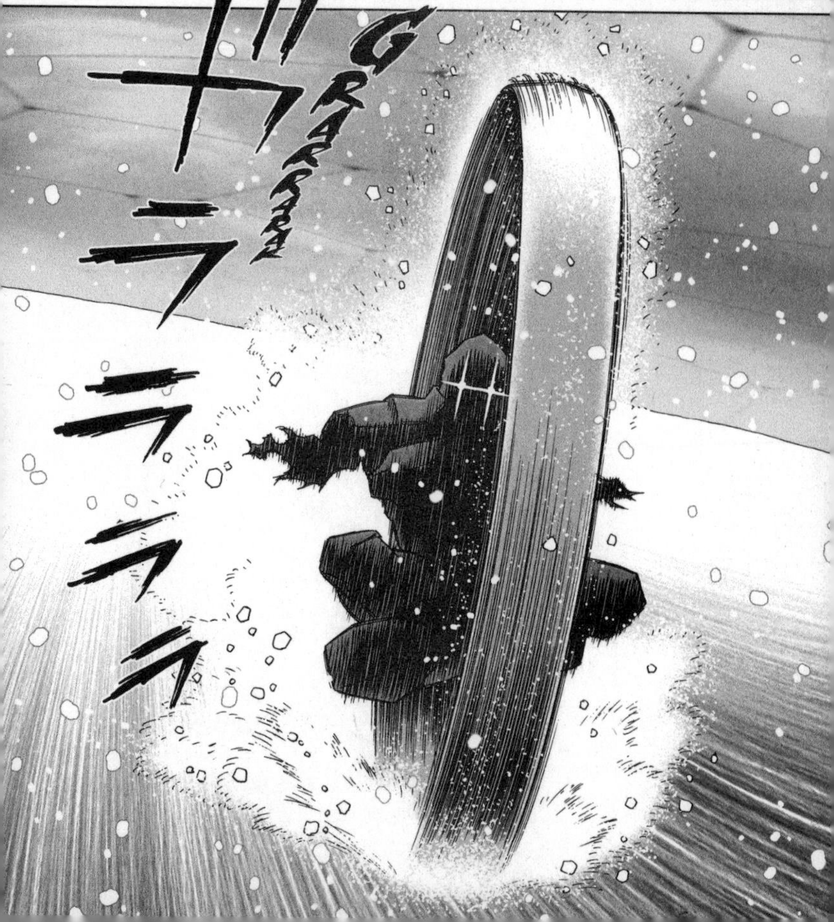
ザララララ
GRARARARA

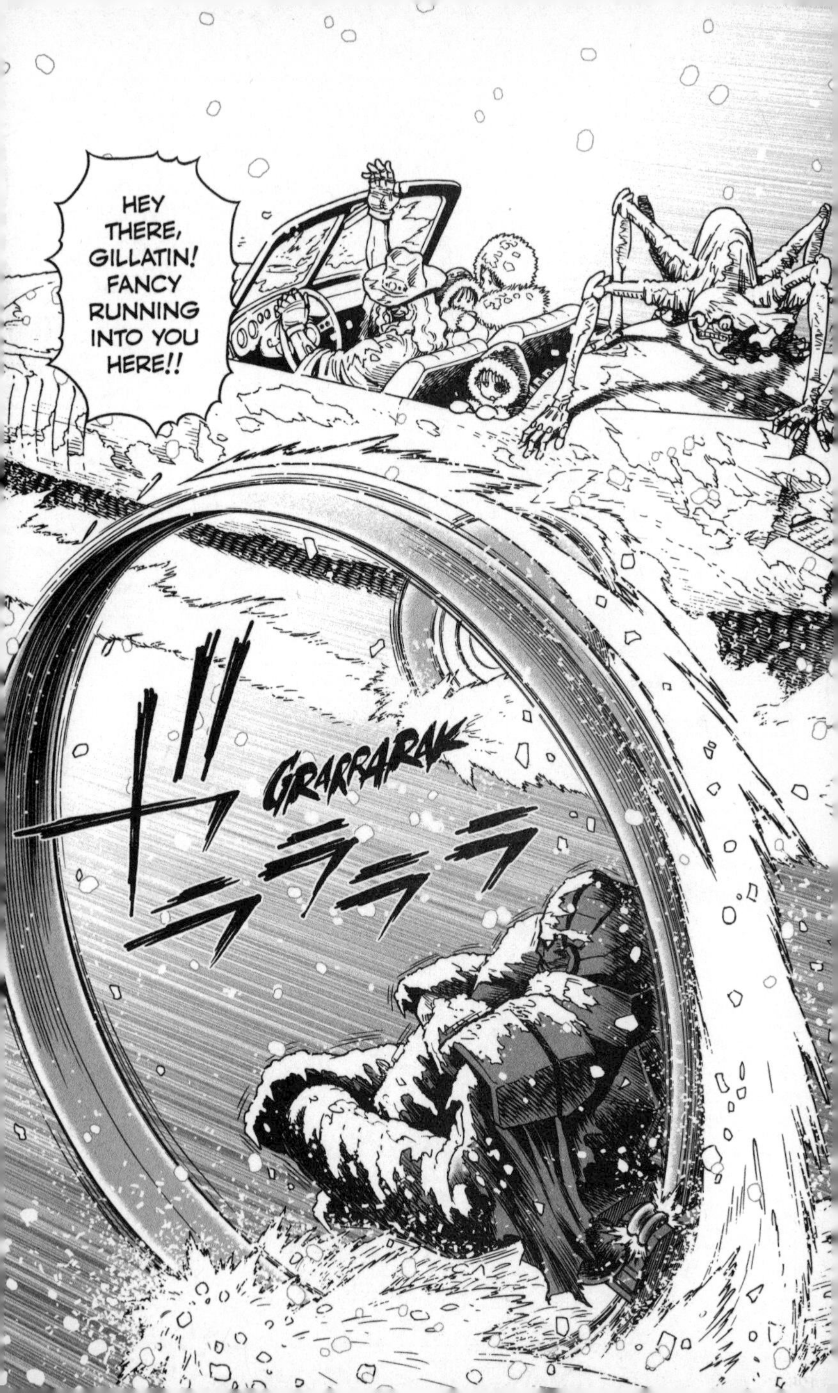
HEY THERE, GILLATIN! FANCY RUNNING INTO YOU HERE!!
GRARRARAK
ザララララ

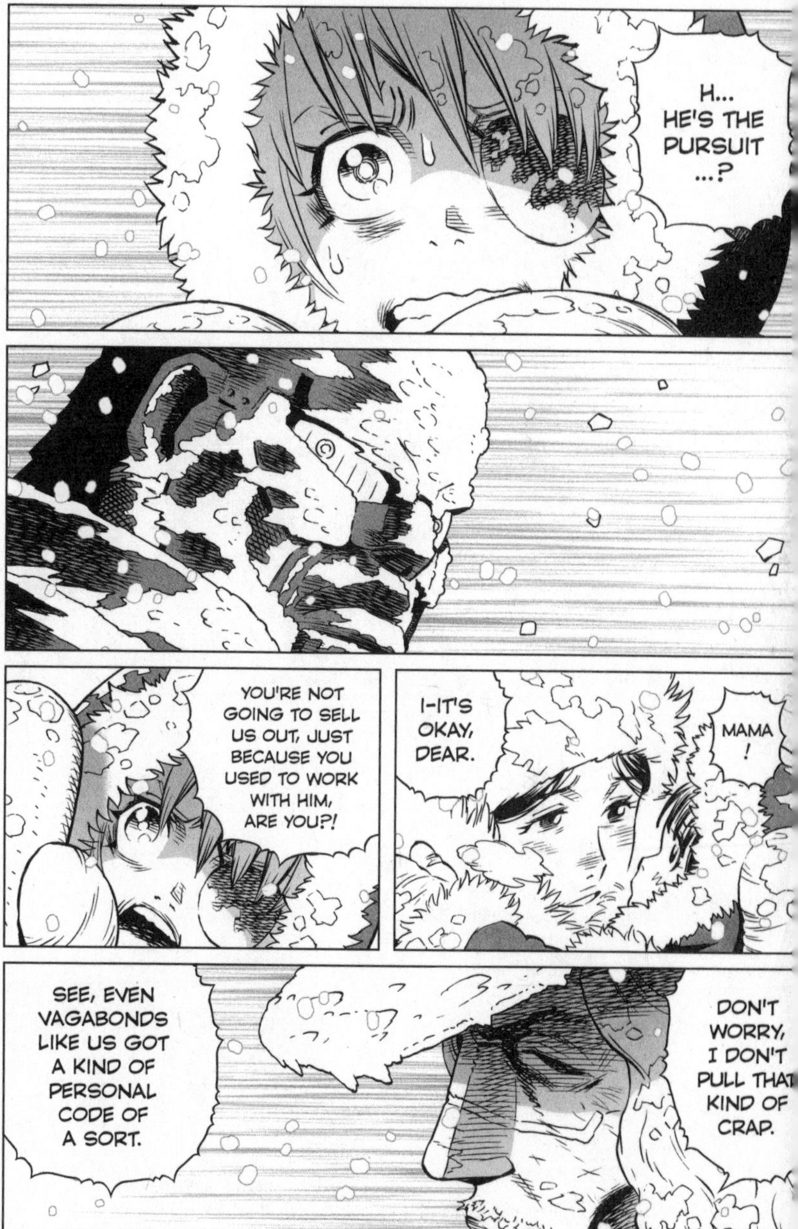
H... HE'S THE PURSUIT ...?
MAMA !
I-IT'S OKAY, DEAR.
YOU'RE NOT GOING TO SELL US OUT, JUST BECAUSE YOU USED TO WORK WITH HIM, ARE YOU?!
DON'T WORRY, I DON'T PULL THAT KIND OF CRAP.
SEE, EVEN VAGABONDS LIKE US GOT A KIND OF PERSONAL CODE OF A SORT.

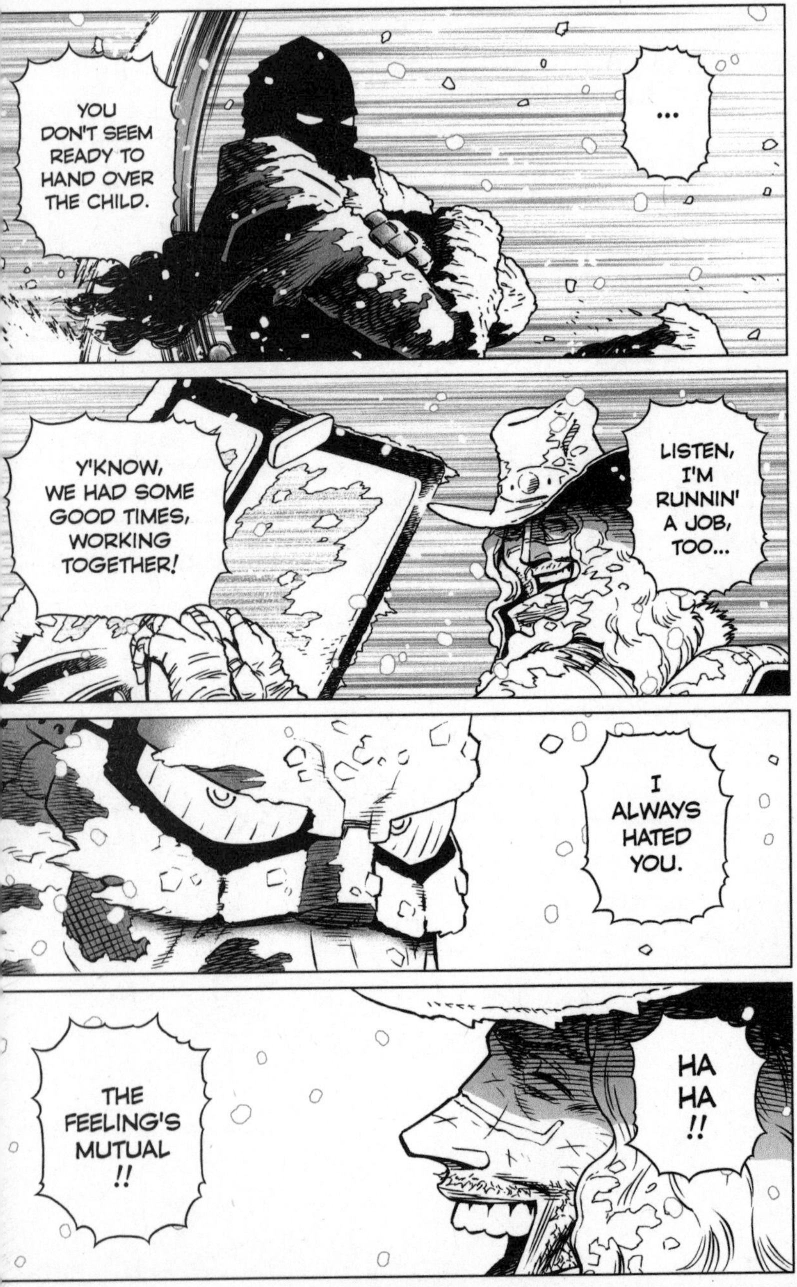
...
YOU DON'T SEEM READY TO HAND OVER THE CHILD.
LISTEN, I'M RUNNIN' A JOB, TOO...
Y'KNOW, WE HAD SOME GOOD TIMES, WORKING TOGETHER!
I ALWAYS HATED YOU.
HA HA!!
THE FEELING'S MUTUAL!!

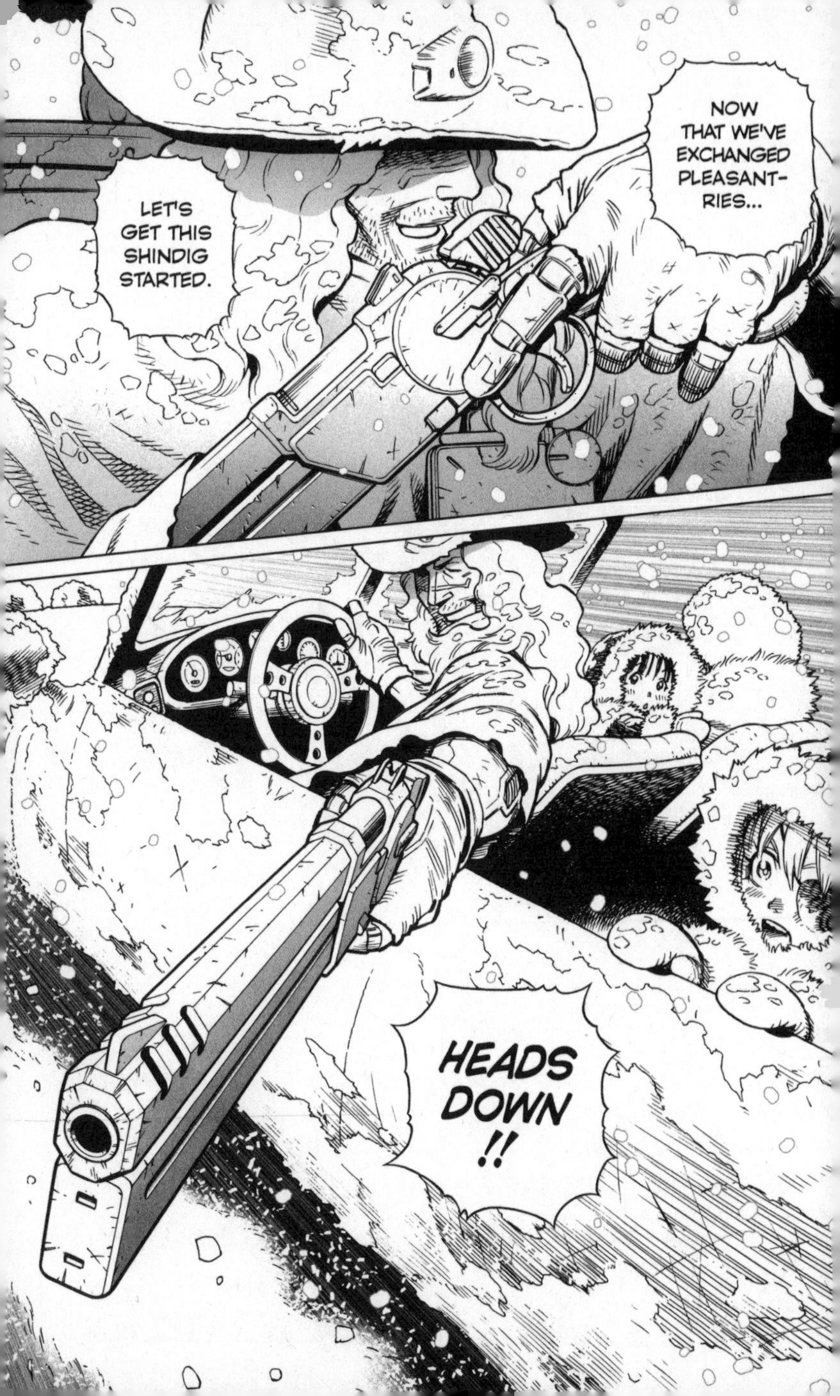
NOW THAT WE'VE EXCHANGED PLEASANT-RIES...
LET'S GET THIS SHINDIG STARTED.
HEADS DOWN!!

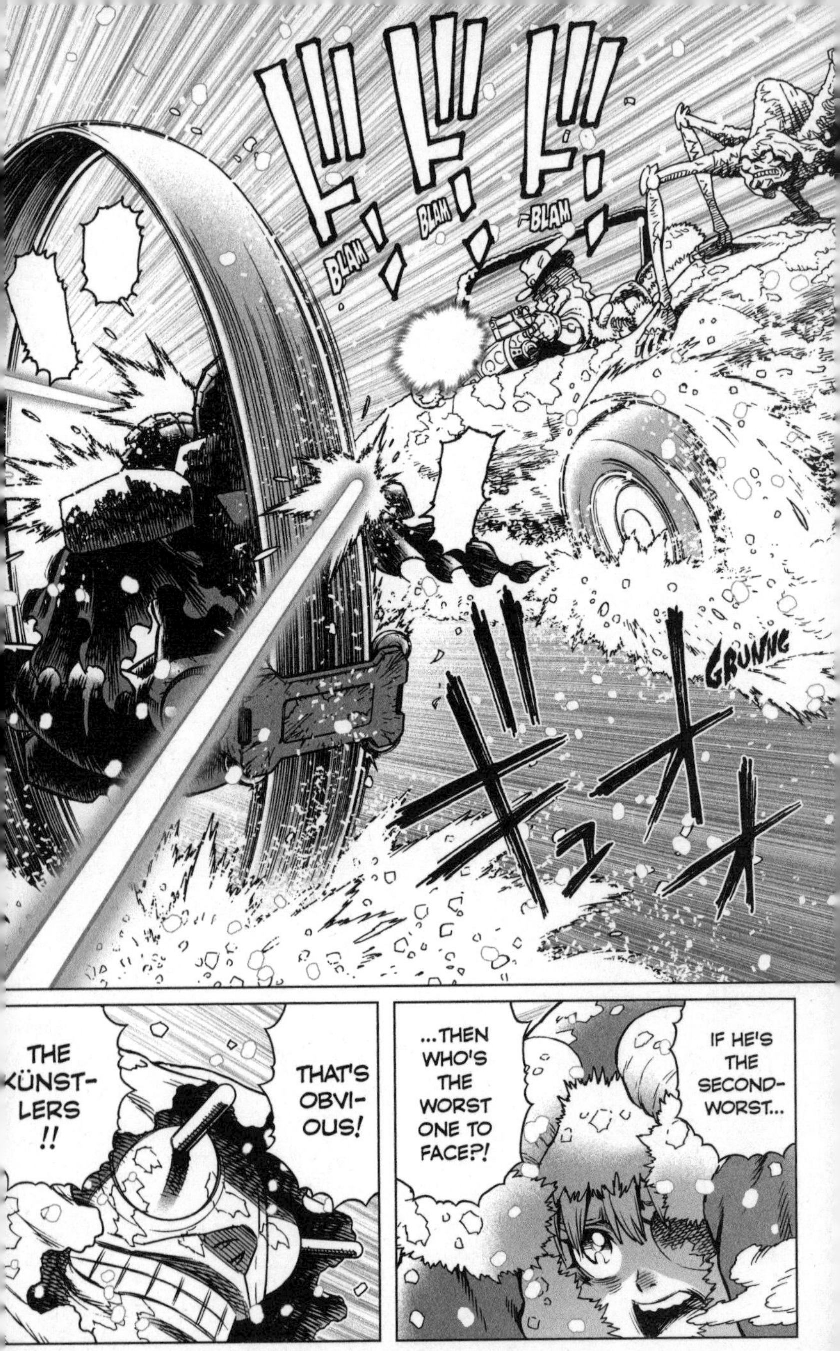
BLAM
BLAM
-BLAM
GRUNNG
IF HE'S THE SECOND-WORST...
...THEN WHO'S THE WORST ONE TO FACE?!
THAT'S OBVI-OUS!
THE KÜNST-LERS!!

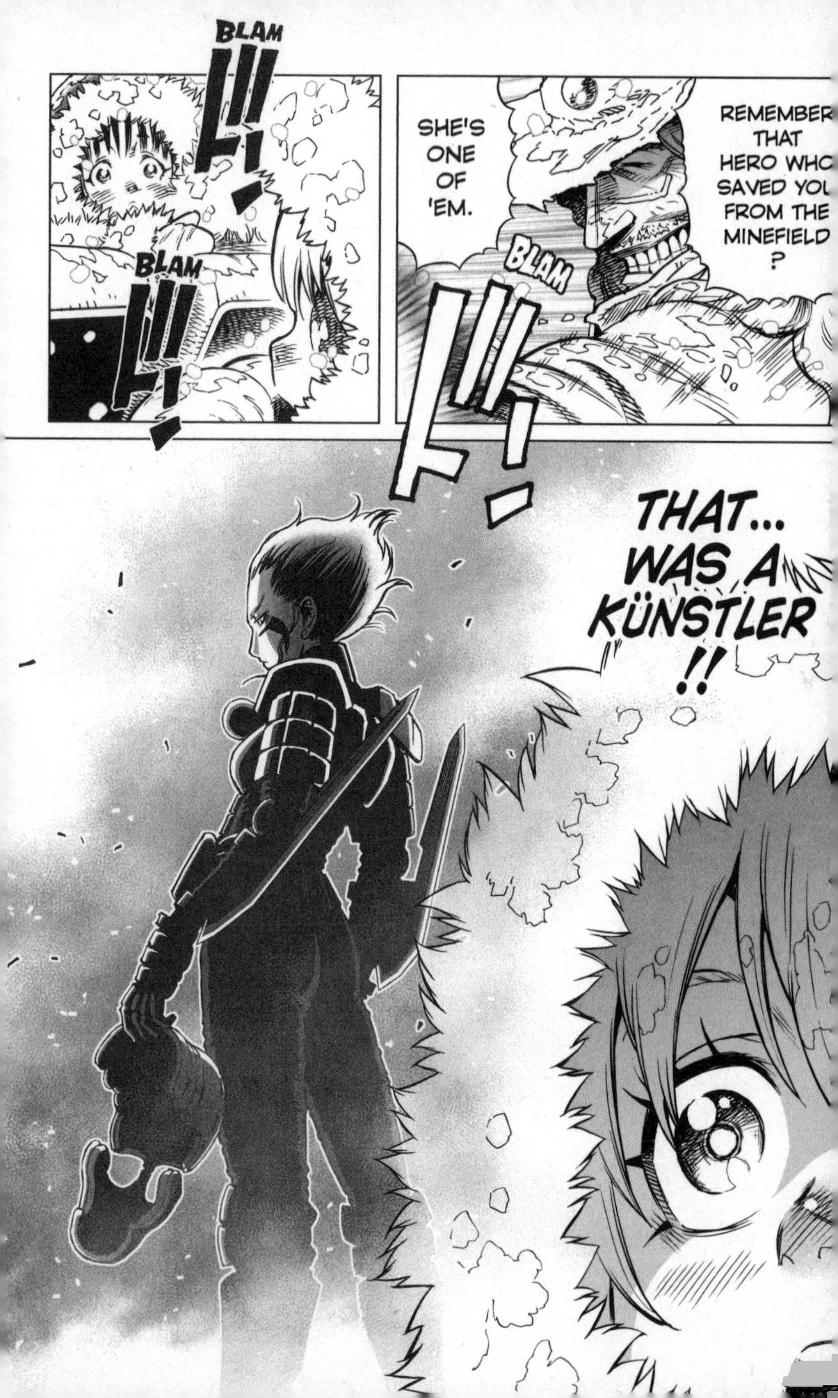
REMEMBER THAT HERO WHO SAVED YOU FROM THE MINEFIELD?
SHE'S ONE OF 'EM.
BLAM
BLAM
BLAM
THAT... WAS A KÜNSTLER!!

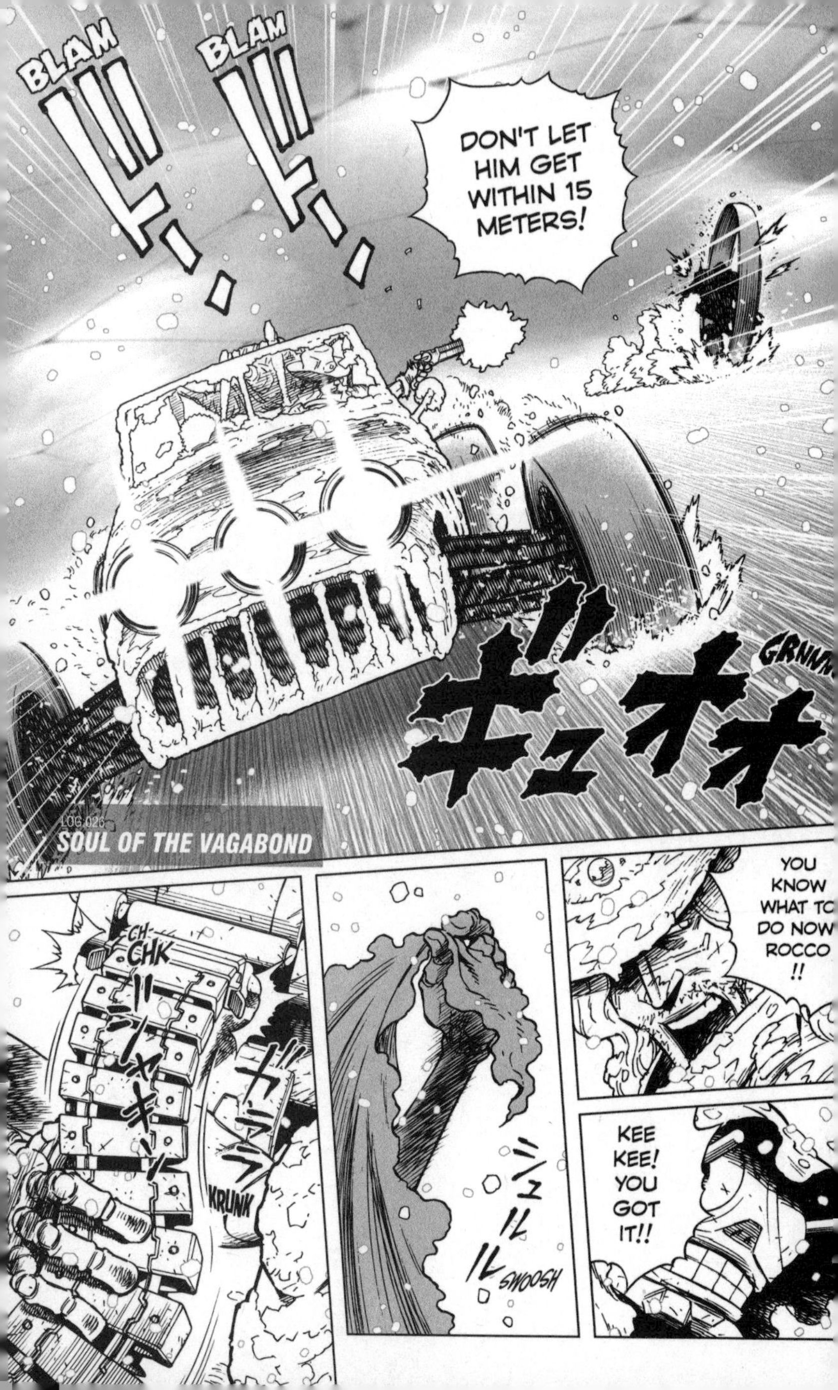
BLAM
BLAM
DON'T LET HIM GET WITHIN 15 METERS!
GRNNN
ギュオオ
LOG 026
SOUL OF THE VAGABOND
YOU KNOW WHAT TO DO NOW ROCCO !!
KEE KEE! YOU GOT IT!!
シュルル
SWOOSH
CH-CHK
KRUNK

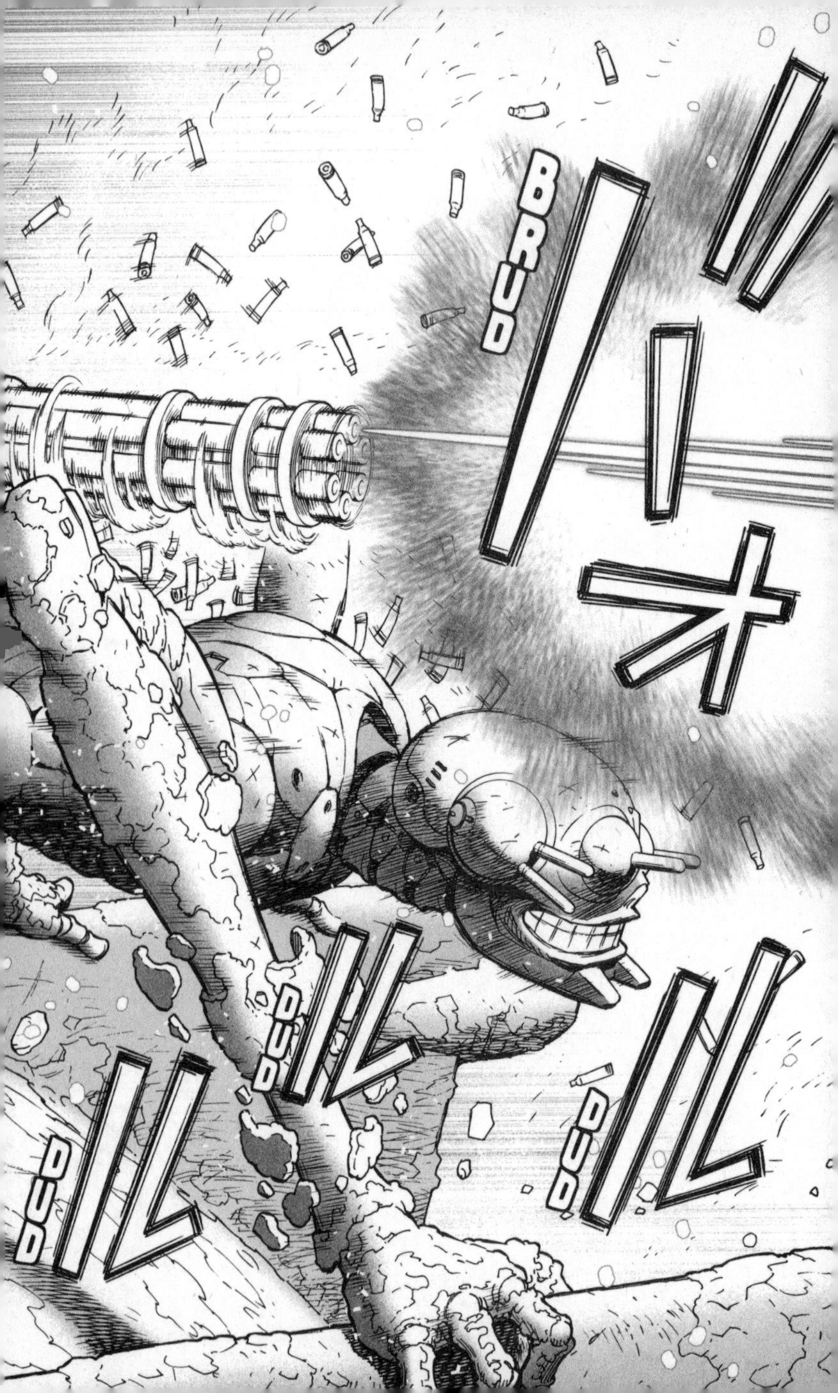
BRUD
DUD
DUD
DUD

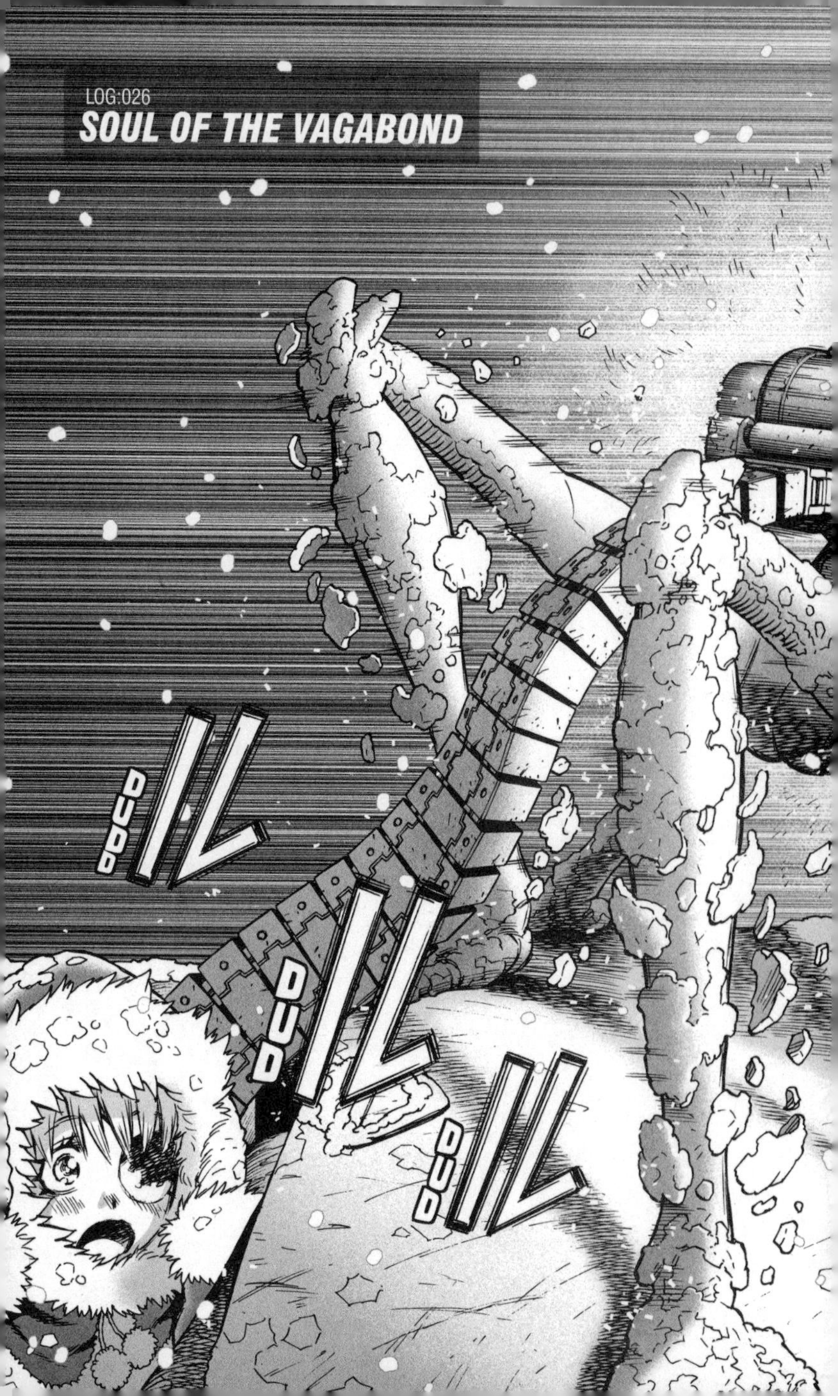
LOG:026
SOUL OF THE VAGABOND
DUD
DUD
DUD

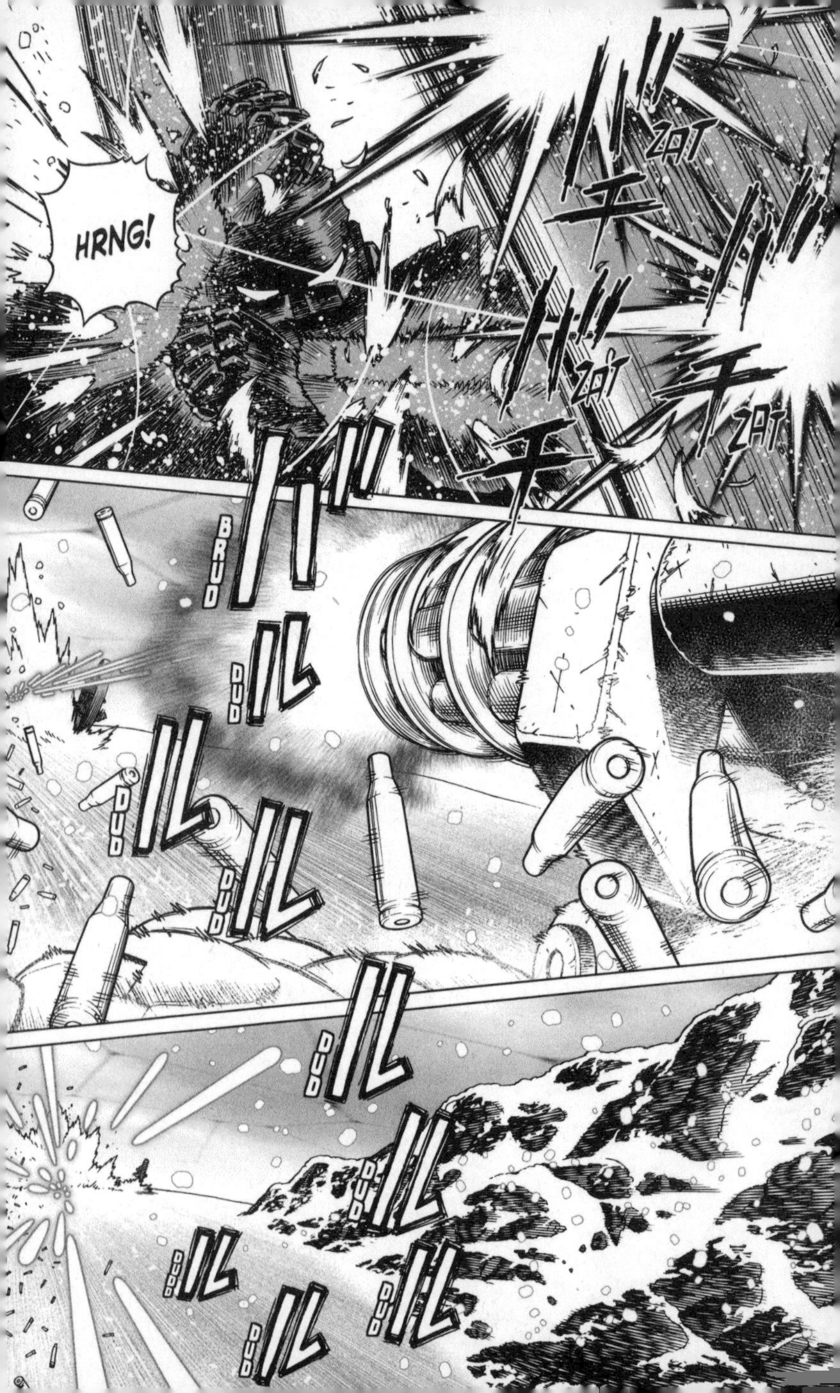
ZAT
ZAT
ZAT
HRNG!
DUD
DUD
BRUD
DUD
DUD
DUD
DUD
DUD
DUD

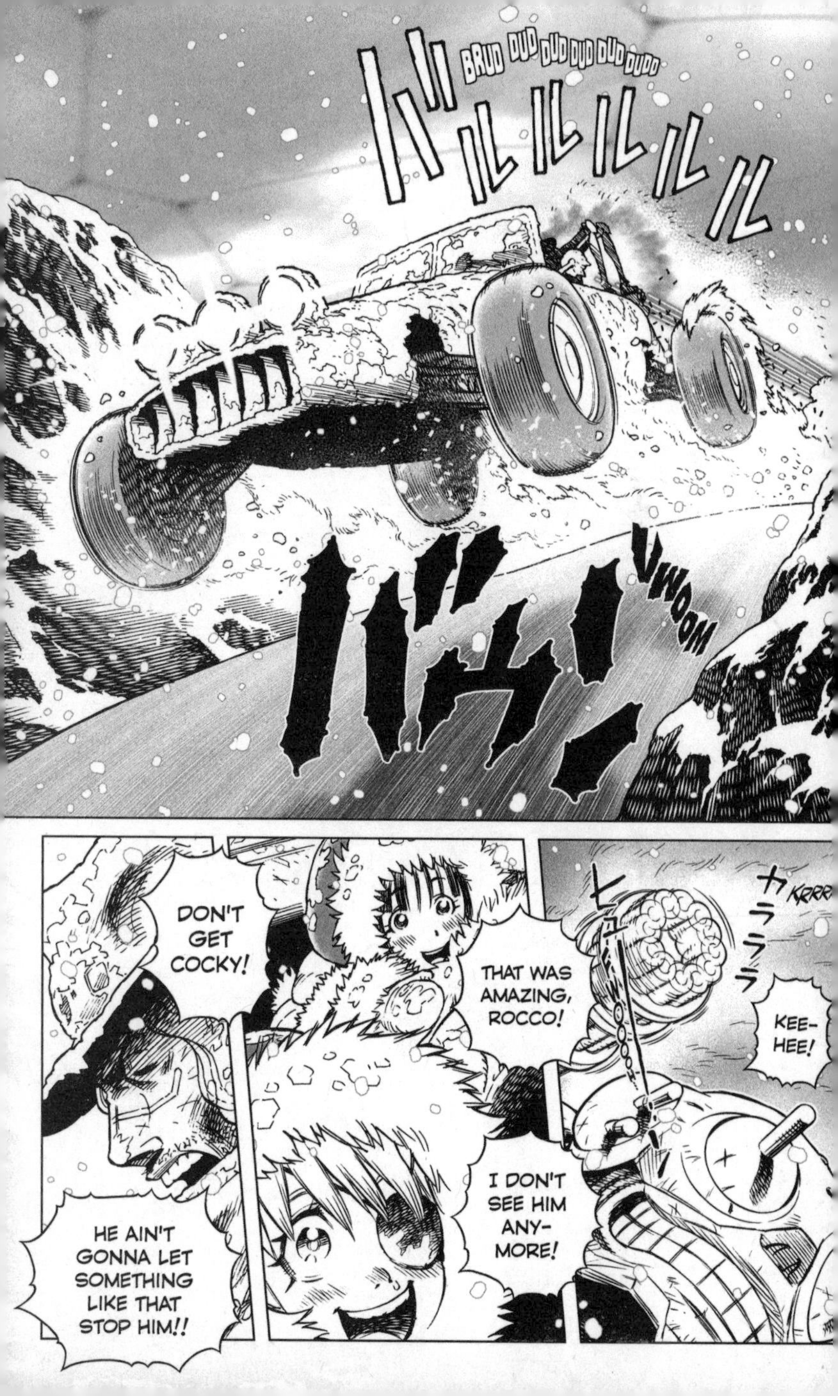
BRUD DUD DUD DUD DUD DUDD
VWOOM
KRRR
KEE-HEE!
THAT WAS AMAZING, ROCCO!
I DON'T SEE HIM ANY-MORE!
DON'T GET COCKY!
HE AIN'T GONNA LET SOMETHING LIKE THAT STOP HIM!!

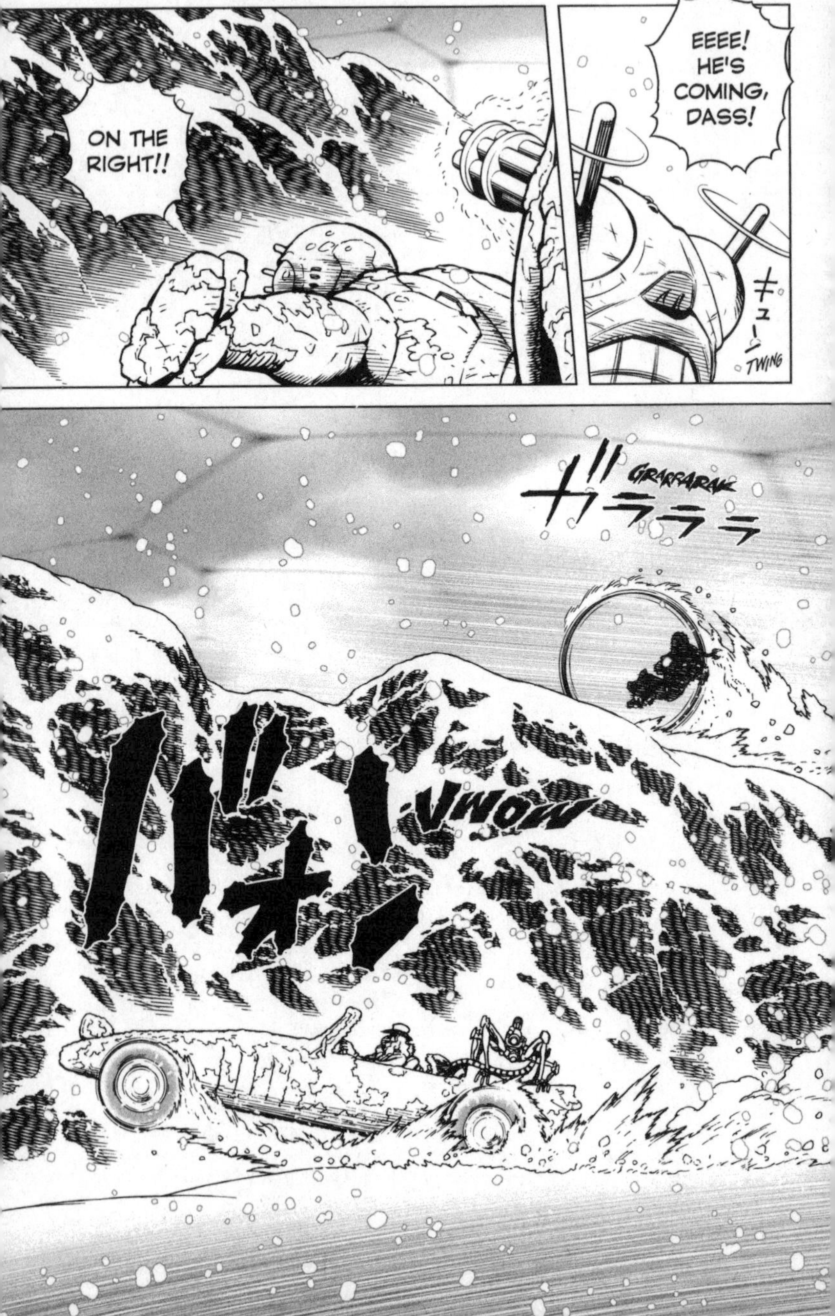
EEEE! HE'S COMING, DASS!
キュー
TWING
ON THE RIGHT!!
ガラララ
GRARRARAK
バォン
VWOW

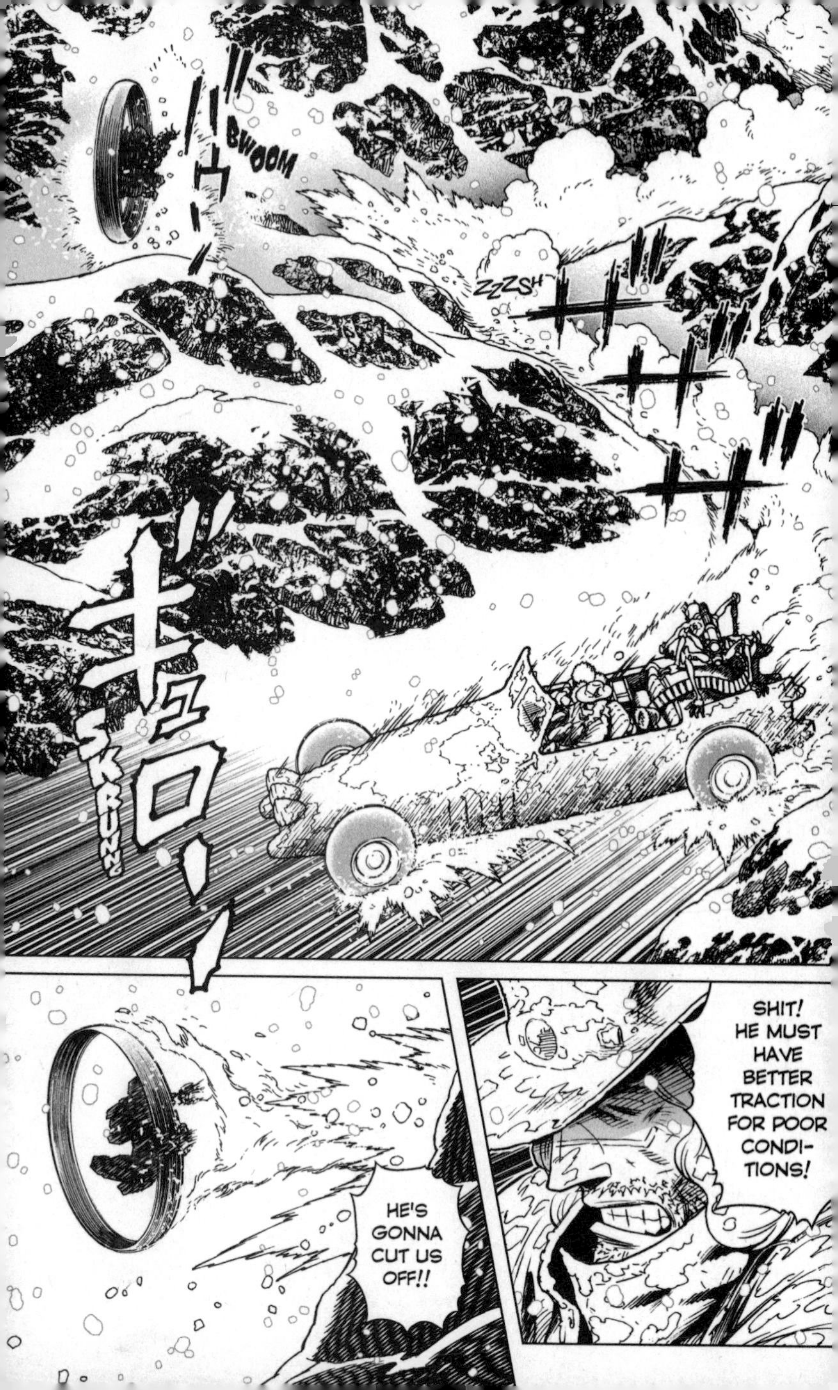
BWOOM
ZZZSH
SKRUNN
SHIT! HE MUST HAVE BETTER TRACTION FOR POOR CONDITIONS!
HE'S GONNA CUT US OFF!!

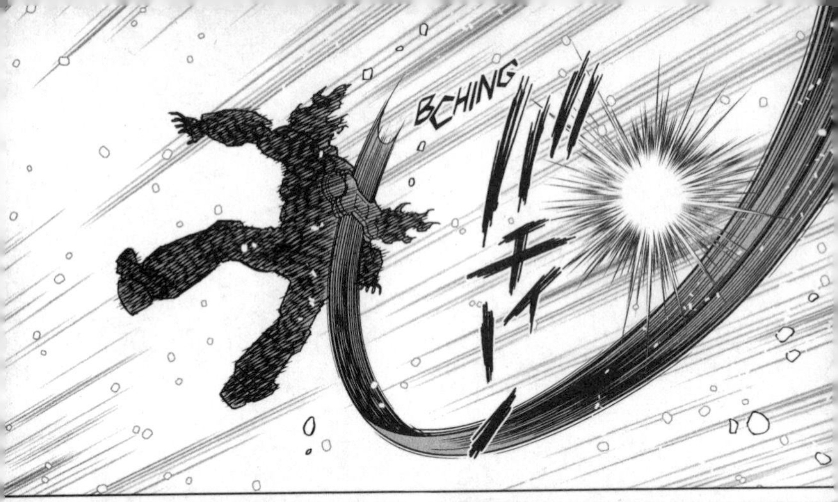
BCHING

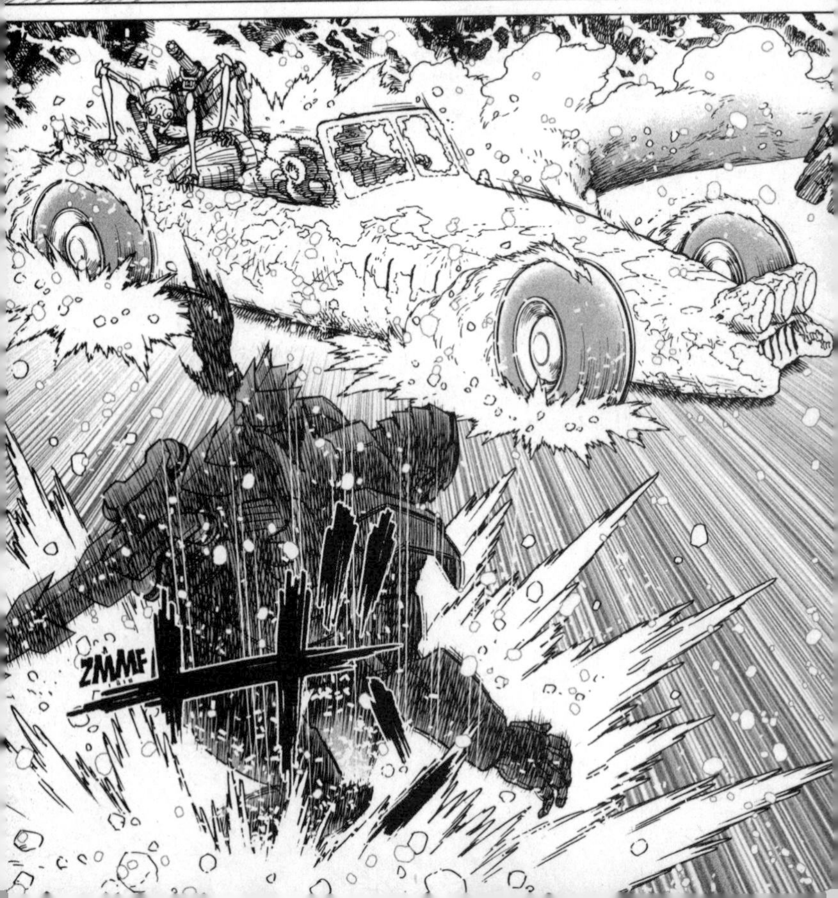
ZMMF

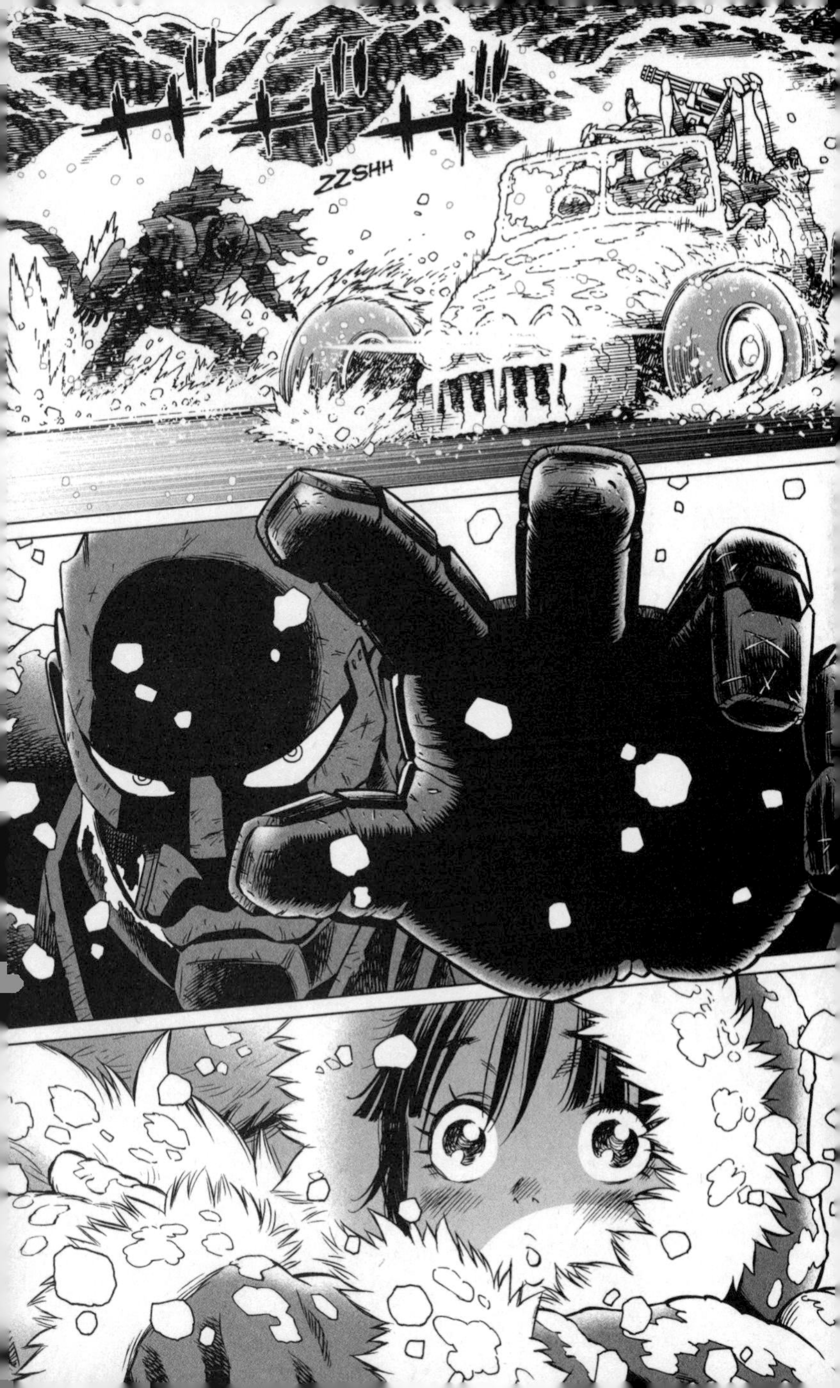
ZZSHH

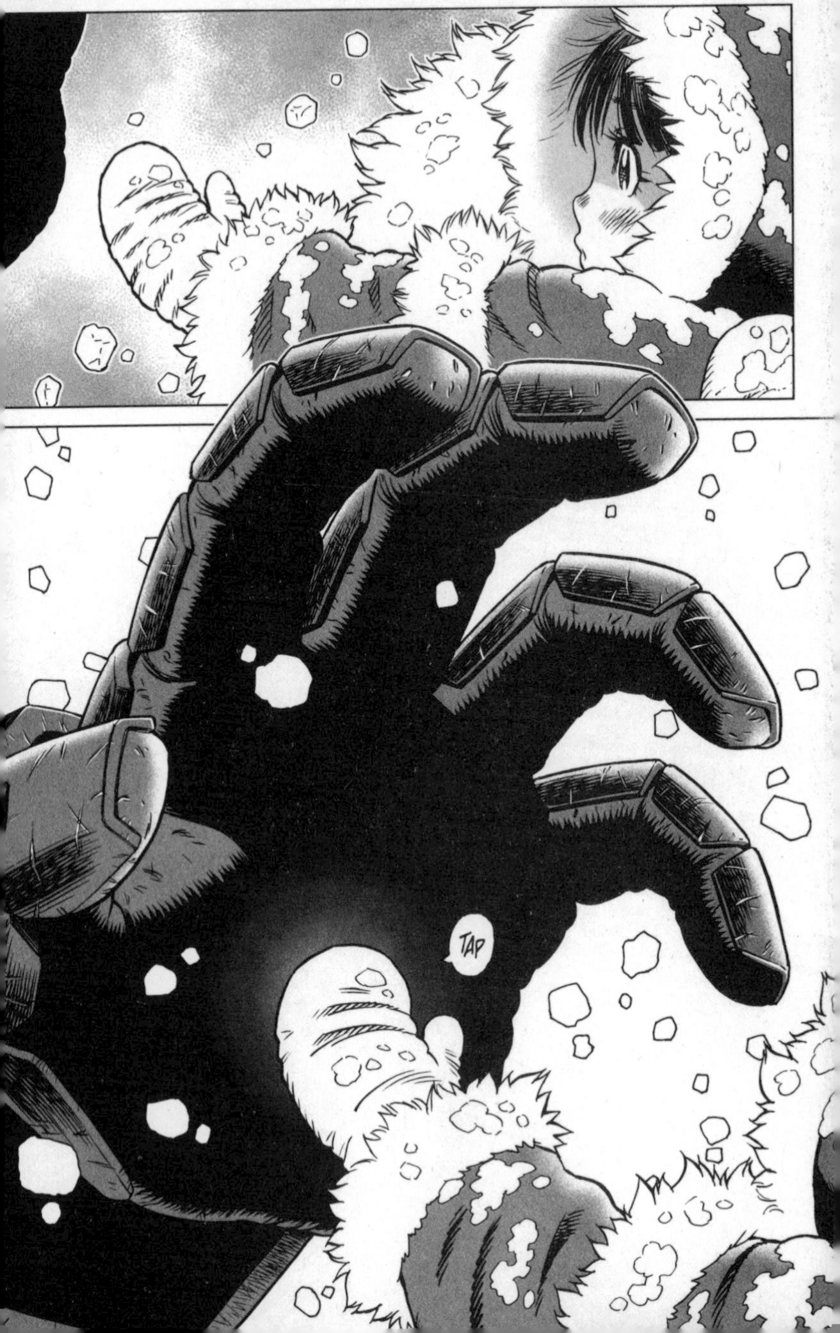
TAP

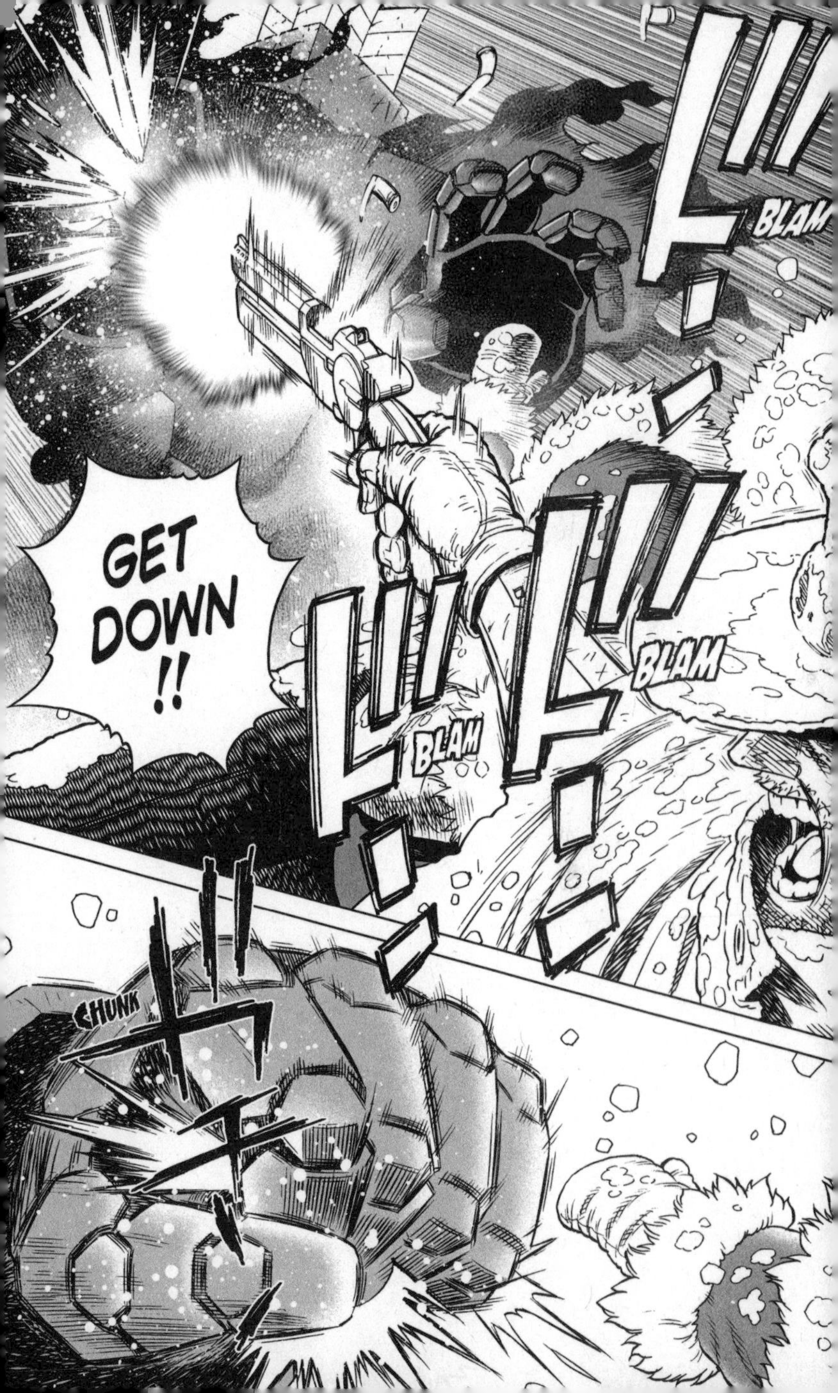
BLAM
GET DOWN !!
BLAM
BLAM
CHUNK

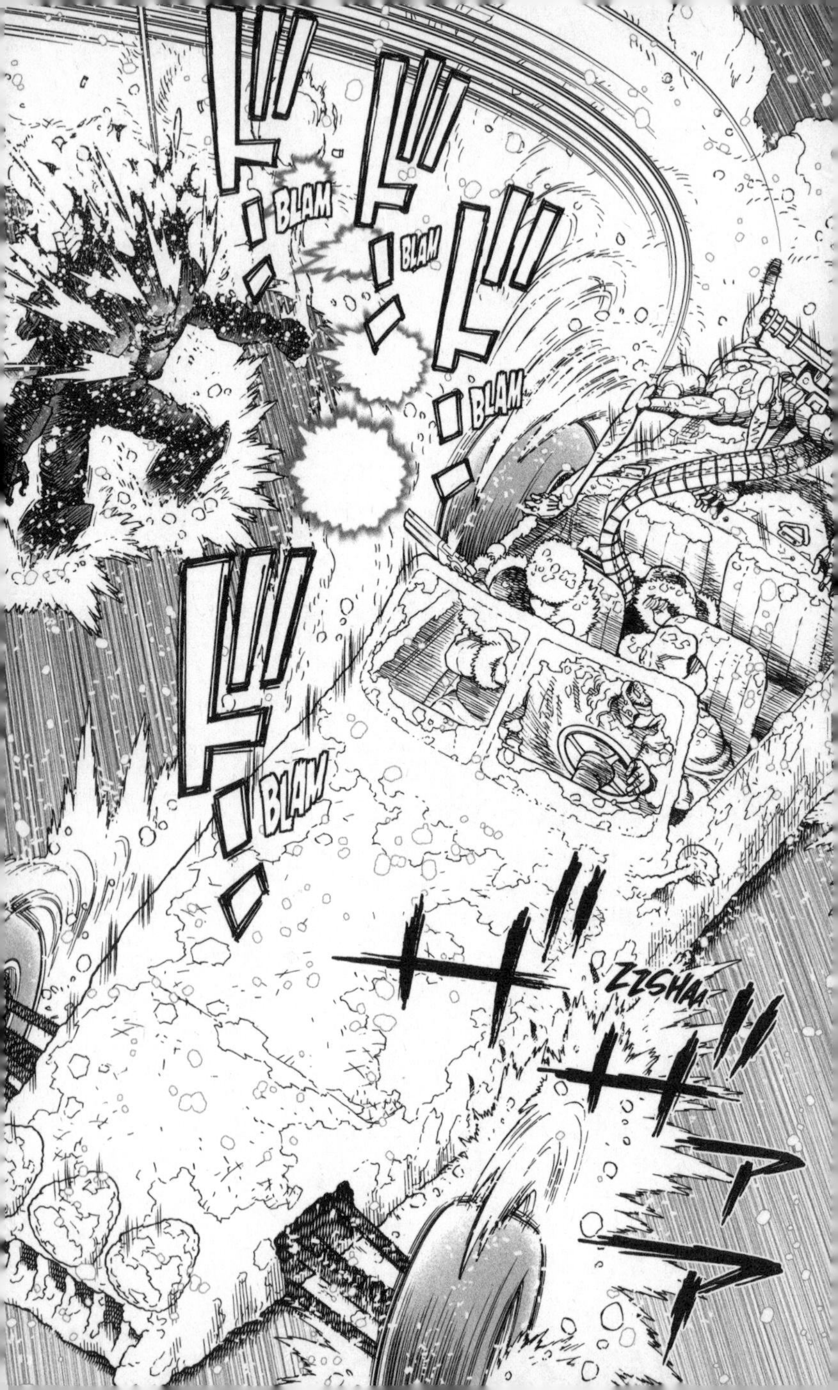
BLAM
BLAM
BLAM
BLAM
ZZSHAA

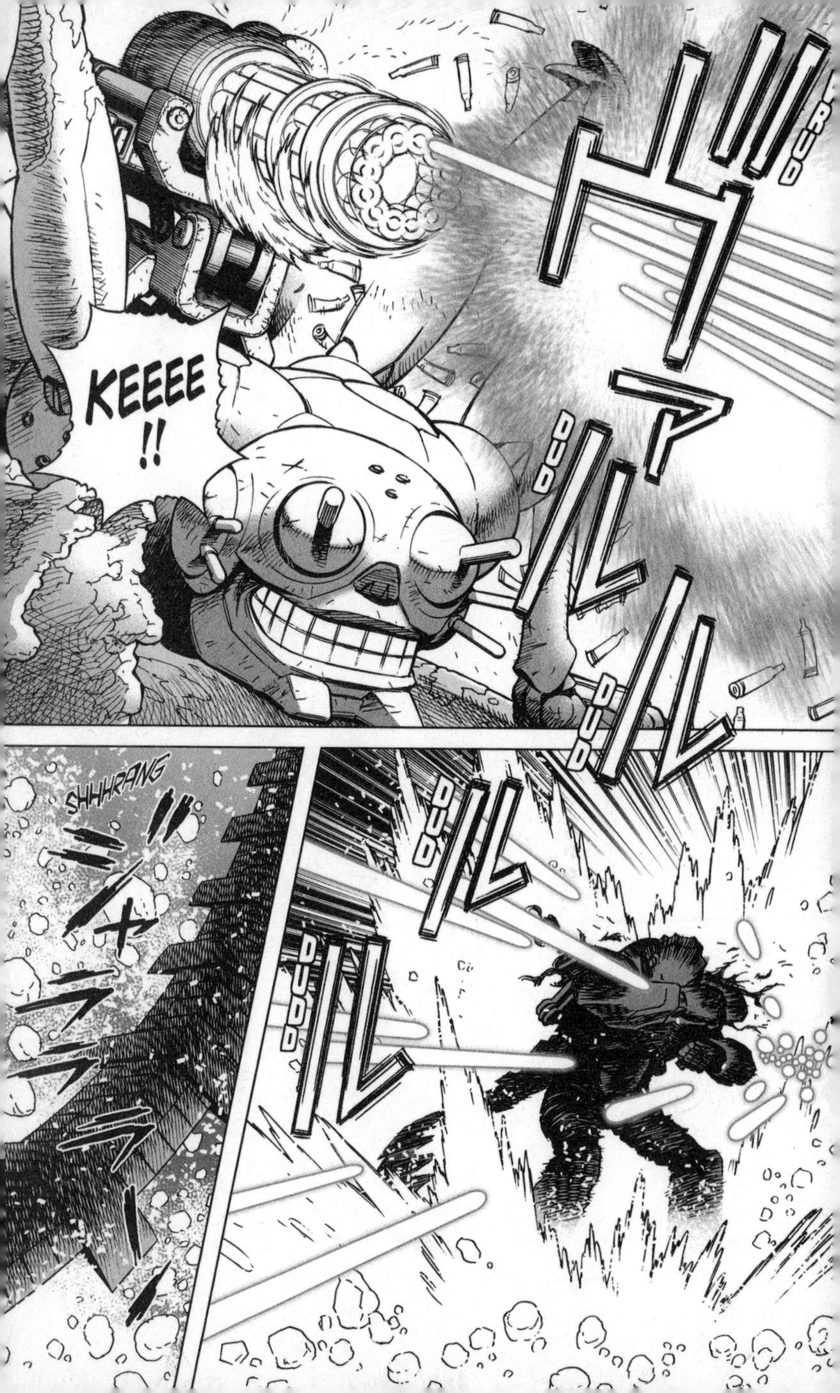
RUD
DUD
KEEEE!!
DUD
DUD
DUD
DUDD
SHHHRANG

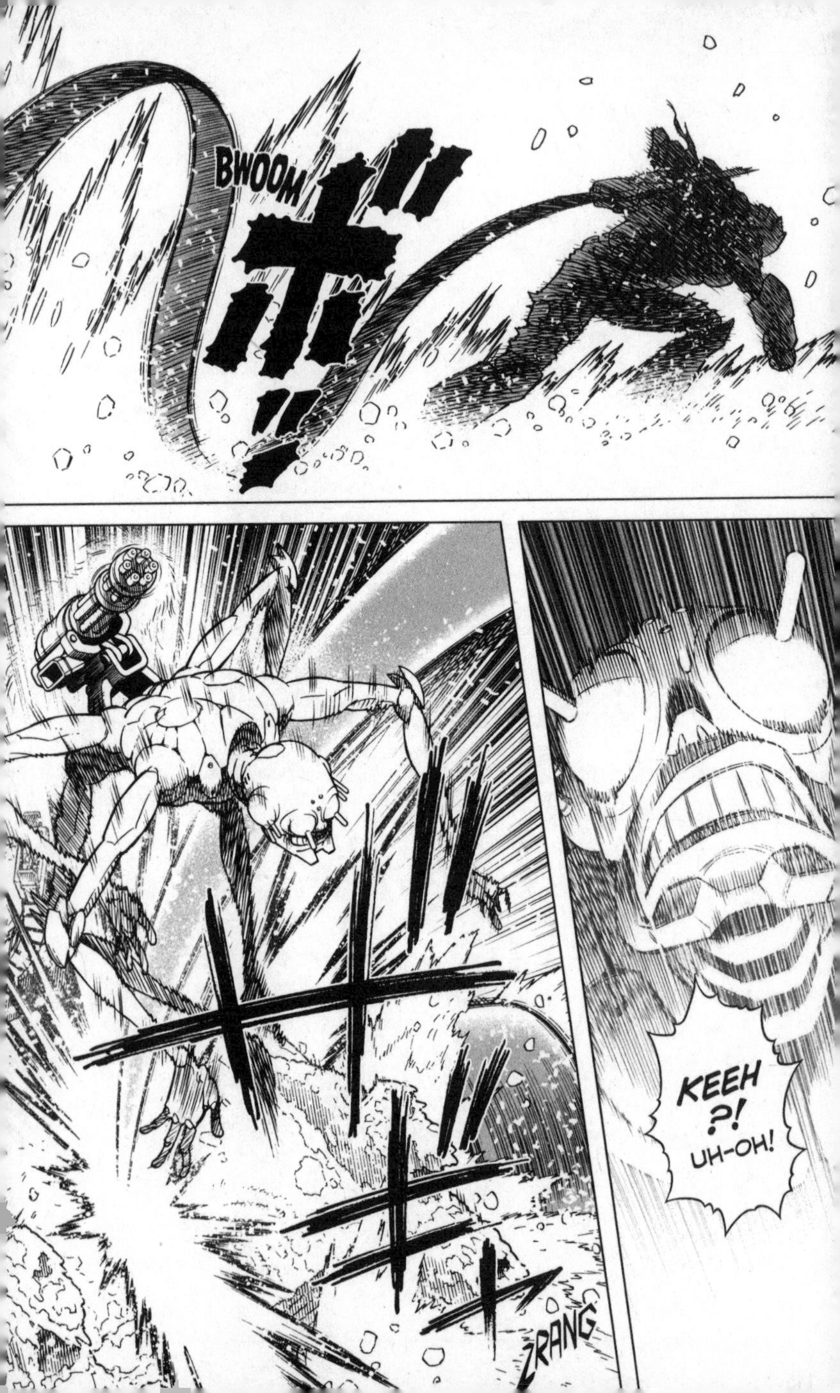
BWOOM
KEEH ?!
UH-OH!
ZRANG

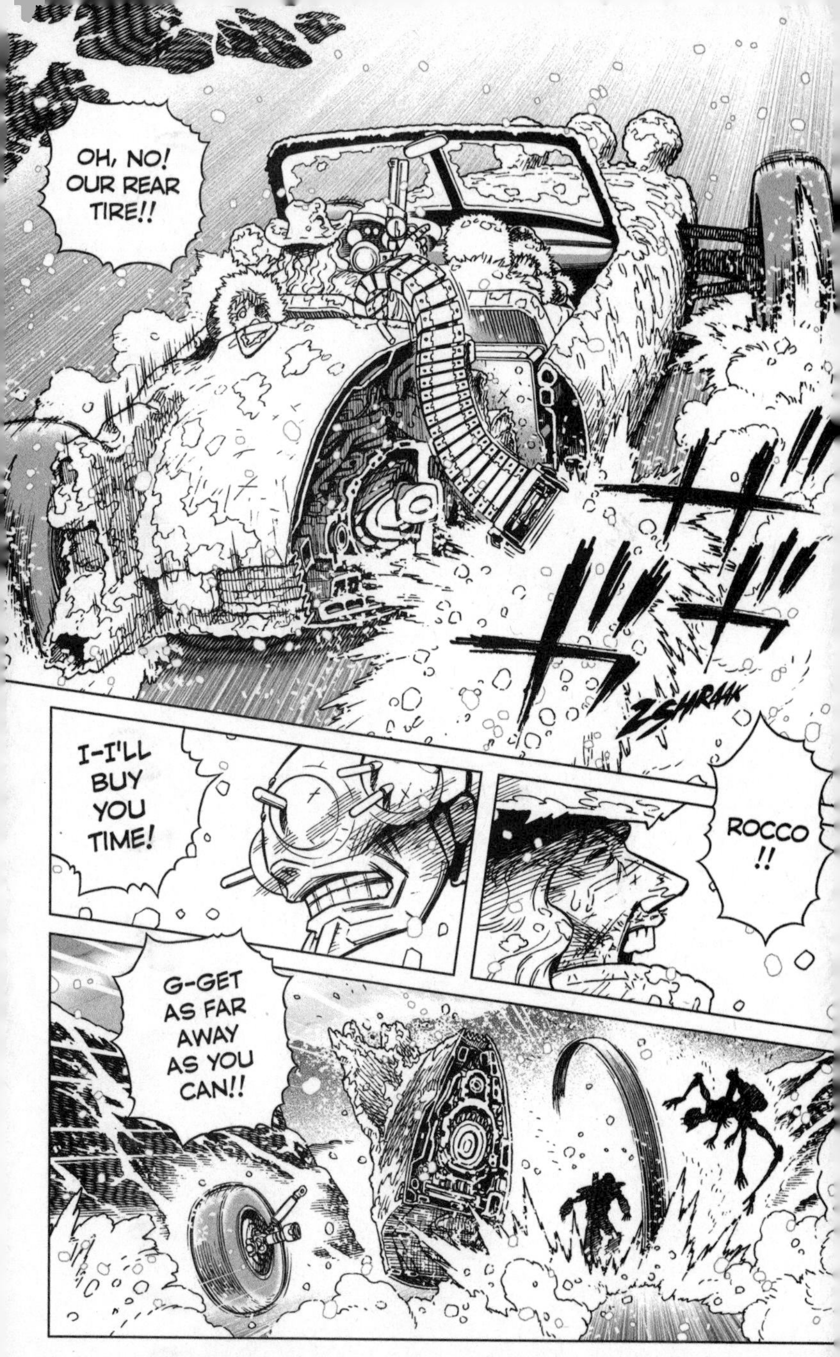
OH, NO! OUR REAR TIRE!!
ZSHRAAK
ROCCO !!
I-I'LL BUY YOU TIME!
G-GET AS FAR AWAY AS YOU CAN!!

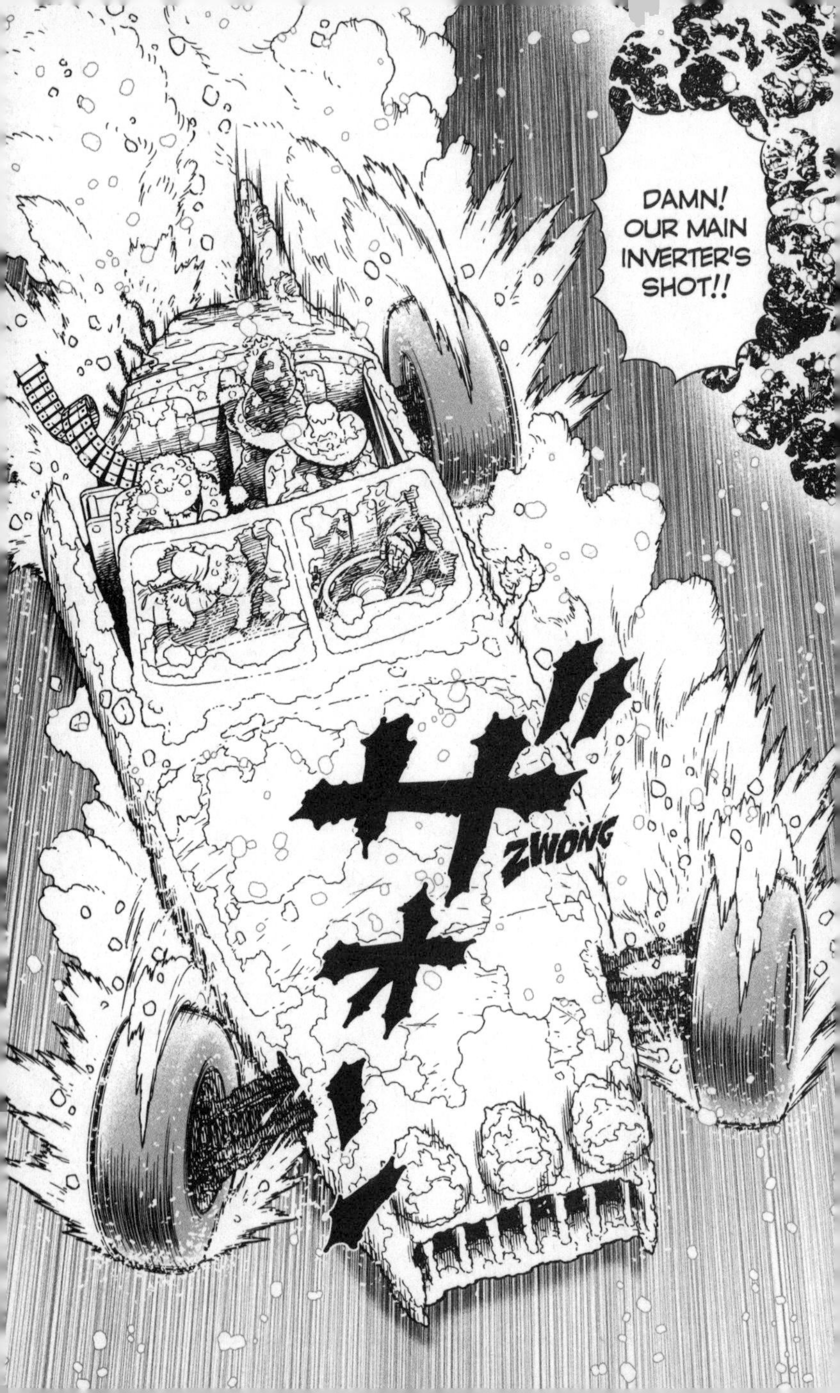
DAMN! OUR MAIN INVERTER'S SHOT!!
ZWONG

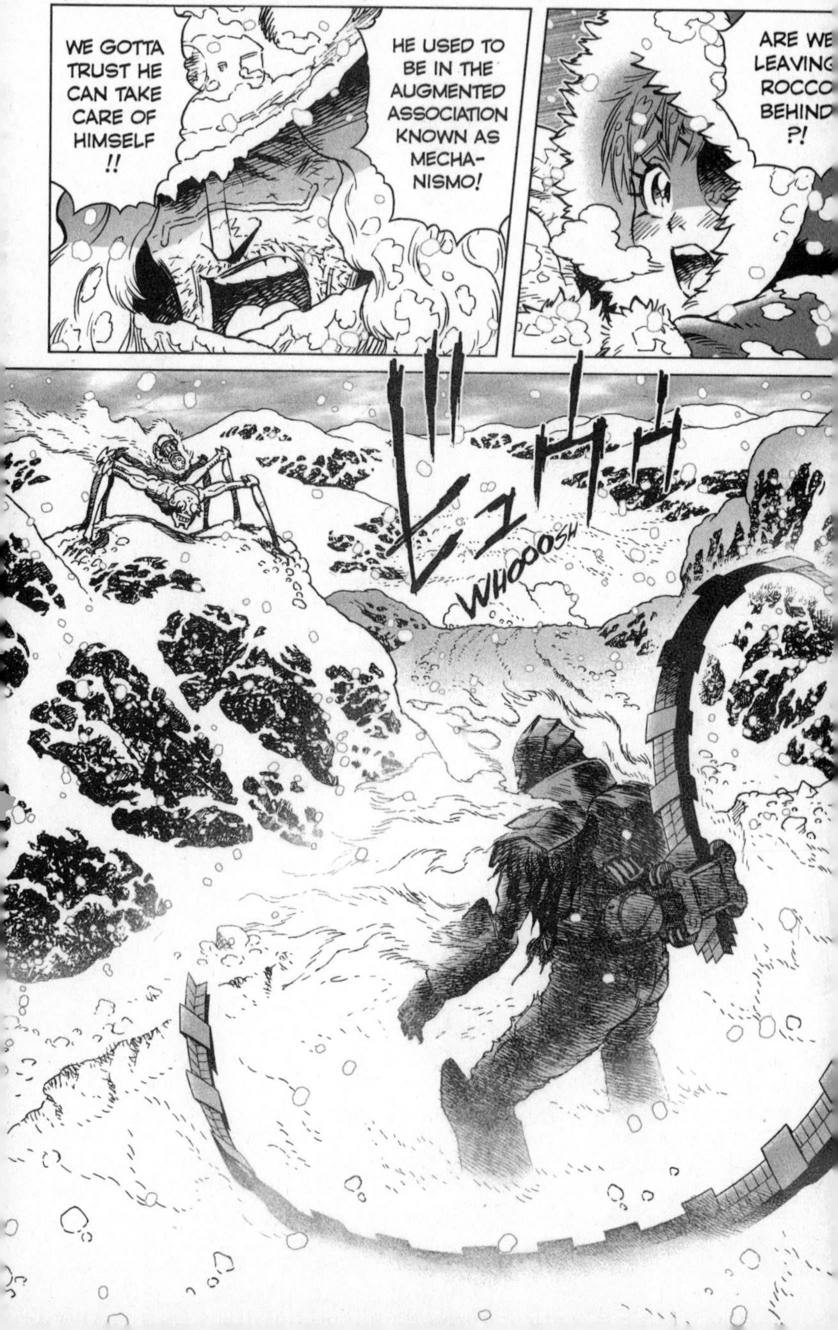
ARE WE LEAVING ROCCO BEHIND ?!
HE USED TO BE IN THE AUGMENTED ASSOCIATION KNOWN AS MECHA-NISMO!
WE GOTTA TRUST HE CAN TAKE CARE OF HIMSELF !!
WHOOOOSH

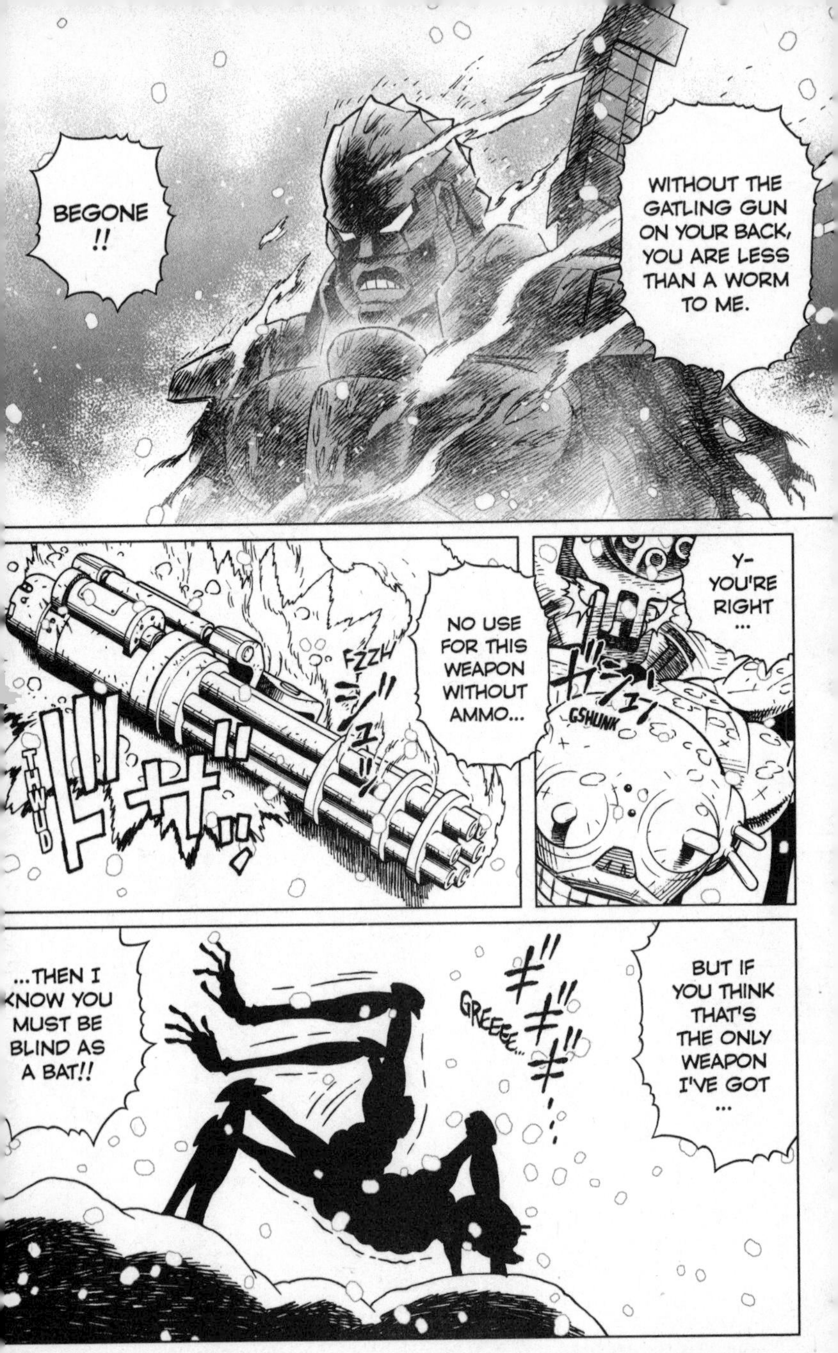
WITHOUT THE GATLING GUN ON YOUR BACK, YOU ARE LESS THAN A WORM TO ME.
BEGONE !!
Y- YOU'RE RIGHT ...
GSHUNK
NO USE FOR THIS WEAPON WITHOUT AMMO...
FZZH
THWUD
BUT IF YOU THINK THAT'S THE ONLY WEAPON I'VE GOT ...
GREEEE...
...THEN I KNOW YOU MUST BE BLIND AS A BAT!!

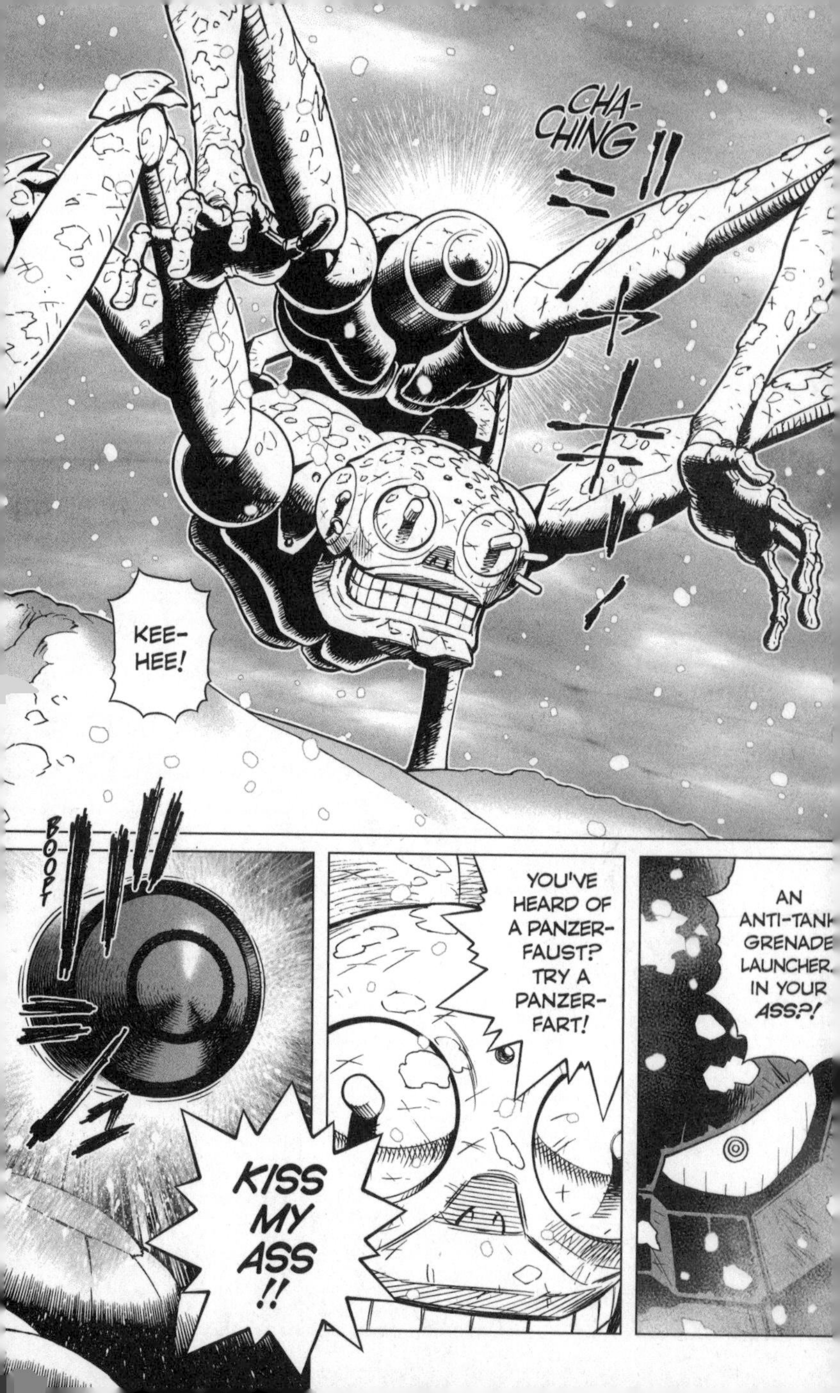
CHA-CHING
KEE-HEE!
AN ANTI-TANK GRENADE LAUNCHER IN YOUR ASS?!
YOU'VE HEARD OF A PANZER-FAUST? TRY A PANZER-FART!
BOOP
KISS MY ASS!!

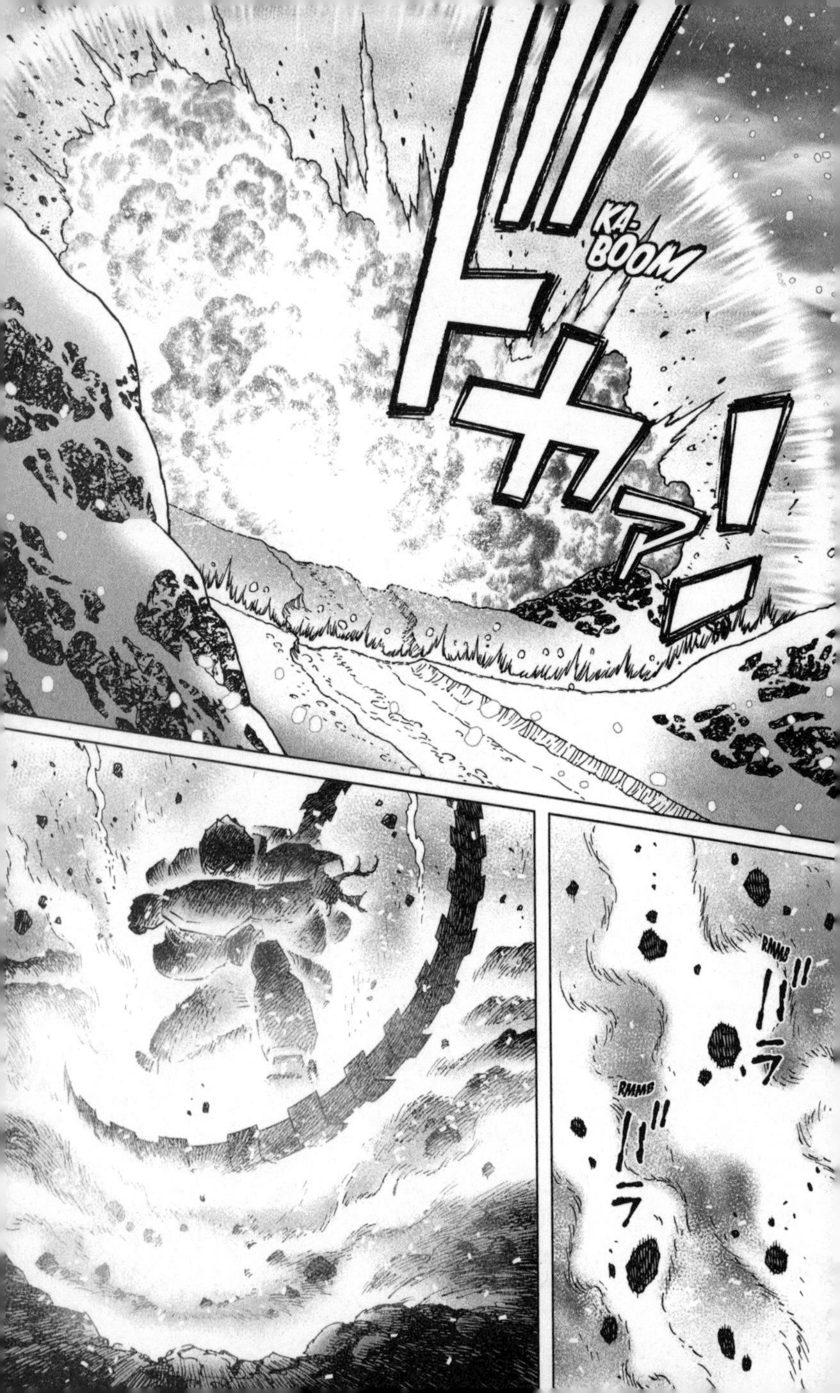
ドカァン!
KA-BOOM
バラ
RMMB
バラ
RMMB

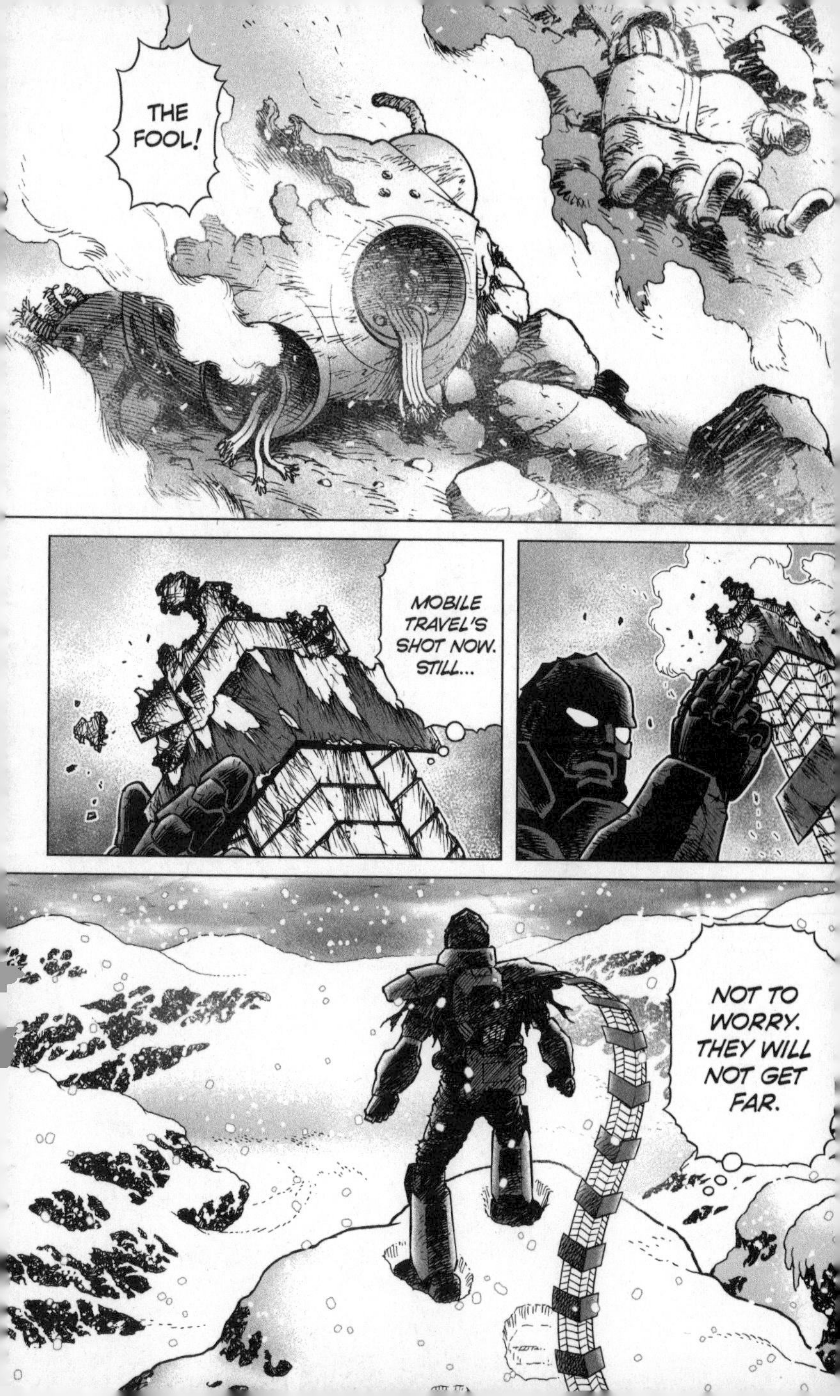
THE FOOL!
MOBILE TRAVEL'S SHOT NOW. STILL...
NOT TO WORRY. THEY WILL NOT GET FAR.

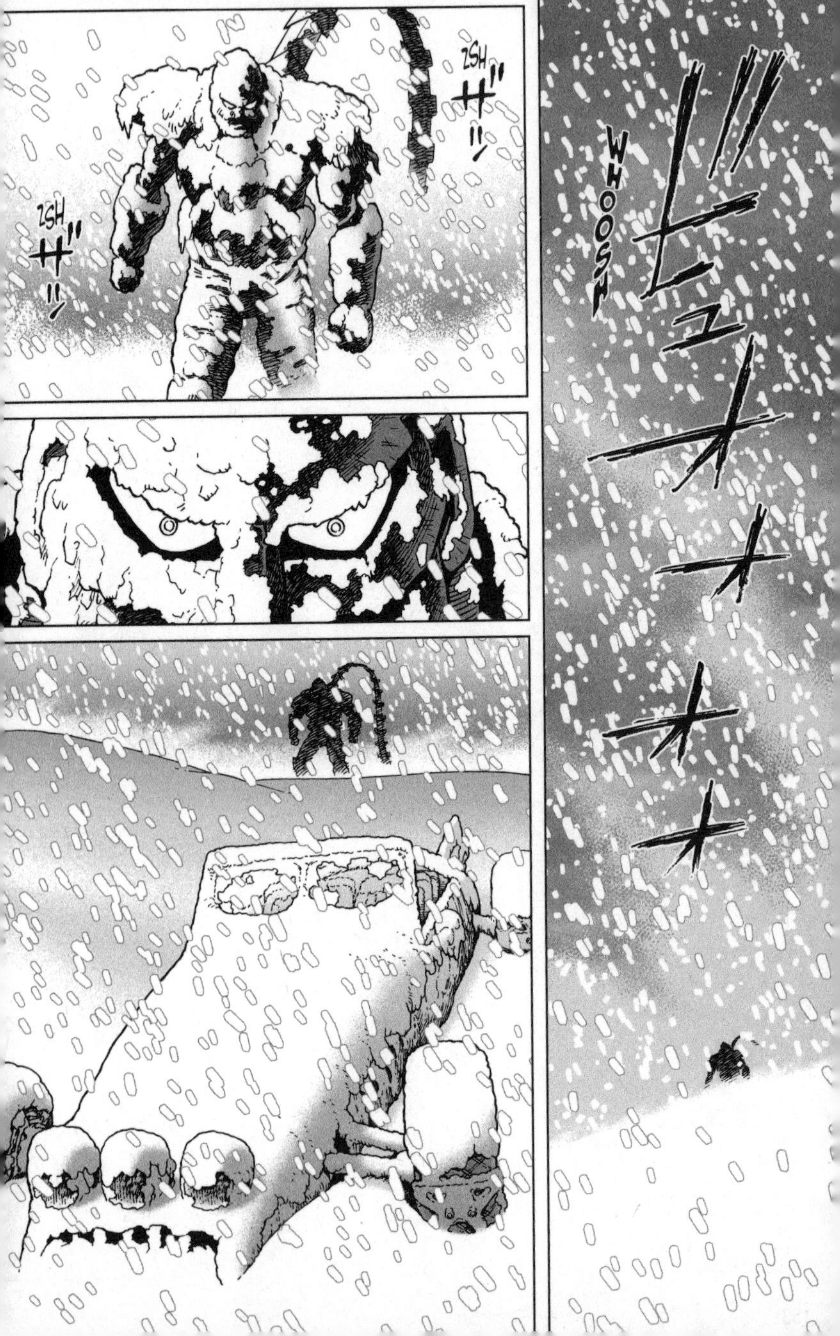
WHOOSH
ZSH
ZSH

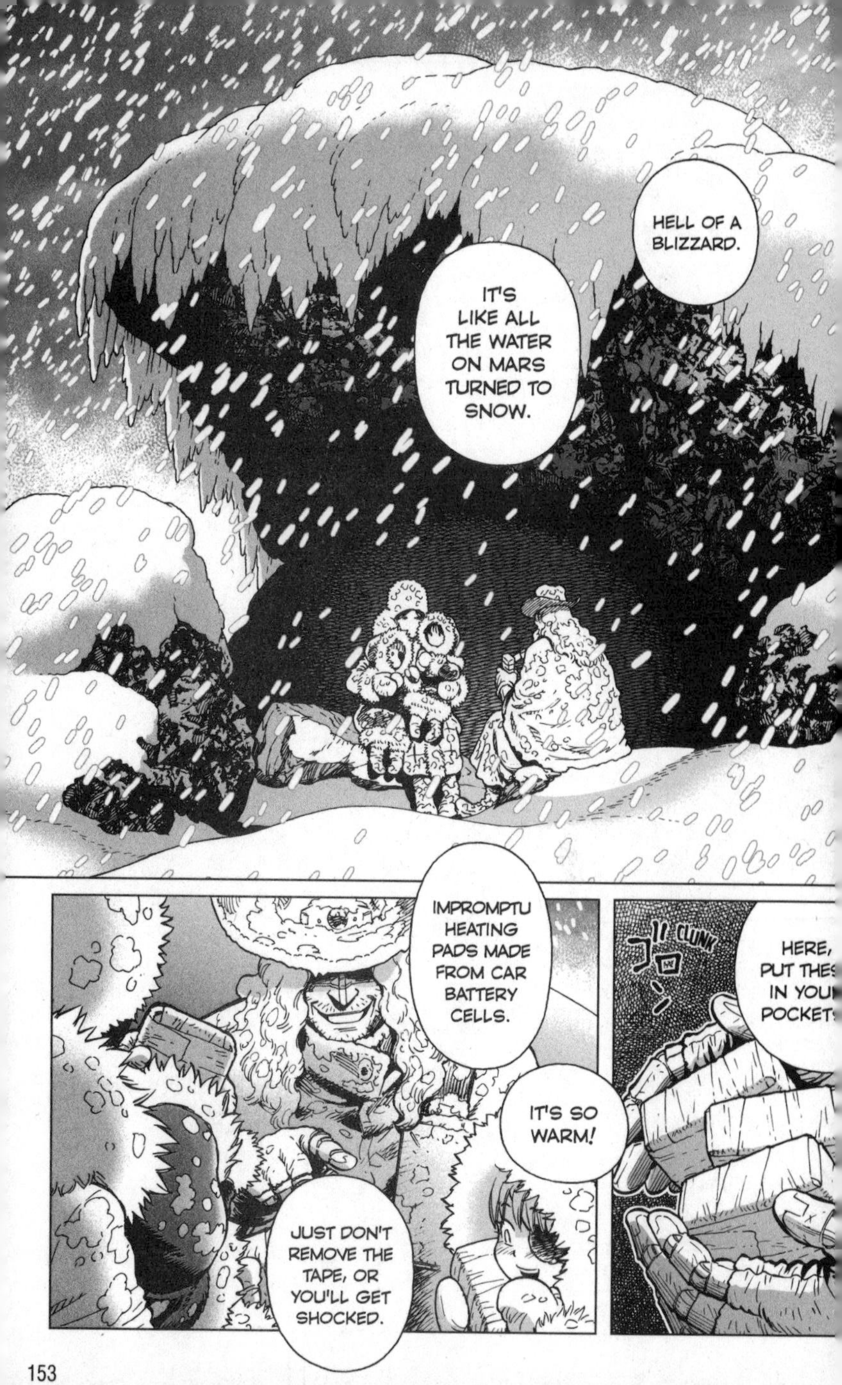
HELL OF A BLIZZARD.
IT'S LIKE ALL THE WATER ON MARS TURNED TO SNOW.
CLUNK
HERE, PUT THES IN YOU POCKET
IMPROMPTU HEATING PADS MADE FROM CAR BATTERY CELLS.
IT'S SO WARM!
JUST DON'T REMOVE THE TAPE, OR YOU'LL GET SHOCKED.

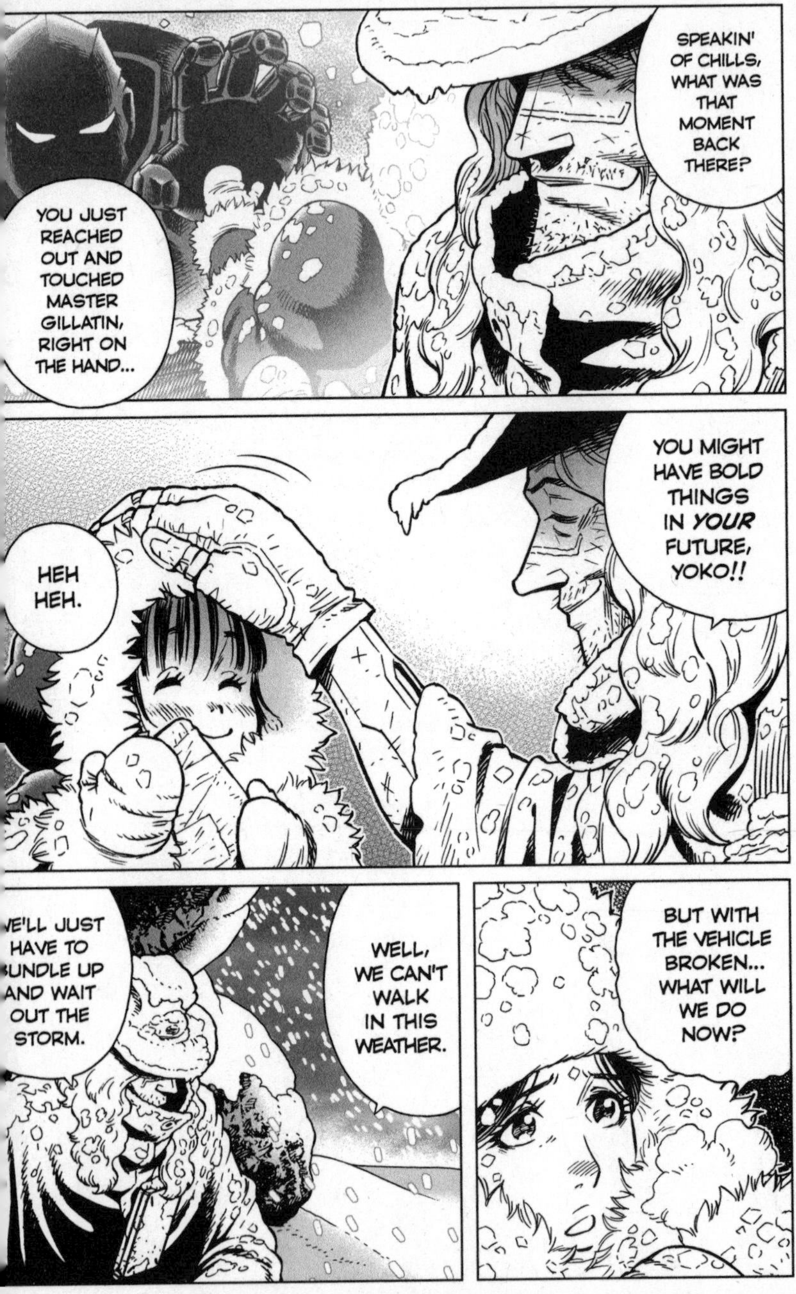
SPEAKIN' OF CHILLS, WHAT WAS THAT MOMENT BACK THERE?
YOU JUST REACHED OUT AND TOUCHED MASTER GILLATIN, RIGHT ON THE HAND...
YOU MIGHT HAVE BOLD THINGS IN *YOUR* FUTURE, YOKO!!
HEH HEH.
BUT WITH THE VEHICLE BROKEN... WHAT WILL WE DO NOW?
WELL, WE CAN'T WALK IN THIS WEATHER.
E'LL JUST HAVE TO UNDLE UP AND WAIT OUT THE STORM.

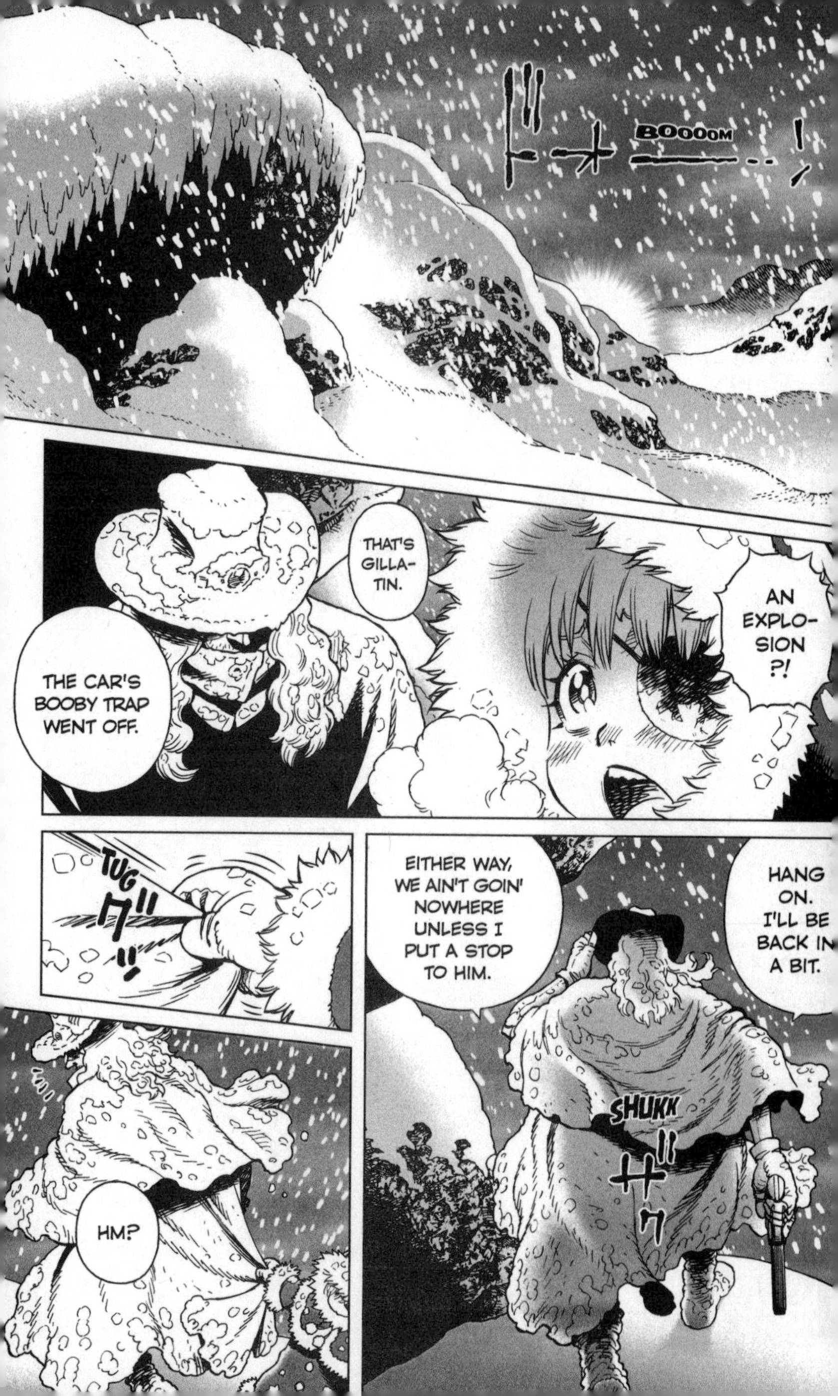
ドォーン
BOOOOOM
AN EXPLOSION?!
THAT'S GILLA-TIN.
THE CAR'S BOOBY TRAP WENT OFF.
HANG ON. I'LL BE BACK IN A BIT.
EITHER WAY, WE AIN'T GOIN' NOWHERE UNLESS I PUT A STOP TO HIM.
SHUKK
TUG
HM?

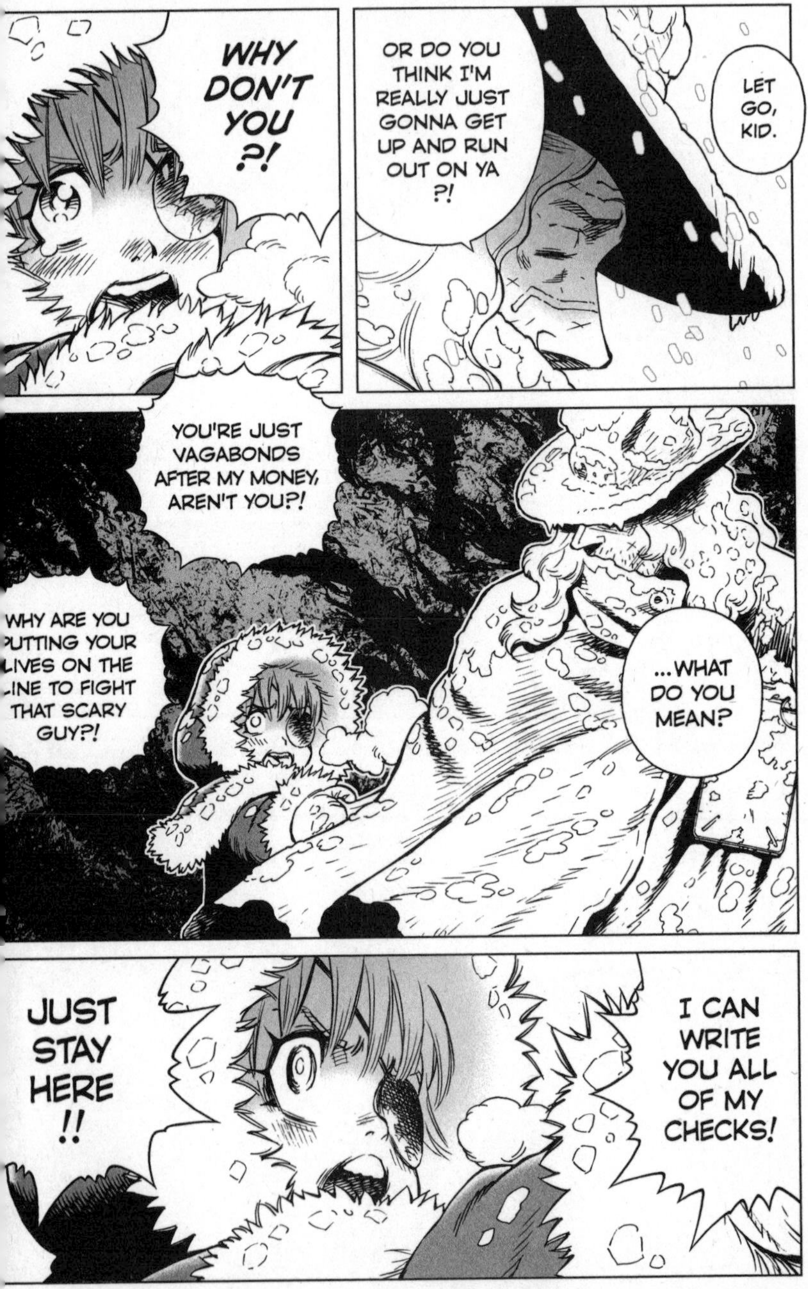
LET GO, KID.
OR DO YOU THINK I'M REALLY JUST GONNA GET UP AND RUN OUT ON YA ?!
WHY DON'T YOU ?!
...WHAT DO YOU MEAN?
YOU'RE JUST VAGABONDS AFTER MY MONEY, AREN'T YOU?!
WHY ARE YOU PUTTING YOUR LIVES ON THE LINE TO FIGHT THAT SCARY GUY?!
I CAN WRITE YOU ALL OF MY CHECKS!
JUST STAY HERE !!

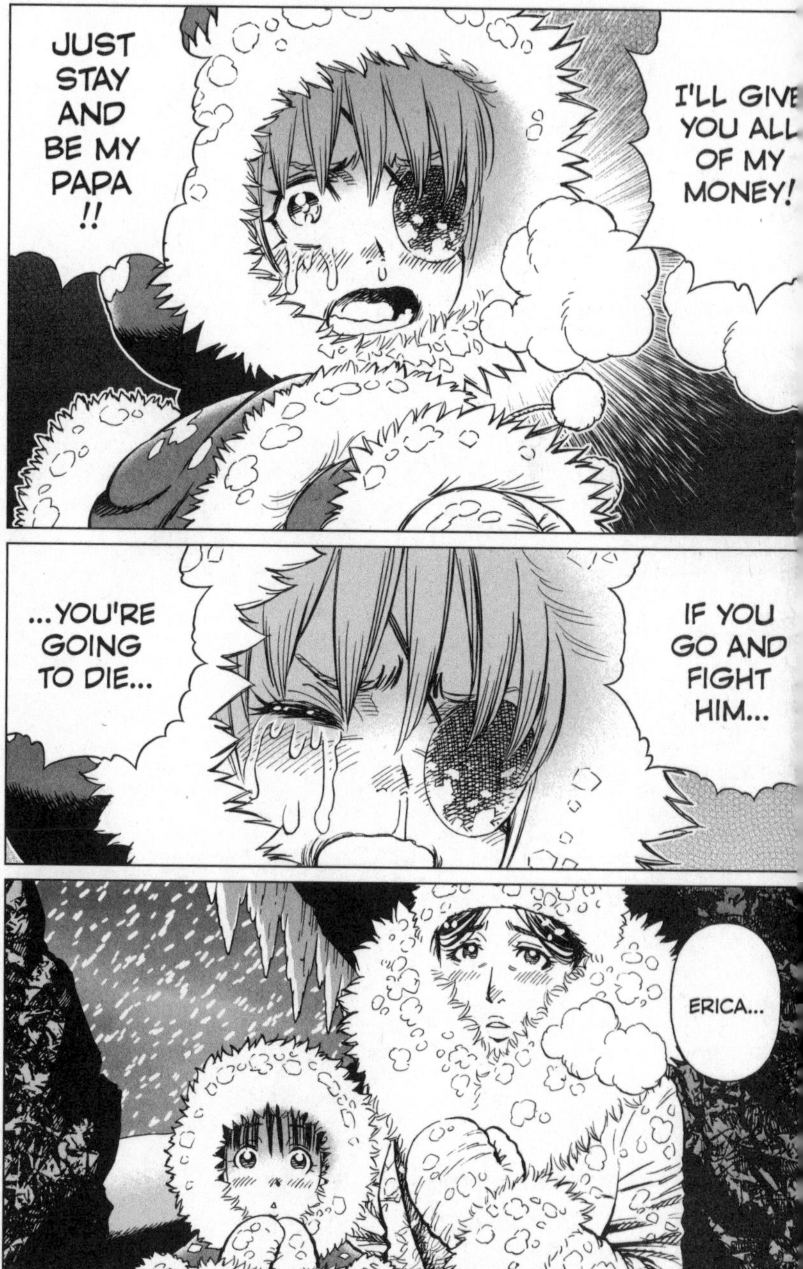
I'LL GIVE YOU ALL OF MY MONEY!
JUST STAY AND BE MY PAPA !!
IF YOU GO AND FIGHT HIM...
...YOU'RE GOING TO DIE...
ERICA...

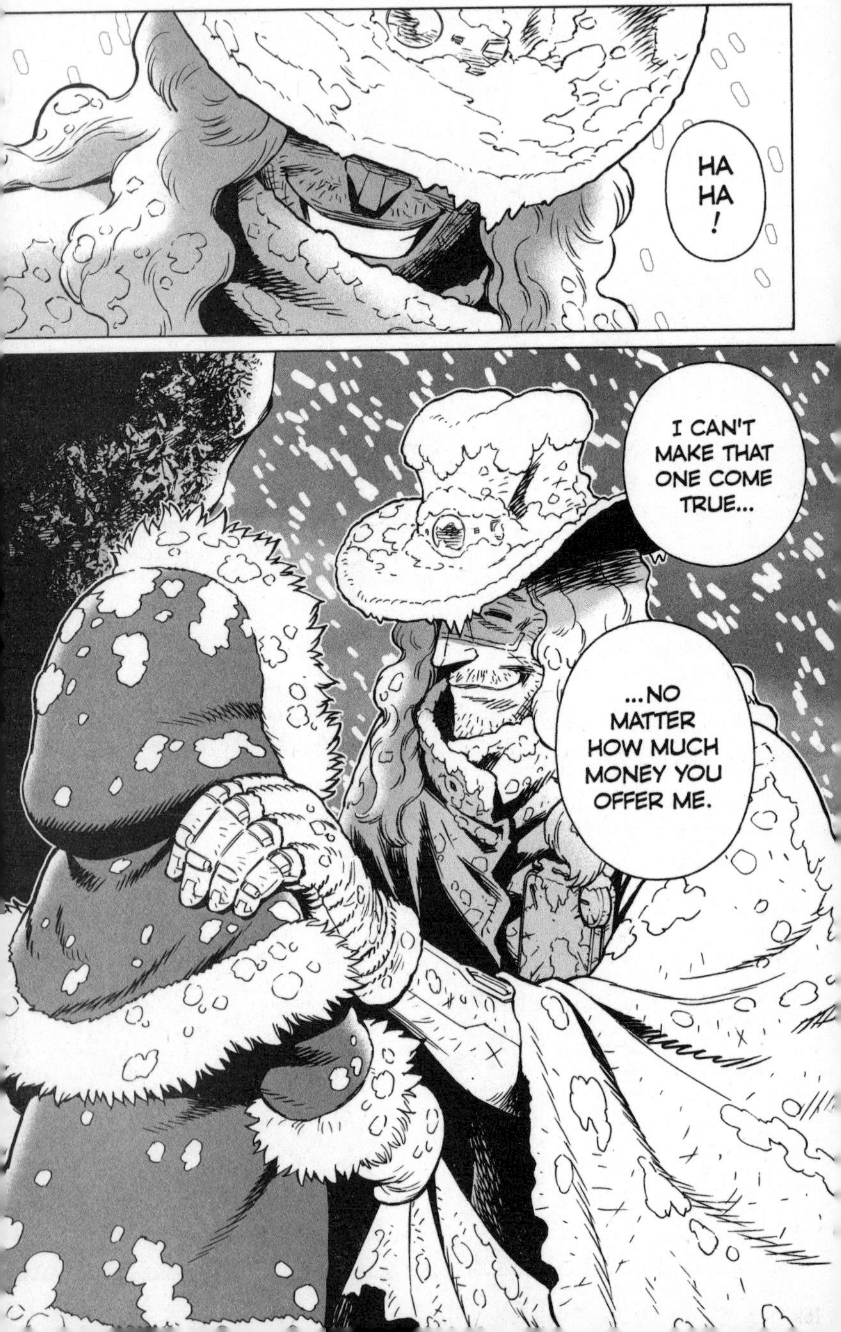
HA HA!
I CAN'T MAKE THAT ONE COME TRUE...
...NO MATTER HOW MUCH MONEY YOU OFFER ME.

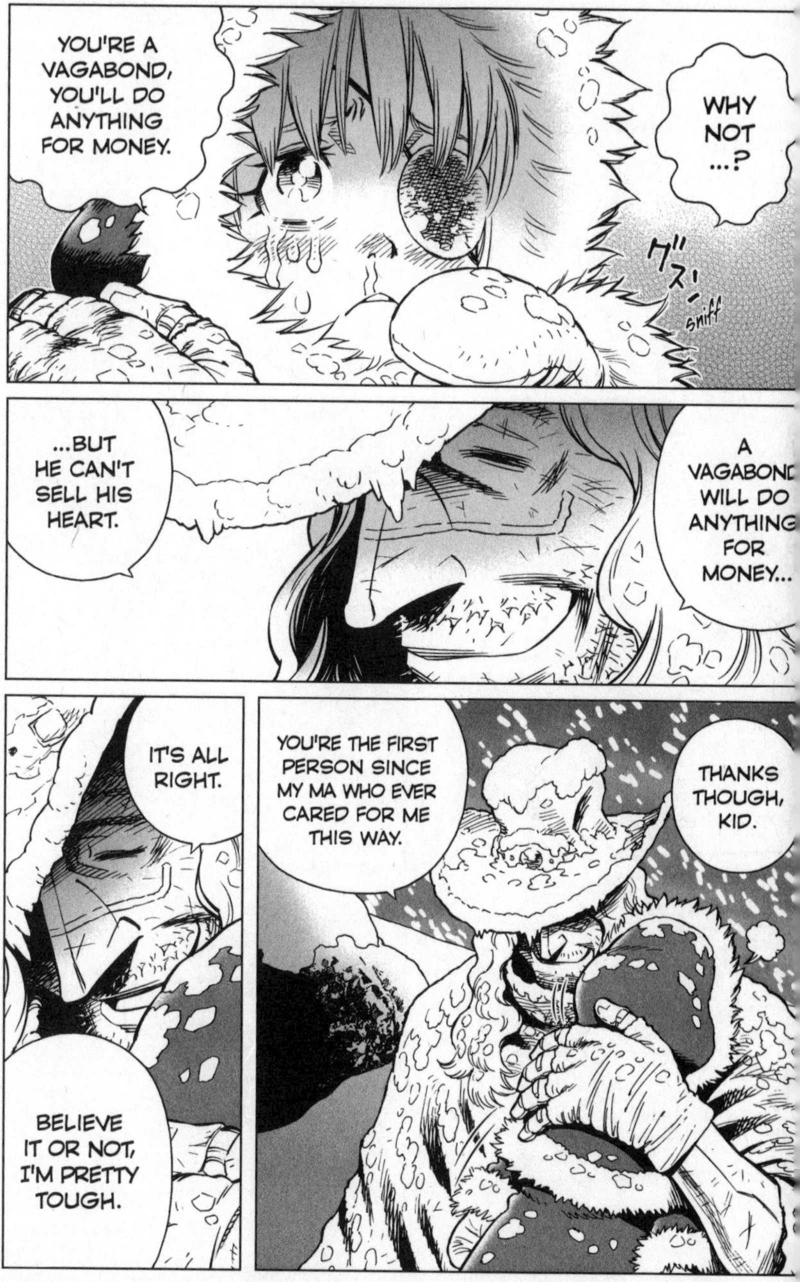

WHY NOT ...?
YOU'RE A VAGABOND, YOU'LL DO ANYTHING FOR MONEY.
グズ
sniff
A VAGABOND WILL DO ANYTHING FOR MONEY...
...BUT HE CAN'T SELL HIS HEART.
THANKS THOUGH, KID.
YOU'RE THE FIRST PERSON SINCE MY MA WHO EVER CARED FOR ME THIS WAY.
IT'S ALL RIGHT.
BELIEVE IT OR NOT, I'M PRETTY TOUGH.

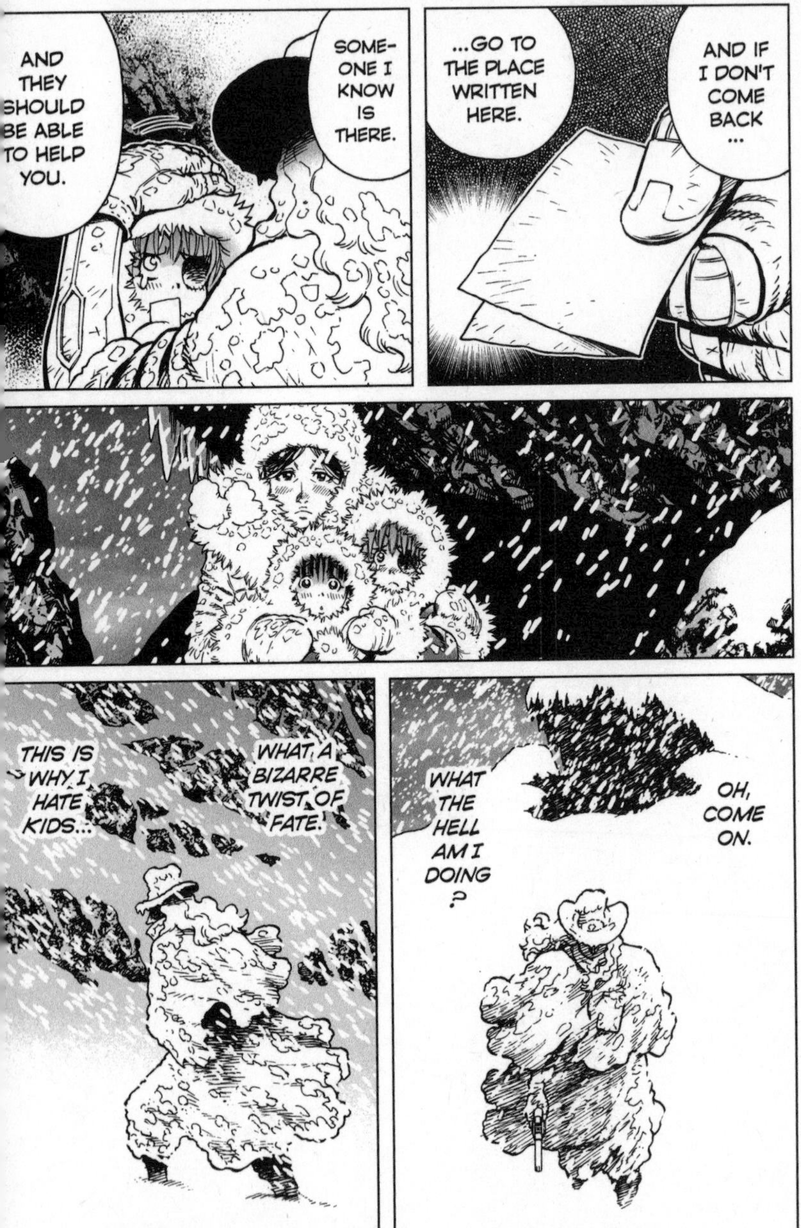
AND IF I DON'T COME BACK...
...GO TO THE PLACE WRITTEN HERE.
SOME-ONE I KNOW IS THERE.
AND THEY SHOULD BE ABLE TO HELP YOU.
OH, COME ON.
WHAT THE HELL AM I DOING?
WHAT A BIZARRE TWIST OF FATE.
THIS IS WHY I HATE KIDS...

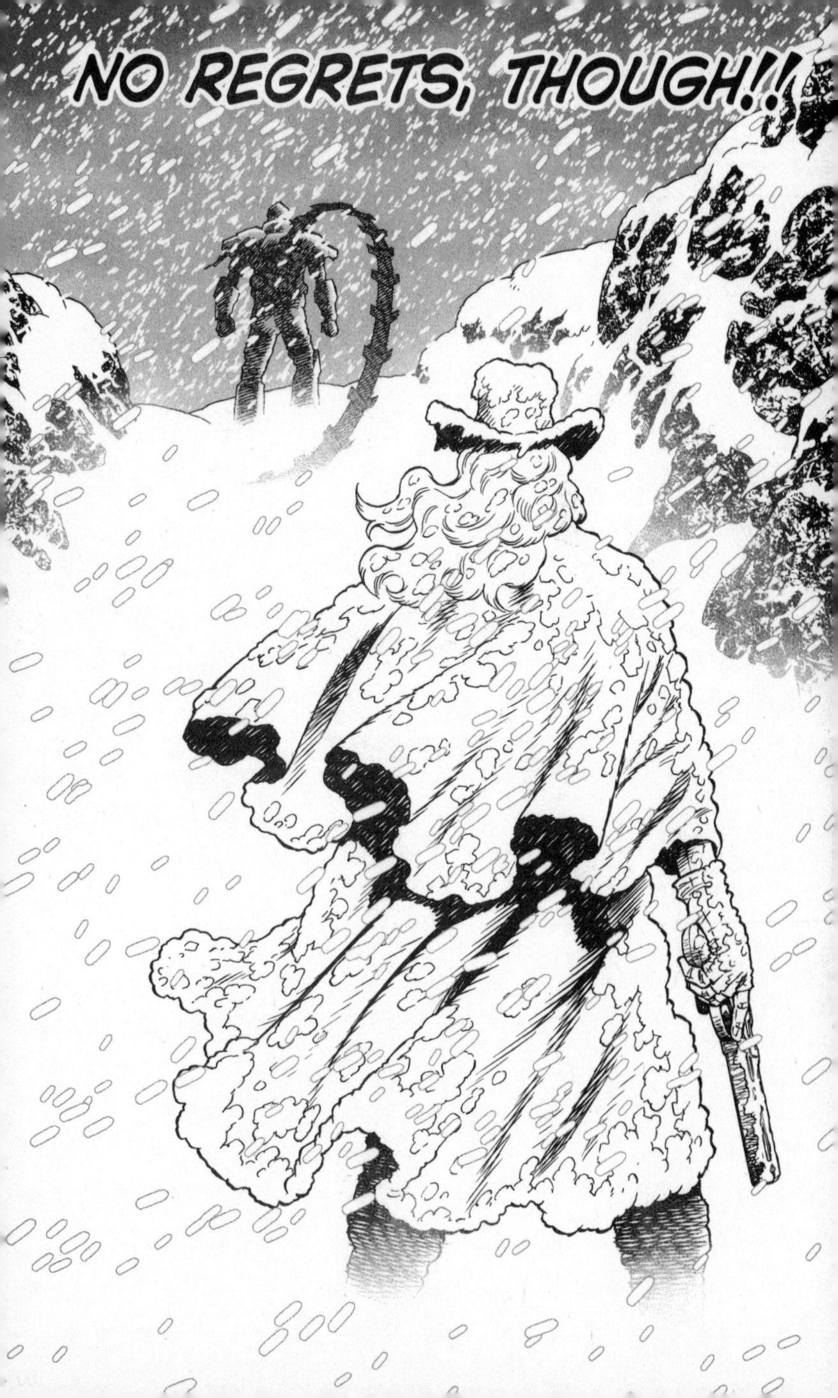
NO REGRETS, THOUGH!!

BATTLE ANGEL ALITA

MARS CHRONICLE

PRESENTED by YUKITO KISHIRO

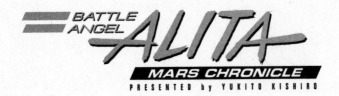

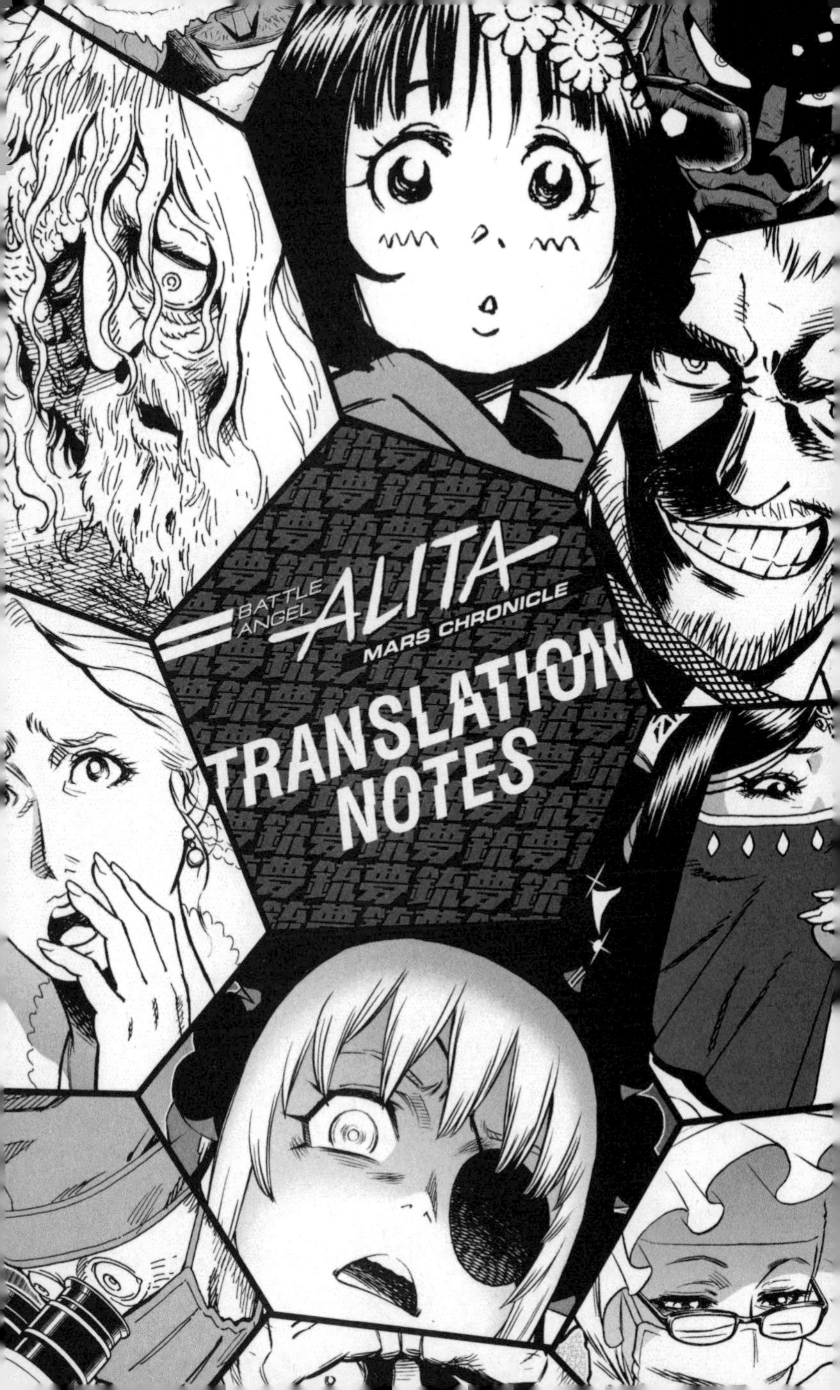
BATTLE ANGEL ALITA
MARS CHRONICLE
TRANSLATION NOTES

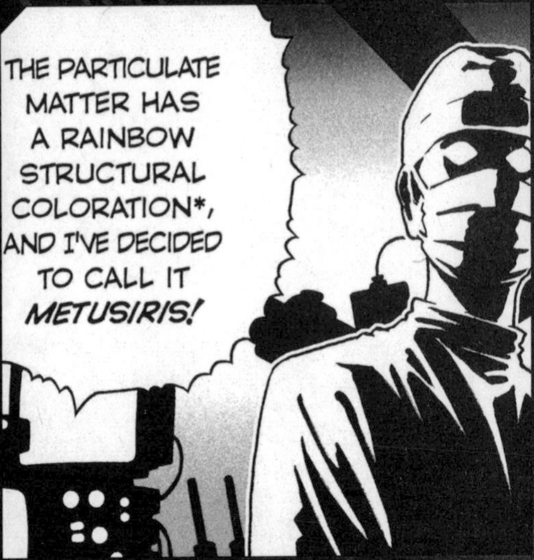
THE PARTICULATE MATTER HAS A RAINBOW STRUCTURAL COLORATION*, AND I'VE DECIDED TO CALL IT *METUSIRIS!*

METUSIRIS pg. 14

This term is made of the Latin words *metus* and *iris*, meaning "terror rainbow."

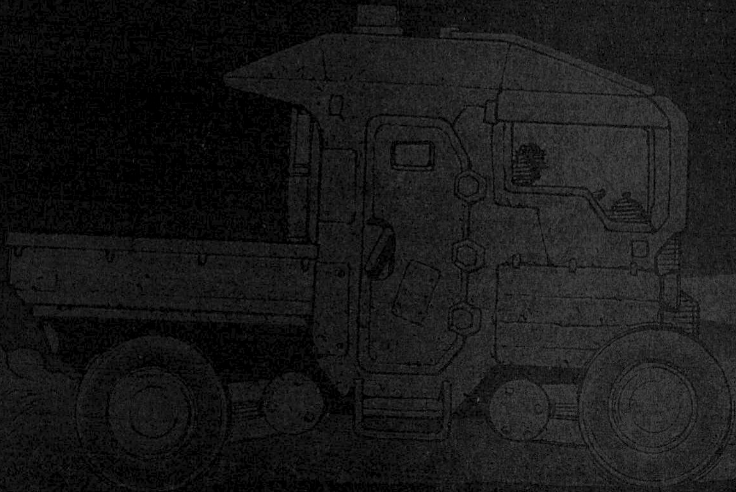

AN ALLIANCE OF GROUPS WHO NORMALLY FOUGHT ONE ANOTHER ROSE UP TO FIGHT THEM. AMONG THEM WERE THE PANZER GRENADIERS, PAPAGEI CORPS, GRENZERS, GRÜNTHAL, YANBARARS...

MILITARY GROUPS
pg. 55

Among the groups mentioned here, the Grenzers are named for a historical infantry force from a military frontier the Habsburg Monarchy (Austria) held against the Ottoman Empire in the 18th and 19th centuries, and the *kanji* in the title indicates the group in *Alita* is a "frontier force." The Yanbarars are described as "mountainous forces," and take their name from Yanbaru, the wilder northern side of the Japanese island of Okinawa.

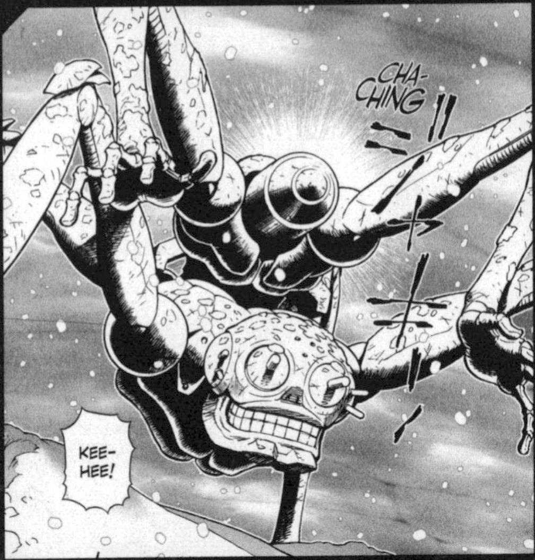
CHA-
CHING
KEE-
HEE!

PANZERFAUST pg. 149

A WWII German anti-tank weapon, essentially a single-use rocket mortar, meaning "tank fist."

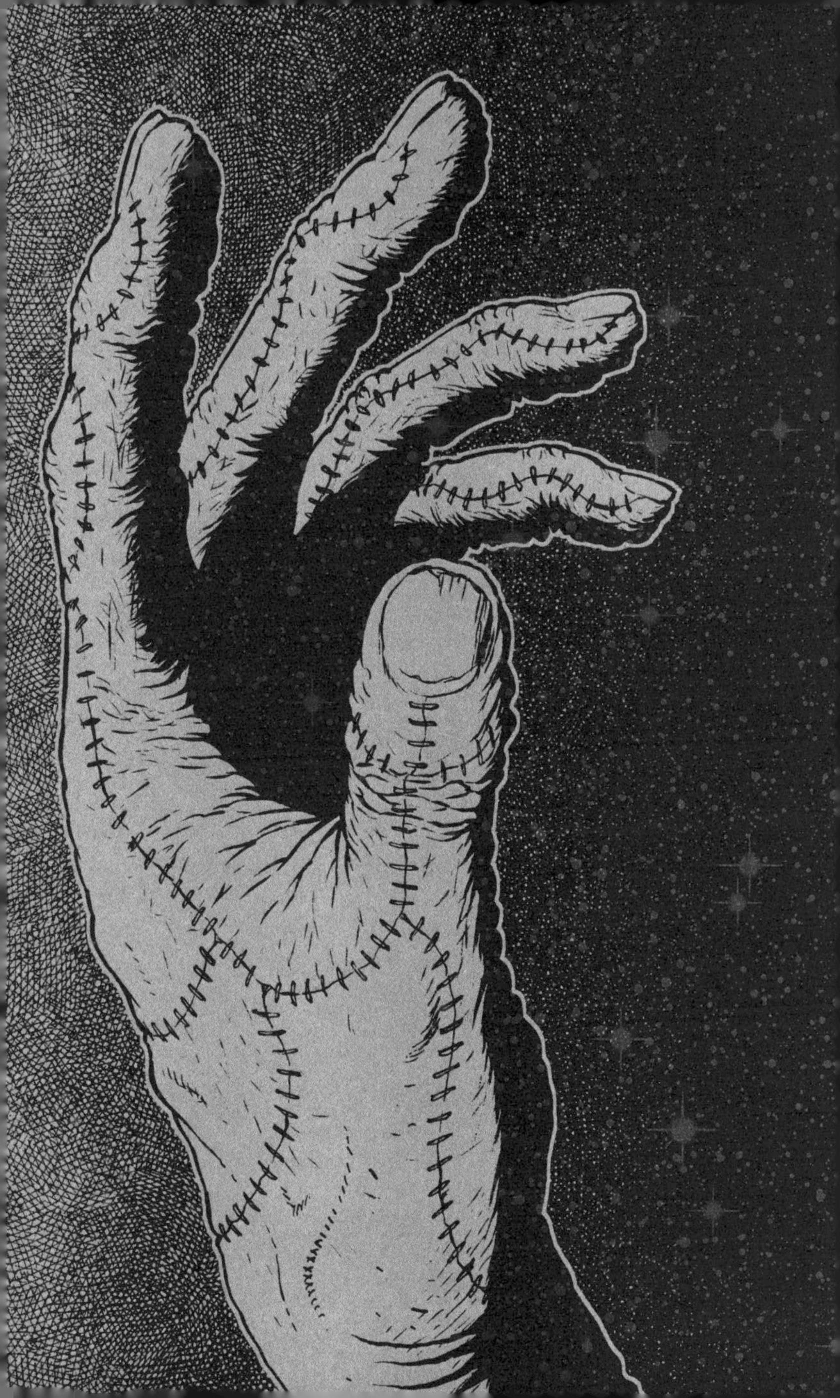

DELUXE EDITION

BATTLE ANGEL ALITA

After more than a decade out of print, the original cyberpunk action classic returns in glorious 400-page hardcover deluxe editions, featuring an all-new translation, color pages, and new cover designs!

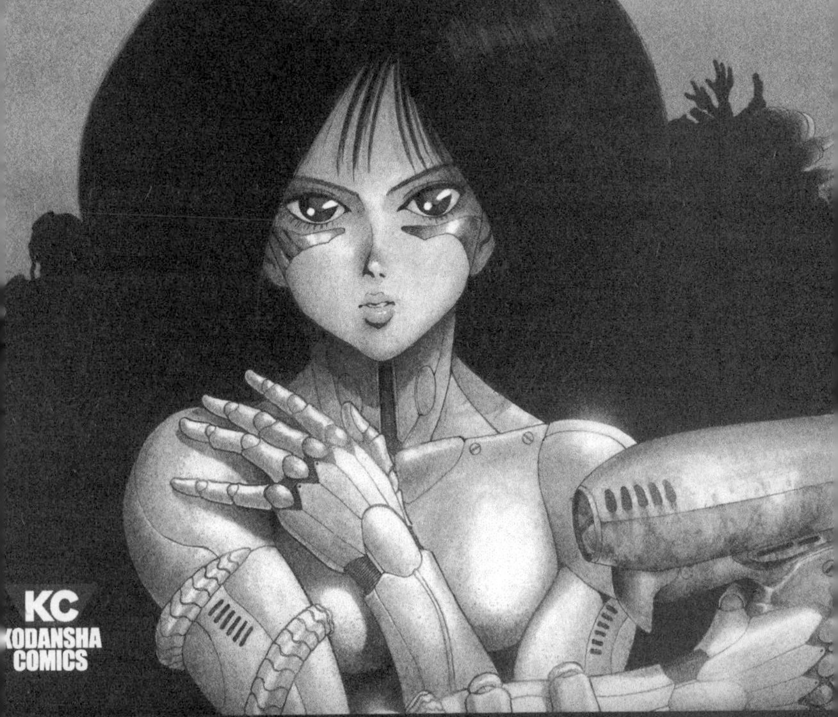
KC
KODANSHA COMICS

Far beneath the shimmering space-city of Zalem lie the trash-heaps of The Scrapyard... Here, cyber-doctor and bounty hunter Daisuke Ido finds the head and torso of an amnesiac cyborg girl. He names her Alita and vows to fill her life with beauty, but in a moment of desperation, a fragment of Alita's mysterious past awakens in her. She discovers that she possesses uncanny prowess in the legendary martial art known as panzerkunst. With her newfound skills, Alita decides to become a hunter-warrior - tracking down and taking out those who prey on the weak. But can she hold onto her humanity in the dark and gritty world of The Scrapyard?

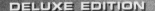

A new series from Yoshitoki Oima, creator of The New York Times bestselling manga and Eisner Award nominee *A Silent Voice*!

An intimate, emotional drama and an epic story spanning time and space...

TO YOUR ETERNITY

An orb was cast unto the earth. After metamorphosing into a wolf, It joins a boy on his bleak journey to find his tribe. Ever learning, It transcends death, even when those around It cannot...

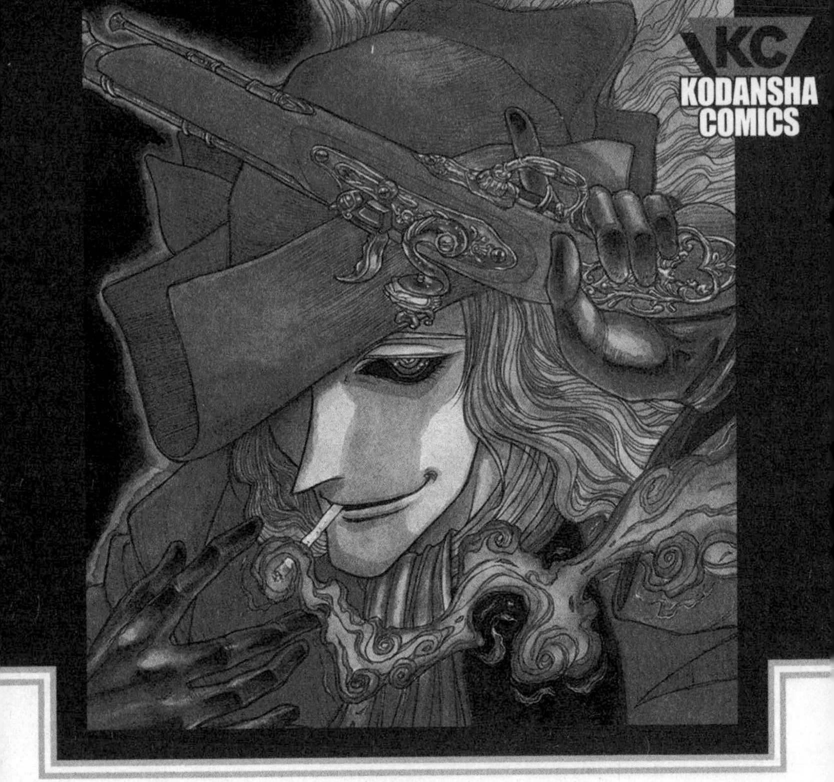
KC
KODANSHA
COMICS

The Black Museum: The Ghost and the Lady

By Kazuhiro Fujita

Deep in Scotland Yard in London sits an evidence room dedicated to the greatest mysteries of British history. In this "Black Museum" sits a misshapen hunk of lead–two bullets fused together–the key to a wartime encounter between Florence Nightingale, the mother of modern nursing, and a supernatural Man in Grey. This story is unknown to most scholars of history, but a special guest of the museum will tell the tale of *The Ghost and the Lady*...

Praise for Kazuhiro Fujita's *Ushio and Tora*

"A charming revival that combines a classic look with modern depth and pacing... **Essential viewing both for curmudgeons and new fans alike.**" — Anime News Network

"**GREAT!** The first episode of *Ushio and Tora* captures the essence of '90s anime." — IGN

HAPPINESS

—ハピネス—

By Shuzo Oshimi

From the creator of *The Flowers of Evil*

Nothing interesting is happening in Makoto Ozaki's first year of high school. HIs life is a series of quiet humiliations: low-grade bullies, unreliable friends, and the constant frustration of his adolescent lust. But one night, a pale, thin girl knocks him to the ground in an alley and offers him a choice.

Now everything is different. Daylight is searingly bright. Food tastes awful. And worse than anything is the terrible, consuming thirst...

Praise for Shuzo Oshimi's *The Flowers of Evil*

"A shockingly readable story that vividly—one might even say queasily—evokes the fear and confusion of discovering one's own sexuality. Recommended." —The Manga Critic

"A page-turning tale of sordid middle school blackmail." —Otaku USA Magazine

"A stunning new horror manga." —Third Eye Comics

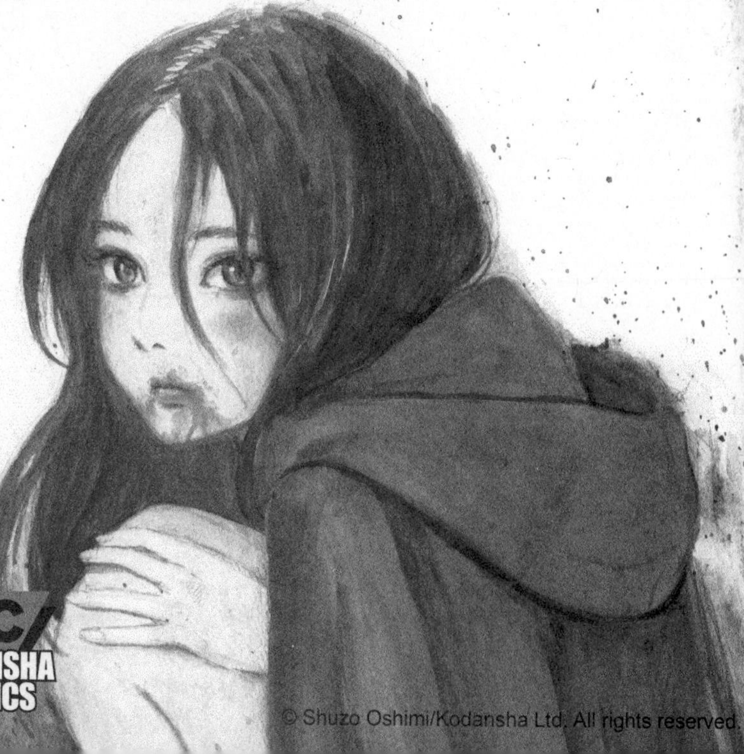

KC KODANSHA COMICS

Japan's most powerful spirit medium delves into the ghost world's greatest mysteries!

Story by Kyo Shirodaira, famed author of mystery fiction and creator of *Spiral*, *Blast of Tempest*, and *The Record of a Fallen Vampire*.

Both touched by spirits called yôkai, Kotoko and Kurô have gained unique superhuman powers. But to gain her powers Kotoko has given up an eye and a leg, and Kurô's personal life is in shambles. So when Kotoko suggests they team up to deal with renegades from the spirit world, Kurô doesn't have many other choices, but Kotoko might just have a few ulterior motives...

IN/SPECTRE

STORY BY **KYO SHIRODAIRA**
ART BY **CHASHIBA KATASE**

KC KODANSHA COMICS

New action series from Hiroyuki Takei, creator of the classic shonen franchise Shaman King!

In medieval Japan, a bell hanging on the collar is a sign that a ca[t] has a master. Norachiyo's bell hangs from his katana sheath, but he i[s] nonetheless a stray — a ronin. This one-eyed cat samurai travels across a dishonest world, cutting through pretense and deception with his blade[.]

NEKOGAHARA

STRAY CAT SAMURAI

By
Hiroyuki Takei

"I'm pleasantly surprised to find modern shojo using cross-dressing as a dramatic device to deliver social commentary... Recommended."

-Otaku USA Magazine

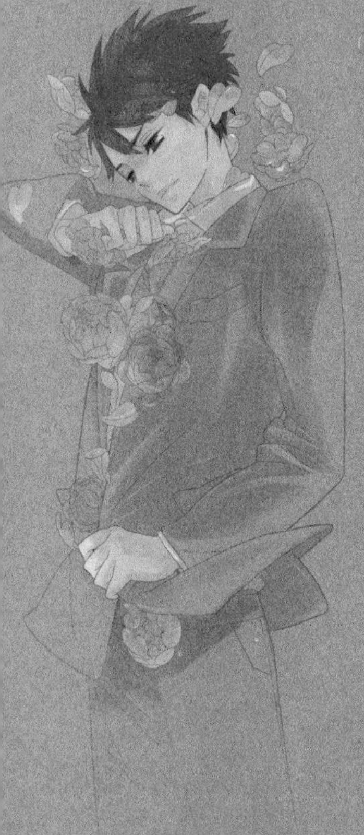

the prince in his dark days

By Hico Yamanaka

A drunkard for a father, a household of poverty... For 17-year-old Atsuko misfortune is all she knows and believes in. Until one day, a chance encounter with Itaru–the wealthy heir of a huge corporation–changes everything. The two look identical, uncannily so. When Itaru curiously goes missing, Atsuko is roped into being his stand-in. There, in his shoes Atsuko must parade like a prince in a palace. She encounters many new experiences, but at what cost...?

aving lost his wife, high school teacher Kōhei Inuzuka is doing his best to raise his young
aughter Tsumugi as a single father. He's pretty bad at cooking and doesn't have a huge
ppetite to begin with, but chance brings his little family together with one of his students, the
onely Kotori. The three of them are anything but comfortable in the kitchen, but the healing
ower of home cooking might just work on their grieving hearts.

This season's number-one feel-good anime!" —Anime News Network

A beautifully-drawn story about comfort food and family and grief. Recommended." —Otaku
JSA Magazine

sweetness & lightning

By Gido Amagakure

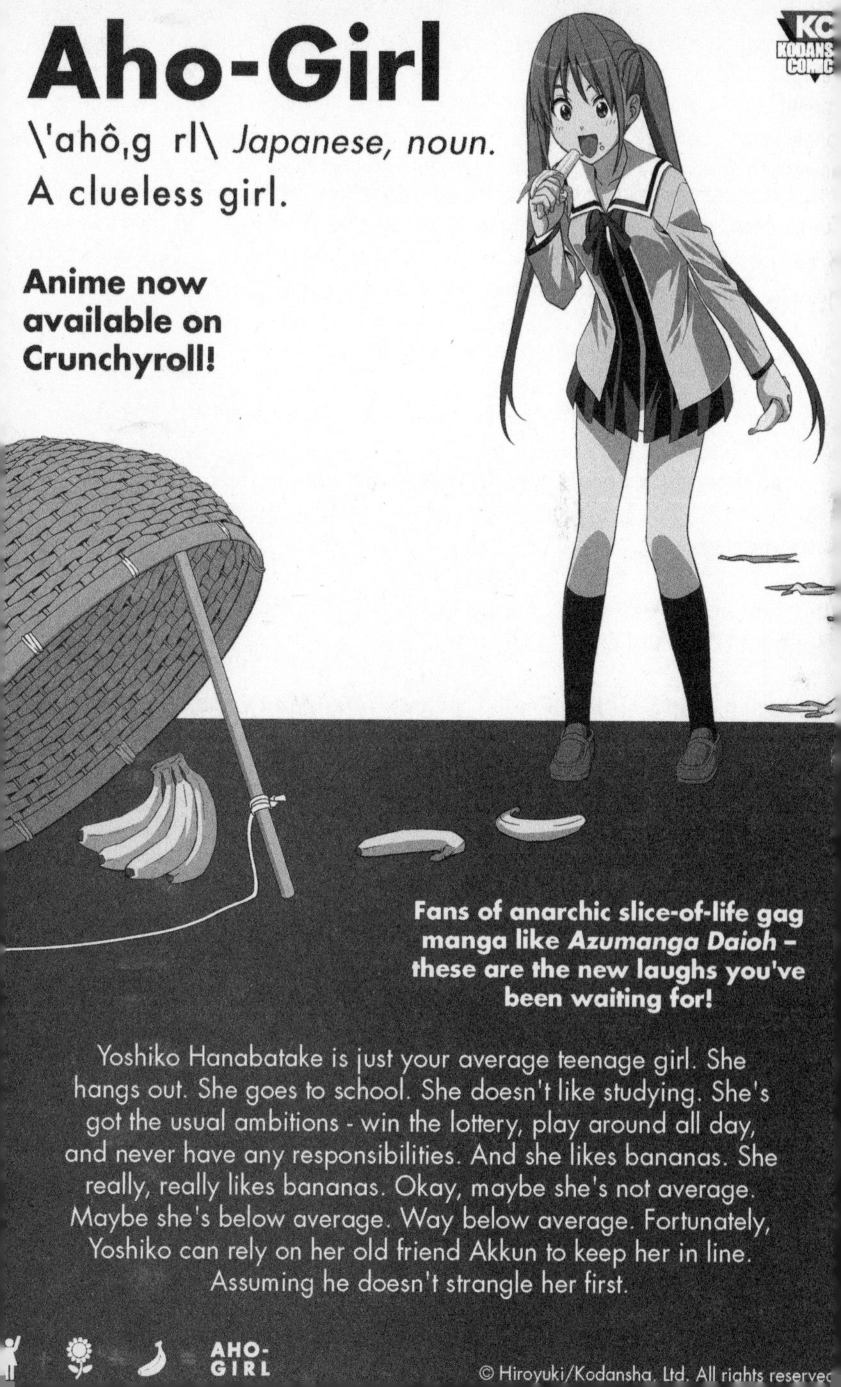

attle Angel Alita: Mars Chronicle volume 5 is a work of fiction. Names, aracters, places, and incidents are the products of the author's agination or are used fictitiously. Any resemblance to actual events, cales, or persons, living or dead, is entirely coincidental.

Kodansha Comics Trade Paperback Original.

ublished in the United States by Kodansha Comics, an imprint of odansha USA Publishing, LLC, New York.

ublication rights for this English edition arranged through Kodansha td., Tokyo.

rst published in Japan in 2017 by Kodansha Ltd., Tokyo, as *Gunnm: lars Chronicle 5*.

BN 978-1-63236-658-0

rinted in the United States of America.

ww.kodanshacomics.com

8 7 6 5 4 3 2 1

ranslator: Stephen Paul
ettering: Evan Hayden
diting: Ajani Oloye
odansha Comics edition cover design: Phil Balsman